On Film-making

also edited by Paul Cronin

HERZOG ON HERZOG

of related interest from Faber and Faber

SWEET SMELL OF SUCCESS
by Clifford Odets and Ernest Lehman

On Film-making

An introduction to the craft of the director

ALEXANDER MACKENDRICK

Edited by Paul Cronin

FOREWORD BY MARTIN SCORSESE

faber and faber

First published in 2004
by Faber and Faber Limited
Bloomsbury House,
74-77 Great Russell Street,
London WC1B 3DA

Published in the United States by Faber and Faber Inc.
an affiliate of Farrar, Straus and Giroux LLC, New York

Typeset by Faber and Faber Limited
Printed and bound by CPI Group (UK) Ltd, Croydon, CRO 4YY

A CIP record for this book
is available from the British Library

ISBN 978-0-571-21125-8

10 9 8

To my sons: Kerry, Mathew and John Mackendrick

Contents

Foreword by Martin Scorsese

How do you teach film directing? I'm not sure if we've come to a consensus yet. Everyone seems to approach the task differently. Which should come as no surprise. After all, the medium is still young – a little over 100 years is nothing compared with the thousands of years it's taken for painting, dance, music and theater to evolve. What are the traditions of film-making? Where do you begin? What do you teach, and in what order?

This collection of writings by Alexander Mackendrick is a good, solid starting point. That it's of great value to students almost goes without saying – anyone who studied with Mackendrick during his long tenure at CalArts, and who received these writings in the form of handouts, can attest to their value. But I can also easily imagine a college without a film program building a curriculum around these writings. They're that clear, that concise, that comprehensive. Mackendrick knew that you couldn't reduce film-making to any one thing. He knew that it was about storytelling and that it was also about images, that it was about acting *and* editing, action *and* words. And that more than anything else, it was about practice. Theories are fine, but practice is everything. "Though it will be only a couple of weeks before you are familiar with the basic mechanics of film-making, it will take a lifetime of hard work to master them." As someone who feels like he's still just beginning, who has to start all over again with each new movie, I can attest to the truth of Mackendrick's words.

Mackendrick had practice, and plenty of it. He came up through the studio system – Ealing to be exact – where he did some of the best work in the middle of what is now remembered as the Golden Age of British film comedy. *The Man in the White Suit. The Ladykillers* – the last Ealing film, and one of the best.

For him, they were simply practice.

Mackendrick came to the United States after *The Ladykillers*. Burt Lancaster brought him over to work on a movie called *The Sweet Smell of Success*. Some of you might have heard of this picture – one of the most daring, startling, savage ever made about show business and power in this country. "I cannot recommend the film for student study on aesthetic grounds," writes Mackendrick, by way of introducing a section on the screenwriting process and the varying contributions of Ernest Lehman and Clifford Odets to that film. It may sound like false modesty, since *Sweet Smell of Success* is now recognized as a milestone in American movie-making. But for Mackendrick, it was simply more practice. It takes a lifetime, and even then it shouldn't feel like enough. He knew this.

"Process, not product" was his mantra to his students. The creative process – not the creative method, or the creative system. The process. Which never stops. Even when you're resting, letting an idea take root. Mackendrick knew this.

I'm not implying that he was an anti-intellectual Hollywood pro – all you have to do is leaf through this book, with its references to Ibsen and Sophocles and Beckett and Levi-Strauss, to dispel that notion. This book takes on everything from Dramatic Irony to Mental Geography, the relationship between the director and his actors to the structural soundness of *Last Year at Marienbad*. But on almost every page, Mackendrick lets the reader know that all of it, from the lessons about crossing the axis and the condensation of screen time to the techniques for cultivating ideas ("Collecting Data . . . Organizing the Data . . . Incubating the Material . . . Preserving the Spark" – sounds right to me), are worth nothing without practice.

As for the differences between art and entertainment, narrative and non-narrative film-making, they are simply matters of taste and temperament. You can only find out through . . . practice.

This book – this *invaluable* book – is the work of a lifetime, from a man who was passionately devoted to his craft and his art, and who then devoted himself to transferring his knowledge and his experience to his students. And now it's available to all of us. What a gift.

Top: Alexander Mackendrick (left) directs Joan Greenwood (second from left) and Alec Guinness (centre) in *The Man in the White Suit* (1951). Courtesy of The Joel Finler Collection.

Bottom: Mackendrick contemplates a miniature made for *The Maggie* (1954). Courtesy of The Joel Finler Collection.

Introduction

Film writing and directing cannot be taught, only learned,
and each man or woman has to learn it through his or her
own system of self-education.
  Alexander Mackendrick

Alexander 'Sandy' Mackendrick, after retiring from his career as
a film director in 1969, spent twenty-five years teaching his craft
at the newly established California Institute of the Arts in
Valencia, where he produced hundreds of pages of class notes
and sketches. These texts cover a wide range of subjects, from
the intricacies of story structure to the technicalities of directing
and acting, from the mythical significance and history of cinema to the science of visual perception. For Mackendrick, all
were indispensable skills for the student of film-making, without
which the ability to succeed would be limited.

Mackendrick's distinguished and influential body of work as a
director is not the principal reason why his writings are worthy of
study, but it is one reason why we might pay attention to what he
has to say about cinema. By the time he arrived at CalArts,
Mackendrick had many years of film-making experience behind
him. During the Second World War, he produced propaganda
films for the Ministry of Information, and as a member of
Eisenhower's Psychological Warfare Branch shot footage of the
Allied invasion of Italy. During his early days at London's Ealing
Studios in the 1940s he worked on a number of scripts and sto-
ryboarded several productions before directing five films there
(of which his comedies are generally considered among the finest
films the studio produced): *Whisky Galore* (1949), *The Man in
the White Suit* (1951), *Mandy* (1952), *The Maggie* (1954) and
The Ladykillers (1955). Mackendrick went on to make the

1. See Philip Kemp's *Lethal Innocence: The Cinema of Alexander Mackendrick* (Methuen, 1991). For a history of Ealing Studios, see Charles Barr's *Ealing Studios* (University of California Press, 1998).

2. 'The Mackendrick Legacy', *American Film* (March 1976).

3. From an unpublished interview at Mackendrick's CalArts office, 8 March 1990, conducted by John McDonough, to whom I am indebted for his permission to cite from this conversation.

legendary and much revered *Sweet Smell of Success* (1957) in Hollywood, followed by *Sammy Going South* (1963), *A High Wind in Jamaica* (1965) and *Don't Make Waves* (1967).[1]

For students of film, more important than Mackendrick's nine features is his excellence as a writer and pedagogue, a role he was to play until his death in 1993 at the age of eighty-one. Copies of his notes remain prized possessions among CalArts graduates who speak of their mentor with veneration. Designed to guide students through the disciplines Mackendrick called Dramatic Construction and Film Grammar ('the narrative and visual devices that have been developed through inventive direction and performing during cinema's short history'), the notes are masterful studies of the two primary tasks confronting the film director: how to structure and write the story he wants to tell, and how to use those devices particular to the medium of film in order to tell that story as effectively as possible. Devoid of obscurantism, concentrating on the practical and tangible rather than abstract concepts of cinema as 'art', they reveal that Mackendrick had the talent not only to make films, but also to articulate with clarity and insight what that process involved.

The reasons why Mackendrick chose to quit directing and become a teacher are not difficult to understand. By the late 1960s, as Patricia Goldstone has noted, he 'found himself spending more energy on making deals than on making films'.[2] Mackendrick admitted that, after Ealing Studios was sold, 'I had a disheartening time in many ways as a freelance director on the open market, something I was never really suited for.'

At Ealing there was a father figure – producer Sir Michael Balcon – who along with his administration protected me when I first entered the industry in 1946. For ten years I was horrendously spoiled, with all the logistical and financial problems lifted from my shoulders, even if I had to do the films they told me to. The reason why I have discovered myself so much happier teaching is that when I arrived here after the collapse of the world I had known at Ealing, I found that in order to make movies in Hollywood you have to be a deal-maker. Not only did I really have no talent for that, I had also been conditioned to have insufficient respect for the deal-makers. I realised I was in the wrong business, and I got out.[3]

xiv

Mackendrick's widow Hilary remembers that 'however ambivalent Sandy was to the cosy world of Ealing compared to the life of the independent film-maker, he had a regular salary, which relieved him of the pressure of finding income to keep going in between projects.'

Moreover, just before Mackendrick joined CalArts, his long-cherished historical epic *Mary Queen of Scots* collapsed when the film was cancelled.[4] Hilary Mackendrick says that 'Sandy really did feel quite vulnerable, but, in his gentlemanly fashion, declined to take the necessary legal action for the studio to honour its contract. He said, "I'll be paid for making films, but I won't be paid for *not* making films." He suffered from chronic depression throughout his life, and from childhood had been severely asthmatic, which led to the emphysema that eventually killed him. Sandy was desperately worried when he wasn't working and couldn't see a film in sight, and felt bitter about how he'd been treated by the film industry.' At this time, CalArts was seeking to appoint a Dean to the newly established School of Film and Video, and after a number of meetings, Mackendrick was offered a contract that he happily signed.[5]

A CalArts brochure from the early 1970s explains that the Institute had been looking for 'a leader among professional film-makers who is not a prisoner of technology but its creative user, and to whom teaching young film artists is not a way to immortalise his own image'. The *Los Angeles Times* noted in 1969 that Mackendrick originally contemplated the offer 'with no clear knowledge of the operating philosophies that were in the making [at CalArts]. But after eavesdropping at three or four days' worth of faculty meetings, at which [members] kicked around their freewheeling interdisciplinary ideas, Mackendrick says, "I was hooked: I didn't know if they wanted me, but I knew that I wanted them."'[6]

Although he had studied at the renowned Glasgow School of Art for only one year (leaving to take up work in the art department of the J. Walter Thompson advertising agency in London), Mackendrick found the overtures from CalArts intriguing, remarking in 1977 that 'the idea of starting as Dean of an art school when you haven't completed art school yourself seemed too funny to resist.'[7] After having spent so many years as a film

4. See Philip Kemp's article 'Mackendrick Land', *Sight and Sound* (Winter 1988/89).

5. For several weeks in the late 1970s, Mackendrick taught at the National Film and Television School in Beaconsfield, near London, where his students included writer and director Terence Davies.

6. Charles Champlin, 'Putting It On Film Key to New CalArts Program', *Los Angeles Times* (31 August 1969).

7. 'The American Film Institute Workshop with Alexander Mackendrick' (1977).

8. An early CalArts brochure explains that Mackendrick joined the Institute faculty in 1969, two years prior to the arrival of the first students. In those two years he was 'instrumental in the development of the Institute's program in Film and Video', and played a 'major role in the overall design of the Institute'. To this day the School of Film and Video is run on the structural lines that Mackendrick laid down nearly thirty-five years ago.

director, Mackendrick believed CalArts was the place where he could best channel his energies and indulge his 'present passion': the 'unanswerable question' of whether or not film-making could be taught, one with which he was to become increasingly fascinated. 'I find myself absolutely riveted to this particular thing I'm doing now by a strange and unbeatable mixture of exasperation and curiosity,' Mackendrick explained, 'and I'm absolutely devoted to finding out how it works.' Noting that he found being associated with his students' rites of passage 'very touching', he explained that during his first years at CalArts he wasn't in the least scared of learning how to teach, 'because I think that is essentially what a film director does most of the time.'

Michael Pressman, now a producer and director, was in Mackendrick's first class at CalArts. 'Sandy loved teaching, and we really could feel how excited he felt about it,' says Pressman. 'He had several careers: illustrator and cartoonist, graphic artist, screenwriter, then a director, and then a teacher. He had walked away from the film industry, and there were many people in the business who couldn't understand why. I was twenty years old and I certainly couldn't understand it. Today, after twenty-five years in the business, it makes sense to me: Sandy just wasn't interested in the machinations of Hollywood. CalArts was the perfect environment for him, a place where he could give students the invaluable benefit of his knowledge.' Hilary Mackendrick says that 'it was as a teacher that Sandy found his true *métier*, and I suspect his remarkable critical faculties were more appropriate to teaching than to film-making. I know his last ten years at CalArts were his most fulfilling.'

Regarded by many as one of America's most progressive schools of higher education, the California Institute of the Arts, as its current brochure notes, 'was incorporated in 1961 as the first degree-granting institution of higher learning in the United States created specifically for students of both the visual and the performing arts. The Institute was established through the vision and generosity of Walt and Roy Disney and the merger of two well-established professional schools, the Los Angeles Conservatory of Music, founded in 1883, and the Chouinard Art Institute, founded in 1921.'[8] Under Disney's guidance, degree programs in dance, theatre, design, critical studies and film/video (including the influential experimental animation course[9]) were added to those in art and music. Richard Schickel has written that for Walt Disney, CalArts was 'on a grand scale, his own dream of an artist's utopia reconstituted; it was the old studio art classes grown up. A good deal of Disney's estate went to this, his last monument, which he saw as a place where all the arts might mingle and stimulate one another.'[10]

Established 'with the dream of starting a tradition of academic unorthodoxy',[11] CalArts has always viewed the 'industrialisation' of the arts with a healthy disregard. Though it has fed Hollywood its best and brightest students from its inception, the Institute was originally conceived as 'a facility in which students could make films as an artist paints pictures, a creative setting neither vocational nor academic.'[12] Jack Valero, one of Mackendrick's first teaching assistants in the early 1970s, remembers that CalArts 'was a very experimental place, a kind of bohemian paradise where the key word was "interdisciplinary". There were never "teachers" and "students" at CalArts, only artists with varying degrees of experience. Though every film school has its own character, being situated just outside Los Angeles and not right in the belly of the beast has always given CalArts more freedom to experiment than other schools, for example USC and UCLA.' As Mackendrick explained, Hollywood studios 'don't dare, can't afford, to try new things. We can.'[13]

This is a group of schools of 'Art'. Art-with-a-capital-A. From the beginning we declared that we were not a trade school: we did not aim to provide the kind of training directed at preparing students for employment in the industry. By industry, of course, we mean the movie business that, in capitalist America (whether or not we like to face the fact), is a profit-motivated enterprise designed to produce a consumer product for a mass market. In general, the teachers at this institute are not in favour of commercialism. Most, if not all of the programs, encourage students to regard the work that they do as self-expression.

Examine the word. *Expression*, in the sense of externalising concepts, and *self* in the sense of feelings and thoughts that are individual. The self-expressing 'Artist-with-a-capital-A' is intent on producing

9. The 'Film Graphics' program, headed by Jules Engel, was born out of the Disney studio's desire to establish a source of animators to fit their needs. It soon became clear that Engel's students were not being sufficiently geared toward commercial animation, whereupon the 'Character Animation' department (from where some of CalArts' greatest film successes have emerged, including directors Tim Burton and John Lasseter) was established.

10. Richard Schickel, *The Disney Version* (Discus, 1968), p. 306.

11. 'Putting It On Film Key to New CalArts Program'.

12. 'The Mackendrick Legacy'.

13. 'Putting It On Film Key to New CalArts Program'.

14. 'Putting It on Film Key to New CalArts Program'.

15. *Independent* (8 March 1991).

16. 'The Art of the Film' (BBC Radio, June/July 1955).

work that presents an image of his or her feelings, thoughts, intuitions, and then makes that work publicly available.

'There's something obsessional, compulsive about wanting to make films and we should go with it, not discipline it,' said Mackendrick in 1969.[14] As such, rather than working to 'commercial standards', something they would probably end up spending their entire working lives doing if they chose to enter the film industry, Mackendrick urged students to toil over their 'own personal projection' of who they were.

Nevertheless, although CalArts concentrated on 'what's called independent film-making, as distinct from movie directing',[15] Mackendrick was reluctant to speak of cinema as an 'art', suggesting that unlike the film director and his multitude of colleagues, 'the true artist works alone'.

There's quite a profession sprung up these days of people who write and lecture about what they call the Cinema, spelt with a capital 'C'. It means 'Film as an art form'. To people like myself who work in film studios, the cinema is more understandable when spelt with a small 'c' and when it means something concrete, often literally concrete: a rather ugly building with lurid posters outside.[16]

As Mackendrick explained in one handout to students:

When I joined CalArts, I quickly realised I should try to conceal a very embarrassing truth. Though I have, throughout a long and lively career, seldom had any really close friends who were not in some fashion involved with painting (with sculpture, with writing novels, plays or poetry, or with acting either on the stage, in films or both), it never occurred to me to refer to myself as an 'artist'. What I thought of myself as was a 'professional'. First in advertising, subsequently in the cinema with some interludes in theatre. A 'professional', at least in the common usage of this term, is one who is very far from being 'independent'. If the artist seeks – indeed demands and must have – 'freedom', then the industry professional has to face that what he needs and wants is 'dependence', the mutual and reciprocal support of others in what is an industry that produces a product designed for mass consumption in the hopes of massive profits.

For Mackendrick, the job of a director was a 'craft' that could be learned by anyone willing to undergo the necessary rigorous

xviii

training. He was anxious to spell out to CalArts students – many of whom prided themselves on being 'artists' yet dreamt of gainful studio employment as Hollywood 'professionals' upon graduation – that there were very definite skills they needed in order to become efficient storytellers within that system, or indeed *any* area of film production.

17. 'A Film Director and His Public', *The Listener* (23 September 1954).

One would not banish pianos from a music school on the grounds that an ability to play is merely a technical skill. We expect you to be able to read a light meter, focus a lens and use an editing machine, because these instruments of the craft are inseparable from the practice of the 'art' of the film-maker.

Writing in 1954 about the studio system, he noted that

[the] whole elaborate industrial plant is a piece of machinery and it cannot turn over until one or two appointed people have fed into it the most tenuous raw material in existence – a creative idea. I have used that word 'creative' with some misgivings. I have referred to art and self-expression. The surest way to cause embarrassment among people who actually work in film studios is to use these words. They sound slightly indecent. This is not humility on our part. It is tact. When we know that someone is risking vast sums of money we think it is bad manners to brandish our artistic temperaments. It makes the business men nervous. And since the money we are gambling is mostly theirs, the least we can do is to act as if we were reliable and responsible characters: not artists but craftsmen, highly paid craftsmen who can be guaranteed to turn out goods of standard quality.[17]

Though Mackendrick was respectful of innate 'creative' ability, he believed it was ineffectual if not accompanied by this 'reliability and responsibility' and a sound technical knowledge base from which to draw. Only with such qualities, alongside the obligatory commitment and toil, would CalArts students achieve their full potential. 'Though it will be only a couple of weeks before you are familiar with the basic mechanics of film-making,' wrote Mackendrick, 'it will take a lifetime of hard work to master them.'

Owing to his convictions about the necessity of some form of training for students of film-making, Mackendrick's approach was perceived by many at CalArts as being somehow antithetical to what the Institute strove to be: an arena for complete freedom of self-expression, an experimental laboratory devoid of any commercial considerations for the industry. Mackendrick was aware of the appeal of experimental storytelling and actively encouraged students to follow such paths by ensuring there was a wide spectrum of teachers at the film school. Don Levy and Nam June Paik taught avant-garde film, Jules Engel tutored students of experimental animation, and Terry Sanders and Kris Malkeiwicz instructed those interested in documentaries. But he nevertheless felt that many of the methods of the avant-garde were at best controversial, at worst an evasion of students' real tasks as film-makers. 'Sandy constantly pushed students to ask themselves exactly what it was they wanted to be *avant* of,' says Lou Florimonte, who taught at CalArts with Mackendrick for many years.

If they didn't have a grasp of how story structure and film functioned at the most rudimentary level, just what was it they were experimenting with? Sandy believed there were certain 'rules' that serve as the bedrock of narrative storytelling, a good knowledge of which would help students master their craft. But he encountered many students over the years who felt that stories needed to have something of a magical and unknowable element to them and who were resistant to the way he reduced narratives to their nuts and bolts. Consequently, Sandy's ideas were seen by some as being old-fashioned, unadventurous, and rather commercially orientated, a perception that came from his emphasis on discipline and structure.

Writer and director James Mangold was Mackendrick's teaching assistant for two years. He explains:

Art schools often attract the kind of people who are resistant to learning certain things. Sandy was the one person at CalArts who said to students, 'By coming here and ignoring those things, you are missing out on things you *need* to know about.' Though he liked to explore the work of so-called 'experimental' film-makers, Sandy represented the old guard and believed there were certain skills that storytellers needed to acquire before flushing their psyches out through their art. Because he could be resistant to people who wanted to make some kind of passionate mess before they could render even the most

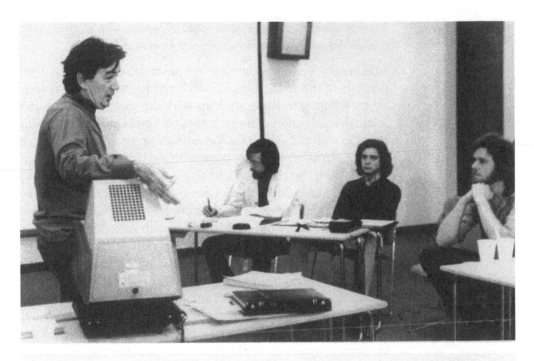

18. *Scope*: 'Alexander Mackendrick', BBC TV (1975).

basic shapes, Sandy was sometimes in conflict with students who thought he was blocking their personal expression.

Mackendrick, driven by his acute understanding of the grim realities of life in the film industry, felt he was doing no such thing. Wanting to equip students with the most functional and adaptable collection of tools as possible before sending them out into the world of work, the key to his approach was simple: to train students 'so they can cope with *anything* that might happen'.[18] With the rudiments of film grammar applicable to *all* forms of cinema, Mackendrick believed that pushing students to familiarise themselves with the concepts he discussed in class would help them express themselves with maximum clarity in whatever realm they chose to work in.

After nearly ten years as Dean, Mackendrick resigned to concentrate solely on his teaching at CalArts where he was, by all accounts, a hard taskmaster. 'Sandy's ideas were quite advanced for some students, and it's perhaps fair to say he wasn't a natural teacher for beginners,' says film historian Philip Kemp. 'In the classroom, where he wielded impressive authority, his way of teaching was to be very tough, on the grounds that if students were talented and motivated – if they had a genuine need to make films – they would get through regardless.' But though he had a certain aggressiveness and intellectual arrogance about him, Mackendrick elicited fierce loyalty and respect from his protégés who fought to study with him. 'Sandy wasn't intimidated by anyone, yet could be very intimidating himself,' says Lou Florimonte.

It was difficult to relax when you were with Sandy as he was constantly turning things upside down in a challenging and provocative way. He never set out to offend, he just wanted to keep things alive, and as a teacher was extremely mischievous and unpredictable in a very creative way. For Sandy, good was never good enough, and he would accept a student's deficiencies only after every effort had been exhausted – long sessions of guiding, illustrating, arguing, pleading and threatening. His real gift was being able to see with incredible clarity the work that was presented to him, and one simple comment to a student often meant his ideas would fall into shape. If a student did finally get Sandy's approval, he knew he had a project ready to take out into the world.

Mackendrick had various methods of pushing students in the right direction. One of the most rudimentary was repetition, an important cornerstone of his system of instruction. Many students recall his aphorism 'Process, not product' and belief in what he called 'repetition directing', the practice of small throw-away exercises that would place students on the steep learning curve that a mastery of film-making requires. Another, tied to the idea that student films were either 'too long' or 'much too long', was to place an egg-timer on his desk just as a student was about to tell his story in class. A third was based was based on the series of cards on the walls around his office upon which were written various principles. David Brisbin, a former student and now a production designer, explains that

In our groups of six or eight people each of us would write a scene and give it to our classmates. We would all be responsible not so much to critique, rather to come up with ways to solve various structural problems as they became apparent. We'd be sitting there talking, and when a mistake was made Sandy would point to a card and we would all immediately know what kind of changes the script needed. Our student lives very much revolved around what was on the walls of that room. The simplicity of the 'slogans' was very helpful to us all, and the mistakes we all made were usually so standard that the cards stayed up there for years.

But perhaps the simplest and most effective way Mackendrick got the very best from his students was by expecting them to work hard. He wrote about how tirelessly students needed to persevere in order to realise their ambitions, and about how he himself had much sympathy with students

who try to avoid the exhausting, time-consuming and boring work involved in gathering data, reading masses of background information, travelling to talk to people and exploring places. It's not easy, but it is the grist for invention and an essential step of the creative process.

'Creativity' will always look after itself if you are prolific in production, which means starting off by turning out masses of work that is relatively unoriginal, derivative and imitative. When productivity has become second nature, you will find you have acquired a freedom in which your particular and personal individuality emerges of its own accord. One of the things I find most frequently missing in students as they arrive at CalArts is not imagination itself, rather the knack of making a disciplined effort in the development of fertile invention.

Intelligent and critical students are all too apt to use 'thinking' as a substitute for the much harder work of 'imagining' at the intuitive, emotional and sensory levels. People who talk about things instead of doing them tend to use analysis as a substitute for creativity. But a statement about the kind of effect you want to achieve is never a substitute for the often exhausting labours that must go into actually creating that effect. Work is the only real training.

'I remember more than once writing a three-page screenplay and showing it to Sandy,' says James Mangold.

The next day he would hand me seven pages of notes and drawings about it. As a lazy seventeen-year old who had cobbled together those few pages the night before my meeting with him, I was amazed at what Sandy was willing to do as a teacher. He worked so hard for us, much harder than we deserved. He was never a nine-to-five teacher, and we never felt when he closed his office door behind him in the evenings that he had left his ideas and students behind. His response to our work was so incredibly *un*-lazy and passionate, and there was always a kind of warning bell that I heard whenever I was with him. To me it rang: 'I am the writer and director of films you are still watching thirty years after I made them. The determination and commitment I have shown is something you will need if you are to survive in the world I have left behind.' In retrospect, I have come to understand that within those seven pages that pulled apart and ultimately annihilated my work, Sandy's lesson was that in order to make something good, real diligence is needed.

But however formidable his working methods, for many students their time with Mackendrick proved invaluable. 'Sandy gave me a knowledge base from which to draw, often unconsciously, and not a day goes by in my working life when I don't think about what I learnt in his classes and from his notes,' says former student and film critic F. X. Feeney.

I've never met anyone who has as universal and as integrated an understanding of how you get a written story onto the cinema screen as Sandy did. The highest praise I can give him is that he showed us how superficially we looked at cinema. Through my understanding of his handouts I can intuitively articulate what it is about a film that excites me and – crucially – what is lacking in a bad film. What made Sandy unique was his emphasis on craft and his avoidance of talking about 'art' in abstractions and generalities. He was an instinctive systems builder, combining the soul of an artist with the expertise of an engineer, and with a true renaissance man's sense of detail displayed a profound and systematic understanding of cinema's complex weights and measures. Sandy could look at any apparatus and break it down into its component pieces, and taught that by peeling back the layers and carefully studying something, whether it be an image, a story, a vaudeville act, or a joke, it was possible to unlock the mechanisms that made it work, and just as importantly be able to express what it might be lacking.

Though the selection of Mackendrick's writings presented here is far from complete, it does give a solid overview of his teachings. As he specifically designed his notes to be 'aids to students' memories of our classroom discussions', Mackendrick was always reluctant to make them available to people not enrolled in his courses. This is why several of the handouts constructed around specific scenes from films screened to students are not included in this book. Examples of texts omitted from this collection include the comparative piece entitled 'The Play and the Film: *Oedipus Rex*' that, though fascinating, merely gives a scene-by-scene breakdown of Sophocles' *Oedipus Rex* and Pasolini's 1967 film version (both 'worth studying for pure mechanical structure' notes Mackendrick). Another lengthy handout reiterates ideas detailed elsewhere, then uses them to construct a silent film version of the first half of scene two of Tennessee Williams' *A Streetcar Named Desire* (one that, Mackendrick somewhat proudly explains, 'uses only seven title cards containing a total of eighty-six words'). 'The intention of this exercise', he wrote, 'is not to prove that dialogue is unnecessary in the cinema. Indeed, the reverse. By exploring how film grammar can communicate most of the bare essentials of the narrative without the spoken word, we are able to isolate just how much extra is added by the quality of the dialogue and the actors' performances.'

'The Watergate Hearings' is comprised of Mackendrick's transcripts and storyboards of the televised hearings in the wake of

19. See Lance Lee's
*A Poetics for
Screenwriters*
(University of Texas
Press, 2001), Michael
Tierno's *Aristotle's
Poetics for
Screenwriters:
Storytelling Secrets
from the Greatest Mind
in Western Civilization*
(Hyperion, 2002), and
Ari Hiltunen's *Aristotle
in Hollywood: Visual
Stories That Work*
(Intellect Books, 2002).

the Watergate scandal, and raises pertinent questions about the nature of non-fiction film-making. F. X. Feeney recalls that 'the handout was Sandy's way of getting us to understand that *all* forms of television and cinema should be looked at in terms of film grammar. It was apparent to him that there was someone structuring the narrative of the Watergate broadcasts, just as there is behind the most elementary piece of news reportage, political propaganda or educational film.' But 'The Watergate Hearings', like other texts absent from this book, seems to be very much an adjunct to classroom discussions and screenings, and lacks the energy of Mackendrick's writings included in this collection.

Several handouts dealing with dramatic construction have also been excluded, for example 'From Book to Screen: *The Third Man*' that compares Graham Greene's novella with the screenplay he wrote for Carol Reed's 1949 film, and another that reproduces a particular chapter of John Steinbeck's novel *The Grapes of Wrath* alongside the relevant dialogue from John Ford's 1940 film version. One of Mackendrick's most memorable exercises was created when he took the set of storyboards he had drawn of Orson Welles's *Citizen Kane* – a film told in a series of flashbacks – and re-edited them so they ran in chronological order. ('Needless to say,' wrote Mackendrick, 'it isn't as good, since what has been thrown away is the central thematic idea: the exploration of why the man was the kind of man he was.') And though his lengthy handout on Aristotle's *Poetics* – primarily made up of excerpts from the Greek classic with short commentary interspersed – is also missing from this collection, Mackendrick repeatedly urged students to read the work.[19] Several handouts not reprinted in full are quoted from in this introduction, which also contains interviews with former students and colleagues, as well as extracts from Mackendrick's unpublished (and always undated) notebooks.

In Mackendrick's archive there is a large collection of his Step Outlines and storyboards (often with accompanying dialogue) of scenes from various films. In the days before video and DVD players, these pages must have been treasure-troves for students. But today, however masterful a draftsman Mackendrick was, they seem poor substitutes for the films themselves, titles that include *The Asphalt Jungle*, *Casablanca*, *The Life of an American Fireman*, *On the Waterfront* (opening murder, Johnny Friendly's backroom, taxi cab), *Touch of Evil* (dynamite in shoe box), *Intolerance*, *Shadow of a Doubt* (various sequences, it being a film Mackendrick frequently used in class), *Le jour se lève*, *La grande illusion*, *The Hustler*, *8¹/₂* (Guido's first appearance at the spa) and *North by Northwest* (crop-dusting). Two of Mackendrick's favourite examples were the final scene from Chaplin's *City Lights* and the 1957 Western *3:10 to Yuma*, a film that in Mackendrick's mind was constructed with 'simplicity and economy', full of 'formulaic and archetypical' characters whose dialogue 'has an immediate purpose and effect'.

As producer and former student Thom Mount notes, 'Sandy taught that film is a popular art, not a fine art. The gyroscope that will point your own films in the right direction is a broad understanding of the culture around you.' As such, amongst Mackendrick's papers are his texts on the historical development of theatrical forms and the origins and nature of storytelling and drama, pages that take in Homer, Virgil, Hobbes, Kant, Descartes, Kierkegaard, Kafka, Dostoyevsky, Bergson, Pirandello, Henry James, Oscar Wilde, Freud, Jung, Bettelheim, Ortega y Gasset, Sartre, R. D. Laing, Walter Benjamin, Margaret Mead, Susan Sontag, Noam Chomsky, Jean Piaget, Somerset Maugham, Konrad Lorenz, Harold Pinter, Marshall McLuhan, Northrop Frye, Robert Frost and Mickey Mouse, among others. Mackendrick prepared notes on subjects such as myth (that for 'primitive societies represents what bedtime stories do for us during our childhood'), make-believe ('a curiously subtle and complicated psychological state') and religion. Works he considered particularly beneficial to an understanding of myth and storytelling were Johan Huizinga's book *Homo Ludens*[20] ('a study of what has been called the willing suspension of belief that is involved in "playing", the imaginative act of make-believe'), Lajos Egri's *The Art of Dramatic Writing*[21] and Keith Johnstone's *Impro*[22] (especially Johnstone's work on 'Status'). Mackendrick also produced lengthy summaries of cinema history[23] – from Paleolithic cave painting to Thomas Edison, from George Méliès to Michelangelo Antonioni – as well as handouts on comedy, most of which are drawn from Max Eastman's book *Enjoyment of Laughter*.[24] (Mackendrick

20. *Homo Ludens: A Study of the Play-Element in Culture* (Beacon Press, 1955; first published in German in 1944).

21. Touchstone Books, 1972.

22. *Impro* (Methuen, 1981). See also *Impro for Storytellers* (Faber and Faber, 1999).

23. Mackendrick cites Louis Giannetti's *Understanding Movies*, Gerald Mast's *Film/Cinema/Movie: A Theory of Experience* and Kenneth MacGowan's *Behind the Screen: History and Techniques of the Motion Picture* in handouts relating to the beginnings of cinema. Another book that Mackendrick used in class is C. W. Ceram's fascinating *Archaeology of the Cinema* (Harcourt, Brace and World Inc.,1965), 'the definitive history of the cinema before 1897'.

24. *Enjoyment of Laughter* (Simon and Schuster, 1936).

25. See Richard L. Gregory's *Eye and Brain: The Psychology of Seeing* (Oxford, first published in 1966, now in its fifth edition).

told students that 'If you have ambitions to practise comedy, you won't learn a lot from books.') In a summing up for their final class, Mackendrick wrote to students:

What is it I have been trying to demonstrate for you as we have been vivisecting all these stories – stories as varied as prehistoric myths, ancient epic tales of gods and heroes, classic works of the theatre, folk stories, fairy tales and even anecdotes, and finally as commercial mass entertainment? It's this: they all seem to share a similar anatomy. Though wildly different in their *content*, they are curiously alike in *structure*.

Finally, an important element to Mackendrick's teachings, one he believed to be critical to an understanding of the director's craft, stems from his interest in science and extensive readings in the discipline. Though certainly not the first film-maker to explore such things (in *Painting with Light*, his classic 1949 book on cinematography, for example, John Alton writes that 'the human brain is the most completely equipped television studio there is'), Mackendrick believed students should have an elementary comprehension of how the brain functions in relation to visual perception ('the mental reading of the information coming from the eye'). Students may have looked blank-faced when told they needed to know about image movement in relation to the retina, or wondered why they should study handouts such as 'The Evolution of the Eye and Brain', 'Persistence of Vision', 'The Illusion of Movement in Film' and 'The Neural System and Levels of Awareness'. But Mackendrick was adamant such things needed to be understood, explaining in a notebook how

the principles of the psychology of perception are important to students' understanding of the effects of camera movement, and of their value in the study of film grammar . . . Particularly in narrative/dramatic cinema, the director must rely on the 'tricks' that deceive the eye and the brain. Using these 'flaws' in perceptual processes, he builds out of fragmentary pieces of images and sound a new and persuasive but fictitious 'reality'.

Mackendrick cited the work of neuropsychologist Richard L. Gregory, whose work is summarised in one handout.[25]

Gregory's point is that even our everyday perception of reality is in a sense illusory. Film/video language is a system of visual and aural signals conveying meaning and structure to the mind, not the eye. The mechanism of the eye (not only the camera-like aspects of the physical eye itself, but the nerve-chemistry of rods and cones in the retina) supplies information that passes along the optic nerve to the cortex where the signal is decoded and interpreted. This is a complex process, but what is important for the film director to understand is that the brain (the mind's eye and ear) is active. The eyes may do some of the decoding, but it is the brain that reads the visual and oral information, sometimes relying on information from both, as well as calling on stored memory, to find meaning. In short, perception is not a passive activity: it involves making a decision about the sensory data that is supplied.

26. 'Do Make Waves: Alexander Mackendrick interviewed by Kate Buford', *Film Comment* (May–June 1994).

The many pages on the science of perception and vision are not included here because they are either out of date, or available in a more coherent form elsewhere, or both.

Mackendrick's notes are generally free of personal anecdotes about his own work as a director (the most obvious exception being the lengthy piece on *Sweet Smell of Success* in the 'Dramatic Construction' section). 'A director should never, on any account, try to "explain" himself,' he wrote. 'What's more, the impossibility of being objective about one's own work is what makes it so much more useful and instructive to use as study material the work of other people about whom one can be relatively objective.' But the most important reason why Mackendrick avoided using his films as classroom examples was that he was increasingly convinced of 'the harm done to young folk by what is known as the cult of the director – the director as the figure responsible for everything,' something he was 'dedicated to stamping out'. For Mackendrick, the very word 'director' implied being in control of other people's skills just as much, if not more, than the exercise of one's own craftsmanship. As he explained, 'The true role of a director involves more than having practical experience in various technical skills – it means functioning as a leader who is able to give direction to a group of other talented individuals.' In fact the great directors, he suggested, 'dissolve and disappear into the work' while making 'other people look good'.[26]

27. AFI Workshop.

28. 'As I See It with
Alexander
Mackendrick', *Film
Teacher* (Spring 1953).

I am nothing but the centripetal force that holds these interpretations together. I may privately think I did it all, but in fact I'm kidding myself, because the director is merely the channel of other people's talents.[27]

One of Mackendrick's most ardent beliefs about the collaborative nature of film-making – and a critical link between the two sections of this book – was the importance of writer and director working together in order to bring their visions to the screen within the same film. As far as Mackendrick was concerned, the technical concerns of film grammar were never to be explored independently of story, while at the same time any competent piece of cinematic storytelling was an inevitable example of how 'form can never be entirely distinguished from content'. Mackendrick was keen to emphasise that everything in a film should be at the service of the narrative, whether it was lighting ('What mood and emotional tone can be established through the use of light and shadow?'), editing ('If I cut here, what will be revealed to the audience, what will be left out, and how will this help tell the story?'), framing and shot size ('If I use a close-up here rather than a long shot, what am I asking the audience to think about?'), camera movement ('If I move the camera, from whose point of view will the audience be experiencing the action?'), or acting ('How can I use this prop to convey a particular story beat to the audience without saying anything?'). 'Every bit of a film', wrote Mackendrick, 'ought to be a necessary part of the whole effect.'[28] Simply, the wide array of concepts articulated in the two sections of this book were always intended to reinforce each another.

By plotting, in two intricate handouts, the precise physical moves of characters in various scenes from Orson Welles's *Touch of Evil* and Elia Kazan's *On the Waterfront*, by alerting students to the camera moves and shot sizes used to reinforce thematic content, by demonstrating how the characters interact with each other and with on-set props, Mackendrick was able to show just how unified his notes on Film Grammar, Dramatic Construction and acting are. 'How does one go about planning the camera angles and moves, the staging of the actors, and the decision when to cut away from one shot to another?' he asked in a handout.

It must start with the story, needless to say. When working with a text, the first thing a director must do is break the scene down into moves. This doesn't mean physical moves, rather the dramatic beats that mark the intentions of the characters, the steps of story progression, all of which are only later gradually translated into the staging of the actors. What students must do is think first from the point of view of the performer and only then consider what things look like through the viewfinder.

There exist several practical guides to film production, and many volumes that purport to teach the craft of writing for the cinema.[29] While preparing this collection I read a good number of these texts, something that enabled me to understand what makes Mackendrick's book so distinctive.

First, unlike most books on the subject, *On Film-making* is written by a bona fide film-maker, a man whose cinematic achievements are recognised more than thirty-five years after he directed his final film. Moreover, his insights as a teacher come not only from his years of practical experience, his time spent as a professional writer and director in Hollywood and elsewhere (Mackendrick was nearly sixty years of age when he taught his first class), but also from his subsequent twenty-year study of how film-making might best be taught.

Second, Mackendrick is a lucid, vibrant and invigorating writer. Compared with the overwhelmingly shallow and self-serving prose of the more than three dozen authors I consulted (primarily those claiming to know the secrets of dramatic construction), this volume has genuine literary qualities. It also, thankfully, eschews the 'Believe In Yourself' and 'Maximise Your Creative Powers' approach taken by so many 'how-to-write' books.

Third, most crucially, Mackendrick's belief in the exploitation of cinema's unique qualities as a storytelling medium is something other books on screenplay writing largely ignore. So enthralled by their apparent understanding of how a well-written film script is structured, these authors either totally disregard or breeze perfunctorily over the inextricable links between the work of the screenwriter and the film director. But as Mackendrick explains in the following pages, a writer's ability to do his job is

29. For those who think the publishing industry's slew of didactic texts on dramatic structure (today most evidently applied to screenplays) is a new phenomenon, the 1960 Dover edition of William Archer's *Play-Making* contains a short bibliographical essay by John Gassner entitled 'Books on Playwriting'. Though it makes 'no attempt to be inclusive', thirty-five books published between 1890 and 1958 are cited.

30. David Mamet, *On Directing Film* (Faber and Faber), 1991, p. 71.

severely curtailed if he has only a superficial knowledge of how cinema functions as a medium. Most other books explain that dialogue should be kept to a minimum (the old adage 'show, don't tell' is ubiquitous), while the subtly distinct idea that words be used merely as 'the sprinkles on top of the ice-cream cone'[30] is relatively unexplored. A good example of Mackendrick's characteristic approach is his discussion of 'subtext', a crucial component of any film story. In most of the books I consulted, subtext seems to be confused with 'subplot' and is explored explicitly from the writer's or actor's point of view. Though in the theatre it is the actor's job to render even banal dialogue meaningful (with – as Mackendrick would call it – different 'colours'), with cinema it is the competent director who will use the fundaments of film grammar to turn script pages into effective cinematic sequences. By not taking into account what the camera, lighting and editing machine are able to convey to the audience – regardless of what is being said by the actors – other authors explore only half the story. In fact, most other volumes scarcely touch upon the concept of visual story-telling at all, and when they do they often make what Mackendrick would have considered a fundamental error. For many, a film that contains beautiful cinematography and imagery is 'visual'. But to Mackendrick such works were merely pictorial. A truly visual film, he explained, is one that exploits the medium of cinema to the fullest extent by telling its story primarily with shot-to-shot images.

This volume is not the final word on the craft of film-making, merely one man's carefully considered thoughts on the subject. Much of what follows may be seen by some readers as representing an extreme point of view. But this is probably the point, for Mackendrick was aware that students would pick and choose from his ideas, inevitably combining them with other teachings, as well as their own notions of what cinema is. Always keen that film-makers steer clear of books about cinema ('talking about film is something of a contradiction in terms: it is already in the wrong medium') and reluctant to edit his own writings into a coherent text for publication, Mackendrick was anxious that students concentrate on the practical applications of his classroom teachings.

One of the ideas that pervaded CalArts from day one was that of 'No information in advance of need.' As far as Mackendrick would have been concerned, this book (which is full of information) is perhaps best appreciated by those neophytes who have already experienced their own practical difficulties in writing and directing for the screen. But even for those people who feel the need – erroneously, Mackendrick would have insisted – to read a book or two before they pick up their equipment and start experimenting, it is safe to say that these notes contain much that film-makers and artists might dwell on. Cameras and editing systems are, to paraphrase Jean Cocteau, as accessible and affordable to today's directors as pen and paper are to the novelist. Consequently, once Mackendrick's writings on cinema and storytelling have been absorbed and digested, there can be no excuses for not putting this book down and pushing forward with your projects. It is here that the ideas will cohere, the mistakes will be made, and the real work done.

Mackendrick rewrote his most important notes every year to make them as clear as possible, and because of this there are sometimes three or four different versions of a single handout. My own work involved selecting for this collection from notes, interview transcripts, notebook entries and drawings contained in the many filing-cabinet drawers of material in Mackendrick's archive. Inevitably this means that the texts presented here have been assembled from a variety of different sources. I am appreciative of the assistance given by former students and colleagues of Sandy Mackendrick in the preparation of this mass of paperwork: Thom Andersen, Martha Baxton, John Brice, David Brisbin, Doug Campbell, Roger Crittenden, Terence Davies, Myron Emery, the late Jules Engel, Gill Dennis, F. X. Feeney, Lou Florimonte, John Gianvito, Ed Harris, Mark Jonathan Harris, Mamoun Hassan, John Hawk, David Irving, Bill Jackson, Richard Jefferies, Rachelle Katz, Kris Malkiewicz, James Mangold, Chris Meeks, Francisco Menendez, Thom Mount, Michael Pressman, Terry Sanders, Conny Templeman, Antonio Tibaldi, Andrew Tsao, Jack Valero and Colin Young. Thanks to Denis Cannan, Bernard Gribble, Ronald Harwood, Philip Kemp, Douglas Slocombe and David Thompson, and Dr Howard Gotlieb and Sean Noël of Special Collections at Boston

University (home of the Alexander Mackendrick Collection). Thanks also to Richard Kelly and Walter Donohue at Faber and Faber for their guidance, Marcel Fitzmaurice and Jeremy Freeson for their counsel, Lesley Shaw for her support, and especially Hilary Mackendrick for her trust and generosity.

Paul Cronin
London, July 2003

Prologue

Film is a medium. It is a language of communication that transmits a concept from the imagination of the creator into the mind's eye and ear of those to whom the message is addressed. Nothing, therefore, is absolute. Everything is meaningless until interpreted as having meaning in the imagination of the receiver, something true of all languages and media. A medium is based on an agreement, a contract that has developed over a long period during which the speaker and the listener, the picture maker and the viewer, performer and audience, have established a system of meanings: a vocabulary, syntax and grammar of the language being used. For this reason, language emerges slowly, and will continue to evolve for as long as audiences and authors develop new ways of expressing themselves.

The filmgoer sits before a lighted rectangle on which are projected moving shadows while he listens to playback of recorded sound. The filmgoer reads these images-with-sound according to accepted and learned film grammar. Thus, when a two-dimensional image of the full-length figure of a woman is projected and then abruptly switched off to be replaced by a much bigger image of a man's face, the viewer does not wonder if the woman has become a man, but rather thinks, 'Oh, I am now in another position, looking in another direction at a man who is near, instead of a woman who is far away.' Also, possibly, 'The woman is what this man is looking at.' And so on.

As a teacher of film-making, then, it is my habit to remind students that film is not just something up there on the screen – it's a happening in your head. The film environment is a flat rectangular space in a dark theatre, nothing more than photographic two-dimensional pictures. Film tends to begin as an idea in the mind of a director or writer. It may have to be realised through a complicated sequence of mechanical processes, always involving a number of technicians who make important contributions. But it must finally end as it began: a response in the mind of a single viewer. Initially and in the eventual effect, the thing is intangible, existing only in the realm of imagination. It is an illusion.

At this early stage, let me explain that it is somewhat misleading to call one of the classes I teach 'Film Grammar'. The word 'grammar' suggests there is some kind of language of cinema, when it is probably more useful to consider the basic ideas in these notes as nothing more than a series of visual conventions based on the contract that exists between film-maker and audience. The trouble is I have not found another name that is as simple yet accurate enough. (The semiotics professors use terms like 'syntactic articulations' to describe the way shots and camera angles can be organised to represent a coherent, though imaginary, space/time continuum, but it's rather a mouthful.)

The key to the Film Grammar class is the common-sense notion that if we are living in the era in which children – before they can spell or read – are exposed to the moving-picture image on television, then what we should be doing is teaching people about the images they are reading and instruct them how to speak back in this visual language that is the literacy of today. In short, it is important that citizens become consciously aware of cinema's conditioning influences. It is not, however, enough to be merely receptive to its codes of communication. To be literate in a medium is to be able to write as well as read. To know how film and video communicate (and, in turn, manipulate), one should also be able to speak the 'language' and have some idea of how a film is made. The only true way to reach such an understanding is, of course, through practice.

But before the student film-maker runs out and starts making films, he should make a detailed analysis of particular examples of stories told through the cinematic medium. Exposure to such dramatic structures will help the young director explore the variety of options he himself might choose to use, according to his own needs, as he tackles new problems and explores his own inevitably individual approach to film-making. This is something we will undertake in class with the use of these notes and prints of specific films. But it is also something you should do at home as you sit watching *any* film, whether good or bad. The medium of cinema communicates fast – we 'read' it at considerable speed. This is why one of the best ways to learn about film grammar is first by watching a film at regular speed so as to take in the initial rush of dramatic emotions, then by studying it slowly. By stopping and starting you will be able to analyse the dynamics of image-to-image, shot-to-shot and scene-to-scene in more depth. Your involvement in the story will soon drop away, revealing those individual structural elements that, when pieced together, create the narrative.

Now to the question so often asked about film-making: is it a craft that can be taught? Absolutely not, no more than anything else that is an 'art' can be taught. On the other hand, it may just be possible to call to the attention of the beginner the usages of the 'language' of cinema that have so far developed (and continue to evolve). The best thing I can do as a teacher is to provide an environment within which those who have imagination and sensibility (and the essential energy, concentration and self-discipline) can learn, teaching themselves. Remember: no 'rule' is worth anything until you have discovered it afresh for yourself. Originality consists in taking existing conventions, studying how they govern the medium, and finding utterly new ways to use them. There are no concrete formulas available to the film-maker, or at least none that should not be immediately abandoned if another arises that suits the circumstances. Indeed, it may be fair to say that you will not understand the value of the traditional use of convention until you have experimented with ways in which it can by effectively disregarded. The value of any 'rule' is not apparent until you have studied the exception to it.

Just as Picasso demonstrated his complete command of figurative and illusionist painting before he went on to reinvent the language of visual art, so it is that the artist or craftsman, with each new innovation he instigates, should begin by ensuring he has complete command over all the so-called principles he then subverts. (After all, a demolition expert has to understand every principle of architecture before he can do his job.) Your only mistake, as you work in this medium of communication, is to produce in your audience an effect you didn't intend, or fail to

1. Lev Kuleshov (1898–1970, Russia) was a theorist, teacher and film-maker who played an important role in the development of montage theory, and is perhaps best known today for the so-called 'Kuleshov Experiment' (see Pudovkin's *Film Technique*, George Newnes, 1935, p. 140).

produce the effect you did. If a film works it is never simply because it followed the rules. If it fails, however, it is almost certainly that the breaking of one or more rule is the root cause.

So just how is the knack of film-directing acquired? Allow me to make two general points at this juncture. First, it has been said that the director is like the orchestra conductor, a maestro who must be able to play every instrument competently. Unlikely as it is that you will ever discover real ability in all three fields of directing, writing and acting, I believe you will not be even competent in any single one without a basic comprehension of the other two. Second, it is important to understand that every art form has evolved different histories, conventions and traditions, clearly identifiable aesthetics, values and procedures. Russian film theorist Lev Kuleshov wrote 'That which is a 'work of art' before it is photographed and recorded will not be a work of art when it is put on the screen.'[1] From this we can conclude that when students choose to film, for example, a dance performance, though the result may be a record of a fine piece of dancing, it will most probably be unsatisfactory when presented as a substitute for the experience of the live and present dancers' performance. And it will also probably be dull as film or video, for it makes no real use of the unique qualities film has to offer. As a student of cinema, it is the particular characteristics of the medium you have chosen to work in that you should consider at every stage of the process.

There are also three practical suggestions I can give. The first is intimately related to Kuleshov's ideas. I am often confronted by students who, when practising shooting set-ups, want to use theatre scripts by established writers rather than their own original screenplays. This can be good practice for beginners as it means concentrating solely on exploring the possibilities of film grammar as you use the camera and editing bench. The potential problem in working on a more original piece of writing is that if the resulting film is unsatisfactory, you won't know whether it was your understanding of the grammar (your direction of the film) that was at fault, or whether the writing was inherently unsatisfactory. By saving up for an ambitious project, by delaying your production experience until you have your own dramatic ideas to work with, you are robbing yourself of a valuable

xxxviii

learning experience. Get some experience of directing from existing (and trusted) script material *before* you try to direct something you've written yourself (though as Kuleshov has suggested, repeatedly using only existing material – especially theatre scripts reliant on the spoken word – is plainly not a good idea).

Second, work for an experienced director, doing some job where you are close enough to watch the process. The editor's job is traditionally regarded as the best experience, the assistant's job is a close second, as you will get a chance to keep watching how the other guy does it, what his problems are, and how much better you will do it when you get your break.

Third, write. By planning on your own, then rewriting over and over, even if this is the part of the process you find most difficult (even intolerable), you will learn an incalculable amount.

Having established that teaching the rules of film-making is not possible, I will now, with the help of these notes, attempt to do just that. What this really means is that I will explain to you as best I can my own method of film-making, the one that suits me. If I bully you into trying things my way, it is not because mine is the only way, or even the best way. Certainly it will probably, in the end, not be your way. But I suggest you make a real effort to follow my formulas as a temporary exercise. Not to 'express yourself'. Not yet. You can do that as much as you like, later. So put aside your hunger for instant gratification and creativity, at least for long enough to understand some basic ideas and practical pieces of advice that you are perfectly entitled to discard later.

Anybody who wants out please say so now.

PART ONE

Dramatic Construction

The Pre-Verbal Language of Cinema

Speech involves the rationalising of our feelings and impulses, something film directors of the silent era discovered they could catch at first hand.

Through the use of different screen sizes and the framing of shots, the juxtaposition of camera angles and point of view, expressive music and lighting, and the principles of editing, they found that the camera can, uniquely, photograph thought.[1] Since that time, those directors who have made the best use of the film medium have used the camera to communicate to audiences at a level far more immediate and primitive than the spoken word. By primitive I don't mean more simplistic and less subtle. Far from it. Cinema deals with feelings, sensations, intuitions and movement, things that communicate to audiences at a level not necessarily subject to conscious, rational and critical comprehension. Because of this, the so-called 'language' the film director uses may, in fact, make for a much richer and denser experience. Actions and images speak faster, and to more of the senses, than speech does.

A recurring theme of these notes is that cinema is not so much non-verbal as *pre*-verbal. Though it is able to reproduce reams of dialogue, film can also tell stories purely in movement, in action and reaction. Cinematographic images, particularly when synchronised with recorded sound, deliver such quantities of visual and audible data that the verbal component (even, in the days of silent cinema, title cards) is overwhelmed and becomes secondary. Consequently, the essential and underlying meaning of film dialogue is often much more effectively transmitted by a complex and intricate organisation of cinematic elements that are not only not verbal, but also can never be fully analysed by verbal means. Look at this example, taken from André Cayatte's

1. Mackendrick frequently cited D. W. Griffith to students as one of the most important pioneering directors in this respect. 'Today the "close-up" is essential to every Motion Picture,' wrote Griffith in 1917, 'for the near view of the actors' lineaments conveys intimate thought and emotion that can never be conveyed by the crowded scene'. (*Focus on D. W. Griffith*, edited by Harry M. Geduld, Prentice-Hall, 1971, p. 52).

2. Truffaut's interview book *Hitchcock* (Touchstone, 1985), p. 61.

1949 film *Les amants de Vérone*, as written by Jacques Prévert.

Some visitors are being taken round a glassworks in which the young hero is one of the skilled craftsmen who makes fantastically ornamental goblets, vases and mirrors. One of them is an attractive young actress who is being escorted by an elderly and wealthy man who obviously wants to impress her. She, meanwhile, has taken rather a fancy to the hero. While her escort is buying her a present in the showroom, the hero watches through a glass partition. The girl turns to smile at him through the glass, whereupon he makes a couple of scratches on one of the panes with his diamond glass-cutter and knocks out of it onto her side a small piece of glass in the shape of a heart. She is amused but has to conceal it quickly as her wealthy gentleman friend returns bearing a huge and ornate mirror. He presents it to her proudly. She looks at it and after a moment smiles. But the camera shows us something he cannot see: she is really smiling into the mirror at the reflection of the young man behind.

This entire incident is quick and casual. It probably takes less time in front of the camera than it does to explain in words, and is much more effective on screen than I have told it here. This is the point: it is not the sort of incident a novelist would invent because it is far clumsier to describe than to play out on film. Nor would it make a good piece of action for the stage actor because the effect depends on quick glimpses of detail, the flicker of reactions on faces and a switch of viewpoint by the camera. Prévert is writing for the cinema, and nothing else. The director Alfred Hitchcock has said that during the silent era, the great directors 'had reached something near perfection. The introduction of sound, in a way, jeopardised that perfection.'[2] Hitchcock is suggesting that a good film should be ninety per cent understandable even if dubbed into a language no one sitting in the auditorium understands. Why? Because a well-written, acted and directed film should be able to convey its emotional meaning through the inventive use of film grammar, not words. And it is, of course, the emotional and dramatic content of any scene that really counts.

There is likely to be immediate protest from those students who insist that dialogue is an entirely legitimate component of

DRAMATIC CONSTRUCTION

modern cinema. Needless to say, the spoken word can be an important element of storytelling on film, but because cinema is so well equipped to explore action and movement, together with the emotions behind the words (those physical impulses and reactions that both anticipate speech and are a response to dialogue), it is not so dependent on what is actually being said. As Truffaut writes in his interview book with Alfred Hitchcock, 'Whatever is *said* instead of being *shown* is lost on the viewer.'[3] Truffaut's cardinal 'rule' does not mean that a film's cinematography is the only medium of communication in cinema. He is not suggesting that speech has no value or that dialogue does not contribute. But he is pointing out that in cinema, mute action supplies the most basic information, while verbal information adds another, secondary dimension.

3. *Hitchcock*, p. 17.

Though a gift for lively and playable dialogue is perhaps the skill most likely to assure you of a professional career as a scriptwriter, the dialogue-driven screenplay is actually a wholly misguided blueprint for a film. Simply, dialogue is almost always less effective than visible activity in cinema, and not until the screenwriter understands that good characterisation can be made visible through physical behaviour and the riches film grammar has to offer is he truly writing for the medium. This is one of the first things the screenwriter needs to understand before studying the craft of dramatic construction, for it is the job of the writer, *not* the director, to decide whether his film story will be built with images or merely decorated with them.

The film camera and cutting bench, able to manipulate both space and time so efficiently (just as the novelist can vary point of view, to say nothing of his ability to describe and explain internal feelings and thoughts), can do much to express those things unsaid by the characters. Between internal thought (the uncensored and unselfconscious impulse) and deliberately delivered words there may be some contradiction. What we say inside our heads is private, and by putting it into words and addressing it to others we often rationalise and even distort our original impulses and intentions. The best lines of film dialogue are sometimes those in which the real meanings lie between the words, where the spoken lines mask the true and unadulterated feelings of the speaker.

Such emotions are often visible to the camera, just as they are to an observant human being, because the spoken words frame those revealing and fleeting moments that take place just before the character speaks or as an impulsive non-verbal reaction to what has just been said, seen by the film editor, for example, in shots containing perhaps a barely visible shift of focus in the eyes, an unconscious flexing of jaw muscles, or a gesticulation during a speech. Study, frame by frame, the performance of an expressive actor in close-up and you may be able to find the precise images where the spark of thought or feeling ignites, those impulsive moments that then find expression in the delivery of a line. In the hands of competent film-makers, even the most seemingly inconsiderable dialogue can provide a significance that would be lost if there were more talking. If a scene is genuinely interesting because it is cinematic (in the sense that without speech we can comprehend most, if not all, of what is happening), then the added component of the spoken word will probably contribute something. If the scene is uninteresting in cinematic terms, then layer upon layer of dialogue will only make it more so.

One of the tasks of the director as he transfers a screenplay to the medium of the moving-image-with-sound is almost to forget what his characters are saying and reimagine their behaviour as being mute, so that all thoughts, feelings and impulses are conveyed to the audience through sound and vision – without speech. There is a curious paradox here, for when a scene has been reconstituted in this fashion the director is often able to reincorporate elements of the original dialogue in ways that make it vastly more effective. Moreover, when a script has been conceived in genuinely cinematic terms, its sparse dialogue is likely to be free of the task of exposition and will consequently be much more expressive. A sound principle is to employ expository dialogue as the reaction to events that take place before the lens (remember: movies show and then tell). Invent action or incidents as the provocation for dialogue, because exposition in film is much more interesting after the dramatic event as a comment (or perhaps an explanation) on it. In this sense the dialogue of a well-constructed film will enrich the visuals – it is never merely an extension of what is already obvious to observant audiences (think of title cards in early silent

DRAMATIC CONSTRUCTION

films used as punctuation of what is being looked at, not as a substitute for it).

The senior writers at the film studio in London where I worked for many years used to delight in collecting examples of bad dialogue in screenplays. One of their favourites was 'Look, Highland cattle!' This was a quote from a particularly amateurish travelogue in which a character pointed off-screen, said this line, and the film cut to guess what? Those three words became shorthand for a piece of wholly unnecessary and redundant exposition used when the story was being told perfectly well solely through visual means. A good director will go out of his way, often in the editing process when he has both words and images in front of him, to gradually eliminate all lines that are not absolutely necessary. In the final film, many pieces of dialogue are apt to become redundant because the on-screen action is telling the story with more clarity without them. A scene that on paper might seem to be more effective when full of witty and clever dialogue can often play far more meaningfully and effectively through subtle moments of silent interaction between characters (moments that are, inevitably, not so easy to appreciate when in script form only).

In fact, cinema can be at its most interesting and forceful when images play *against* the literal sense of the dialogue. When what is spoken by the screen actor acts as counterpoint to what is being seen by the audience, dialogue is able to express much more than the literal meaning of the words and so has extra force. In such cases, the uniqueness of the cinematic medium is most apparent. Through this sometimes extremely subtle juxtaposition of words and images, the writer and director are able to focus attention on the rhythm of a scene's subtext. By doing so, and by making use of the fact that the camera is able to relate things to audiences subliminally rather than literally, it is possible to tell more than one story at once.

Consider this simple example from Truffaut, who writes of the 'mundane occasions [such] as dinner and cocktail parties, or of any meeting between casual acquaintances':

If we observe any such gathering, it is clear that the words exchanged between the guests are superficial formalities and quite meaningless,

4. *Hitchcock*, p. 17.

5. One figure cited repeatedly in Mackendrick's Film Grammar handouts whose work gives us a deeper understanding of these ideas is German psychologist and theorist Rudolf Arnheim, author of the 1933 book *Film as Art* (Faber and Faber, 1983). In a handout that elucidates Arnheim's ideas, Mackendrick notes that it was during the first thirty years of silent cinema when the underlying and immutable grammar of cinema – the visual and kinetic 'language' which distinguishes it from theatre and literature – was established by the more imaginative directors. 'It's been claimed that before the coming of synchronised sound most of the important techniques of cinema had already been established,' explains Mackendrick. In this respect, he adds, 'talking pictures' were deemed by some to be a 'retrogressive step'.

whereas the essential is elsewhere; it is by studying their eyes that we can find out what is truly on their minds. Let us assume that as an observer at a reception I am looking at Mr Y as he tells three people all about his recent holiday in Scotland with his wife. By carefully watching his face, I notice he never takes his eyes off Mrs X's legs. Now, I move over to Mrs X, who is talking about her children's problems at school, but I notice that she keeps staring at Miss Z, her cold look taking in every detail of the younger woman's elegant appearance. Obviously, the substance of that scene is not in the dialogue, which is strictly conventional, but in what these people are thinking about. Merely by watching them I have found out that Mr Y is physically attracted to Mrs X and that Mrs X is jealous of Miss Z.[4]

Puzzled by the difficulties encountered by many students as they tackle the problems of writing for the cinema, I wonder if this is because we are educated to think verbally. This conditioning to express oneself in literate word systems can be a stumbling block to young writers and directors, a handicap to those trying to master the pre-verbal structures of narrative cinema. For most students, ideas that spring to mind are so swiftly transformed into words that we automatically equate thought with speech and writing, rather than visuals. It has even been argued by psychologists that thinking is not possible without the capacity to verbalise.

It does certainly appear that during our psychological development through the stages of babyhood, infancy and pre-adolescence, the point at which we are said to be capable of thought and abstract reason seems to date from the period when we are also learning to speak. But I am not entirely convinced by this argument. Just as a cartoonist can tell a story in sequential images of action without captions, so a film-maker can imagine a scene told in the pure language of the cinema, a language invented before the birth of Talkies (sync sound). Nevertheless, to translate certain concepts into cinematic forms comprehensible without words, the student may actually have to unlearn habits of verbal thought and return to patterns that are in some ways more primitive. This can be a ruthless learning experience, requiring elimination of our habits of talking in generalities, of failing to be specific and concrete, and of intellectual concepts.[5]

8   DRAMATIC CONSTRUCTION

What is a Story?

1. S. H. Butcher translation (Dover, 1997), p. 51. Richard Janko's translation makes this point most clearly: 'Impossible [incidents] that are believable should be preferred to possible ones that are unbelievable.'

Can we define the nature of what we call a story? What are the distinguishing characteristics of a story? Is it content or form? Must a story be a work of fiction? Surely not, since there have been documentaries, biographical and historical, that carefully represent only factual material but nevertheless have as gripping a narrative structure as any work of complete invention. Are there characteristic elements? Does, for instance, a story, whether it presents factual reality or imitations of real life, have to be structured in a particular way? And if so, what are the necessary elements of this structure?

One way to tackle these questions is to explore the origins of the impulses of storytelling as they are seen in the earliest human civilisations and then echoed in the psychology of infants emerging into childhood. It has been pointed out that when a child begins to ask a question like 'Where do babies come from?' and the mother explains about the stork that flies over rooftops, carrying a swaddled bundle that it brings as a present to Mummy and Daddy, this is a much more acceptable reply than information about the semen from Daddy that fertilise the ovum inside Mummy. The tale about the stork (told to a child who has never even seen such a bird) is believable. He or she can handle it, while the stuff about fertility is unacceptable because it raises a lot more unanswered questions. Incomprehensible, it becomes implausible and unbelievable. Note that this point was made a few hundred years before Christ by the man who first tried to set down some laws about drama, Aristotle. He wrote that 'a poet should prefer probable impossibilities to improbable possibilities.'[1]

The child, with its limited experience and simplistic comprehension of life, is trying to make coherent sense out of profound mysteries, and needs any explanations to be satisfying at the

2. Claude Lévi-Strauss,
The Savage Mind
(Oxford, 1972), p. 22.

level of his or her understanding. While the stork story is usable,
the biological data must wait till the child can cope with it. One
can argue, therefore, that such a tale – like the myths of prehistoric times – functions as a 'poetic' explanation of concepts that
are beyond the limited intellectual capacities of the listeners to
deal with. This may be how drama began. In his book *The
Savage Mind*, anthropologist Claude Lévi-Strauss says that 'art
lies halfway between scientific knowledge and magical or mysti-
cal thought.'[2]

The Greek mind of Homeric days personified all its beliefs.
Science was conceived in parable form, with abstract concepts
symbolised in the semi-human forms of the gods. This is surely
how the imagination of every one of us functions when we are
small children. Indeed, it is the way we dream, for dreams are the
unconscious mind at work and they have their own language.
Psychotherapists will warn you that a figure in a dream should not
always be thought of as a person in the same way that the waking
mind conceives individuals. Dream-figures are more often personifications of some aspect of the dreamer's psyche. This could be a
clue to the psychological purpose of all stories. A story that has
fictional characters may be using these figments of the imagination or unconscious in order to act out an abstract thought, an
idea, a theme (the underlying dramatic point of the story).

It can be argued that form, in all of the arts, has a mnemonic
purpose. A mnemonic is, in popular terms, a device like a piece
of doggerel verse that helps you remember some information
you might otherwise forget if you could not rattle off the rhyme
without thinking. The scansion and rhymes of poetry, whether
vulgar limericks or Shakespearean blank verse, have this much
in common: they come easily to the lips because the sounds of
the words, their formal qualities, make them easy to recall. In a
way, a story does this too. The pattern of its dramatic unities, an
articulation of connected incidents that function as the plot,
makes it easier to memorise. The contrasts of the characters and
their patterns of antagonism or of affection are the design of a
closed system, the unifying theme of which is, thinking of
Aristotle, 'unity of action'.

Anthropologists argue that this was one of the original functions of rites and myths. Primitive magical rituals use rhythmic

DRAMATIC CONSTRUCTION

movement, repetitive gesture and musical noise to give sensory unity and comprehension to some otherwise disturbing and fearsome mystery. A myth, it is said, is the verbal equivalent of a rite that serves the same archaic need: to help the primitive mind take hold of a mystery. Stories, even in the contemporary context of mass entertainment, would seem to be successful when they, too, fulfil such a need, something audiences need not even be aware of.

One of the essential components of drama is tension. This tension may or may not be the result of conflict between people on the screen – it doesn't necessarily have to be at the level of plot (though plot suspense is no bad thing). It is rather a tension in the imagination of the audience that leads to feelings of curiosity, suspense and apprehension (for example the audience being torn between contradictory elements of a character). Drama, so said drama critic William Archer, is almost always the effect of 'anticipation mingled with uncertainty'. A good director, therefore, is always asking himself certain fundamental questions. What is the audience thinking? In relation to what has just happened and what might or might not happen next, is it approving, disapproving, fearing or hoping?

In trying to invent film stories that have some narrative/ dramatic tension, it can be useful to recognise the factors that work against tension (though this is not to say that these factors are necessarily bad or wrong). Over a period of some years, I have noted elements of storytelling that a would-be screenwriter should avoid, those things that involve evasions of the more demanding task of real cinematic writing. All of these things are no more than variations on the basic point: don't put into a script things that the camera cannot photograph in action.

Passivity in a character is a real danger to dramatic values. 'Protagonist' (the name given to the leading character in your story) literally means the person who initiates the *agon* (struggle). But a figure who does not (or cannot) actually do things or who hasn't got the gumption to struggle in a way that produces new situations and developments is apt – in dramatic terms – to be a dead weight on the narrative. In effect, a bore. A scene of something 'not happening' will usually be undramatic unless it is presented in active terms. This imperative need for positive action to produce tension towards crisis is not (or not quite) as necessary in the literary media. It is generally easier for a literary work than a film to describe non-happenings. A novelist can write several pages about the motives of a character who, in the end, decides to take no action. He can explore the characteristics of his hero and heroine, analyse their feelings past and present, explain their psychology to readers, and act as historian and critic as he interprets the influences that contribute to certain states of mind. A novel or short story can have, in a sense, no story or dramatic progression, no conflict or crisis. Maybe some forms of experimental and personal cinema have little need for dramatic tension, but a narrative fiction film is (more often than not) something else.

Dramatic tension generally requires an element of conflict. The nineteenth-century theorists suggested that conflict requires the presentation of an onstage clash of wills between the hero and his antagonists. Later critics pointed out that in many cases, when a story is really rewarding, the tension may be a matter not of *what* happens, but *how* it happens. This is the effect of tension arising out of aspects of character rather than plot (which we can define, rather untidily, as the sequential progression of incidents with the cause-and-effect connections that have a forward momentum). For example, the suspense in de Sica's *Bicycle Thieves* is really much less the problem of Ricci's stolen bicycle than about his relationship with his son.

With Sophocles' *Oedipus Rex* – a play that can be studied as the first of all whodunnits – we are pretty sure at a very early stage of the solution to the mystery of Laius's murder, and are not surprised to find out that the guilty man is Oedipus himself. The plot consists in the piecemeal unravelling of a mystery upon which tension is built. Pieces of information and narrative exposition are fed to us in very carefully contrived sequences. Piece by piece, the jigsaw builds the picture of Oedipus's crime. The thing to note is that Sophocles was writing of events that Athenian audiences knew by heart. They knew how it was all going to turn out. But to think that surprise is not a factor when audiences are watching or listening to stories they know the ending of is to misunderstand the very nature of drama. In the case of

DRAMATIC CONSTRUCTION

Oedipus, the real surprise (to the extent that there is one) is in the reaction of Oedipus himself, something the audience looks forward to no matter how many times it has seen the story told in previous productions. Any parent who tells bedtime stories to infants will recognise something similar in the way their child insists on hearing the exact same story over and over again, as if each new turn of events were quite unexpected. Indeed, there is apt to be emotional protest if the narrator takes undue liberty with the yarn. When finally Oedipus's reaction is presented to us, tension is resolved and the story ended.

When characters are presented in a static relationship, dramatic tension is apt to be weak (remember: 'drama' means the 'thing done'). The beginner is apt to think of character in terms of outward physical appearance, the age, sex, social class or profession of the person in the story. But this matters very little in the sense of the drama. A dramatic character is definable only in relation to other characters or situations that involve tension. A dramatic scene is usually one in which something happens: an incident or an event takes place, the situation between the characters is different at the end of the scene from what it was at the beginning. The equilibrium has been altered and there is some narrative momentum that drives the characters (and us the audience) to a new situation in the next scene.

Many successful screenwriters have a gift for duologues, two-handed scenes that have the vigour of a singles match between two strong players. There may be one character who is more important to the story, but the other (even if he or she is acting as a foil in order to provoke exposition) is kept in play to sustain the other end of the dramatic tension. An all-too-common weakness of the inept dramatist is to write a scene between two characters who are so much in agreement that there is no real conflict or cause-and-effect dramatic progression. When this happens the result is apt to be that their positions are quite interchangeable, an almost certain indication that the scene will have little tension. As a great deal of television drama seems to prove, two-handed scenes can become so much the ping-pong game of service and return that monotony sets in. Note, however, that for characters to create dramatic tension, they need not always clash. Romeo and Juliet's balcony scene, for example is a

3. Mackendrick was
impressed by adept use
of the foil in all forms
of storytelling. He
would hand out to stu-
dents a selection of
cartoons from the
pages of *The New
Yorker* as examples of
how to tell stories
purely in images, and in
particular commended
Charles Addams's use
of 'the foil, the figure
which has been added
to the scene as the
straight man to the
comic absurdity'.

concordance of wills and yet is certainly dramatic. There is tension not because of any struggle between the characters, but
because the audience understands that the relationship between
boy and girl is going to lead to some later crisis. The powerful
suspense in Shakespeare's story may be absent from the emoting
of the boy and girl, but it is very well established in our minds as
we watch the scene.

Students often exclaim they are uninterested in on-screen conflict, that the most interesting kind of tension is internal, within
the mind of the hero. Why, they ask, is it necessary to have an
antagonist at all? The answer is that a state of mind is something
static. In terms of the camera it is passive, dramatically inopera-
tive and not easy to dramatise in active cinematic terms. When
on-screen characters are frustrated, bored or alienated, the situation is not yet dramatic. A bored character becomes dramatically interesting only in the context of the possibility of some
escape from his frustration, when his state of mind becomes a
catalyst for positive story action. For example, when contrasted
with active characters or placed in certain situations, an inactive
character is liable to create certain tensions. Simply, if your protagonist is passive it may be necessary to create strongly aggressive antagonists or antagonistic circumstances.

The most effective way of doing this is to think of the antagonist as a foil character, a figure who – like the audience – is ignorant of essential information and therefore asks the questions to
which the audience needs to know the answer.[3] These characters
are confidants or interlocutors created especially for the purpose
of contrasting with other on-screen personalities in order to
reveal certain things to the audience (for example Horatio in
Hamlet and the Fool in *King Lear*). In many examples they
externalise the conflicts of the hero, bringing them out into the
open, thus creating active on-screen situations. A good example
is in *Oedipus Rex* where Creon is antagonist to Oedipus. If you
consider that Oedipus's real battle is not with his brother-in-law
but with the Gods who punish him (somewhat unfairly) for
crimes committed in ignorance, then Creon is simply a dramatic
foil. In the Western *High Noon*, the sheriff's crisis of confidence
is externalised not through an antagonist but through his newly
married Quaker wife.

It is sometimes necessary to create dramatic situations that counteract a character's inaction. How, for example, do you show a man torn between the natural instinct to run away from his responsibility and his reluctant sense of duty? In *High Noon* the sheriff bolts from town and then discovers he simply has to return. His negative thought has been characterised by contrasting it with positive action – his inaction has been shown as the direct cessation of an action. In many cases when something is about to happen but for some reason is prevented from taking place, the non-happening can become dramatic. A similar problem is the need to show a character's disinterest with something, often a negative and passive quality of dramatic importance. On the cinema screen the scriptwriter has to contrast this attitude with active interest. Stanislavsky[4] once asked the question: 'How do you play a man who is bored?' If the actor does nothing then the point is not properly made. But as soon as you define the idea of boredom as being 'interested, but not enough', then it become playable. A bored man is an individual who finds everything interesting to a limited extent. As such, the actor should contrive to be interested in so many things that he isn't really interested in anything very much.

Other things students of screenwriting should avoid are generalisations and indeterminate action. Film treatments (basic plot details in prose form, perhaps with the odd line of dialogue) and scripts are almost always written in one tense: the present. Complex as time dimensions in film may be, they are less free than in the novel where the reader will find several tenses (past, present, future, subjunctive). But there is no equivalent in cinema for indeterminate time. While a novelist can write the adverb 'frequently', an event in a film happens only as often as you show it happening. The author of a screen treatment who writes, 'From time to time, she made a habit of . . .' is simply postponing to the screenplay stage the task of presenting this indefinite and continuing action in an economical and dramatically viable way.

Take the phrase 'the cat sat on the mat.' You can say this in words and the meaning is clear, but it is left to the listener or reader to imagine what kind of cat and what kind of mat. Are we to see in our mind's eye an elegant Siamese with blue eyes, white fur and

4. Constantin Stanislavsky (1863–1938), Russian theatre director and theorist, founder of the Moscow Art Theatre.

brown markings as it poses on a Navaho rug of intricate design? Or is it a black tabby squatting on a rubber doormat? Words, whether spoken or printed, can communicate relatively abstract and intellectual generalisations. Not so cinema, for though a picture is (so it's said) worth a thousand words, photography cannot help but communicate to the mind's eye a great quantity of very specific data about precisely how things look and move.

What we might call interpretations and editorial comment should also be viewed with suspicion by the screenwriter. Drama, historians tell us, probably originated from ceremonies that centred on choral recitations of narratives about the Gods. As the first Greek playwrights devised the earliest patterns of dramatic presentations, the choral commentary became a standard device. Within a few centuries the function of the chorus was progressively diminished in favour of exposition through interaction and explanations by characters within the story, until nowadays dramatic exposition has come to mean essentially all explanation made through dialogue.

A novelist might not use the first-person pronoun 'I' but will still allow himself total liberty to describe to his readers all manner of things that belong only to his imagination and not necessarily the characters in his story. By describing the internal feelings and thoughts of a character, the novelist becomes omniscient, with an all-seeing godlike mind that can look into the souls of men and interpret them for the benefit of the reader. But the film and theatre writer – regardless of how often his creative-writing teacher encouraged him to express his ideas, thoughts and feelings directly, as 'the voice of the author' – does not have this privilege. His task is to give expression to all his narrative ideas through action and reaction, things done and said. In effect, when translating into dramatic form a story that has been written only for reading, the first character to be removed is often the author himself. The screenwriter will work through the original text and ruthlessly eliminate all editorial comment, every phrase, adjective or adverb added by the author as a clue to how he himself wishes the action to be interpreted by the reader. He will retain only those adjectives, adverbs, similes and metaphors that are of immediate practical value to the actor, cameraman, editor or any of the other craftsmen whose media of

DRAMATIC CONSTRUCTION

expression are images, gestures and sounds – those things that can be represented on screen.

A narrative is driven by character progression, something that can take more than one form. It can, for instance, be the kind of progression where changes do not take place within a character but rather in the audience's increased understanding of him or her. Or it might be the kind of development in which the protagonist's personality is changed through his or her experiences. The change-of-heart formula is an old one (example: Scrooge in *A Christmas Carol*), though it is often too simplistic and not really believable. It has been pointed out that when character changes are convincing they are likely to be the eventual resolving of two conflicting elements that exist within a single personality. An obvious suggestion, therefore, when you are devising characters: look not only for interesting qualities in their personalities but also for those social masks that hide other dramatically exploitable temperaments. Think of characters who may at first appear in a sympathetic light but are then revealed, thanks to certain active developments in the story, to have uglier traits – or vice versa.

Student film-makers are often uncomfortable with the task of inventing characters not as individual entities but as interactive personages. One suspects this is because in the early stages of experimenting with storytelling, the beginner chooses a protagonist that in psychological terms is something of a projection of his own point of view, someone who clearly represents his own attitudes, feelings and thoughts, a thinly disguised or idealised version of themselves. There are two potential problems that need to be considered here.

First, there is a tendency to surround this protagonist with characters who are not nearly as fully realised. Every protagonist needs an *agon*, a struggle with surrounding antagonists, and the nature of this struggle is rather misunderstood among many student writers. So misunderstood, indeed, that the student will insist it is not necessary to have such conflict (or even a plot).

Second, changes of personality are not envisaged, which means such characters may have nowhere to go in the story. Or, to put it another way, the writer might not be able to envisage the direction his protagonist should move because he cannot conceive of such changes of attitude and emotion taking place

5. *The Third Man* (Faber and Faber, 1988; first published Lorrimer, 1968), pp. 7–9.

6. See 'Exercises for the Student of Dramatic Writing' below.

within himself. But classic patterns work in a very different way. Oedipus comes onstage as proud, noble and more than a little arrogant to open a story that will lead to his disgrace and humiliation. So when planning a character reversal it is important to begin at a different place from the one you want to end up at. If you have in mind as your protagonist a figure with whom you identify, it makes good sense when you start writing to look for (and even accentuate) those aspects in him or her that you would like to see completely abandoned by the story's end.

In a well-told story, every fictional character functions within a network or nexus, a cat's cradle of character interactions. Certain characteristics of the protagonist and antagonist are revealed often only through relationships with each other or with circumstances (either external or internal) and events played out in action and reaction. Under the pressure of situations, conflicts, clashes of will or story tension, the ideas that lie behind a story's themes cease to be merely abstract and become people actually *doing* things to each other or *reacting* to the action. As has been already explained, film dialogue is best when it has an immediate purpose and produces visible reactions in others. This is the essence of drama. Because character is not a static quality that belongs to a specific figure, rather than thinking of individual characters in the world it is far more useful for the writer to consider the notion of character-in-action-and-reaction. A story's energy comes from the degree to which its characters are warring elements, complementary aspects that illuminate each other by contrast and conflict. The only practical reason for a particular character's existence, in fact, is to interact with other characters.

The published screenplay of Graham Greene's film script *The Third Man* contains descriptions (presumably written by Greene after the film was completed) of the story's four principal characters, followed by notes on subsidiary characters, those necessary as foils or for the development of the incidental action.[5] These are worth your study because they serve as a good model for the kind of thing I have asked you to attach to your efforts at writing Step Outlines.[6] When outlining character relationships it is important to be able to distinguish between those characters indispensable to the central theme and those needed only for the smooth mechanical running of the plot and its exposition.

DRAMATIC CONSTRUCTION

One reason why Greene's descriptions are interesting is that he defines his characters not as individual figures or separate elements but strictly in terms of their connections with the other principals. The main roles are envisaged as a web of tensions. Indeed, the pattern is very often a push-pull tug of war, one that takes triangular patterns where character A is torn between opposing connections represented by character B and character C. The pattern is built by successive steps that establish the dramatic interactions and tensions as they grow in force, making for ironies and surprise reversals that lead, by stages, to a final denouement of the main lines of tension. When called on to write similar descriptions of characters for your own story, you should do so as though you were looking from the point of view of the final resolution of their conflicts and relationships.[7]

7. Mackendrick was aware that director Peter Brook had written something similar when discussing *King Lear* in his book *The Empty Space*: 'Experimentally, we can approach *Lear* not as a linear narrative, but as a cluster of relationships.' (Penguin, 1990, first published 1968) p. 102.

Below: Character relationship map: *The Third Man.*

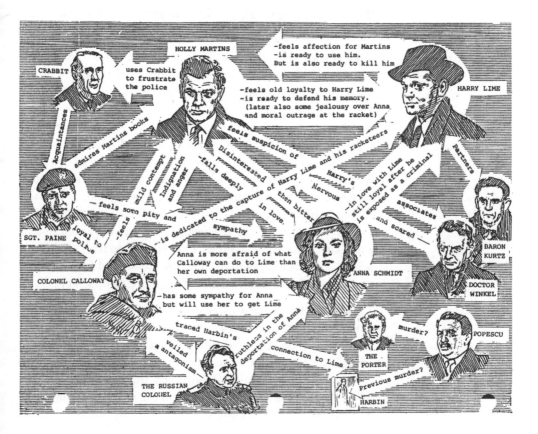

CRABBIT — uses Crabbit to frustrate the police

HOLLY MARTINS

—feels affection for Martins
—is ready to use him.
But is also ready to kill him

HARRY LIME

—feels old loyalty to Harry Lime
—is ready to defend his memory.
(later also some jealousy over Anna and moral outrage at the racket)

acquaintances

admires Martins books

feels suspicion of

feels mild contempt, indignation and anger

—falls deeply

Disinterested

feels some pity and

—is dedicated to the capture of Harry Lime and his racketeers

then bitter

Harry's Nervous

—in love with Lime still loyal after he is exposed as a criminal

Partners

associates and scared

BARON KURTZ

SGT. PAINE

loyal to police

sympathy

in love.

Anna is more afraid of what Calloway can do to Lime than her own deportation.

ANNA SCHMIDT

DOCTOR WINKEL

COLONEL CALLOWAY

—has some sympathy for Anna but will use her to get Lime

traced Harbin's

veiled antagonism

ruthless in the deportation of Anna

connection to Lime

murder?

POPESCU

THE PORTER

Previous murder?

THE RUSSIAN COLONEL

HARBIN

In any project that you have already worked on or that you have scripted and might be planning to make, can you answer these questions? It helps if you can be as specific as possible. (It is also useful to ask these questions of your favourite films.)

1 How many characters are there in your story? Select three that can be considered as principals. I tend to feel uneasy when a student explains that there is really only one character. As we have seen, drama normally involves a conflict between people, therefore you need at least two characters. Often it is more effective to have at least three because this gives the possibility of a triangular relationship, a bind involving a central figure who is pulled in opposite directions by two others. Note that there are examples of characters in films who have dramatic scenes in which no other character is present, but these tend to be of the kind where the environment itself plays the role of antagonist, placing the protagonist in some circumstances that require a reaction from him or her.

2 Who is your point-of-view character? Sometimes it can be difficult to decide between who is the protagonist and who is the antagonist. Though occasionally there are stories in which the audience is not invited to feel identification with any one of the characters, it is far more common to have a figure who represents the viewpoint of the story and who has a final 'objective' of some kind. Ask yourself: by the end of the story what does this character want to achieve? What is required is a character intention that will produce a dramatic action, a visible result on screen. As has been explained, for a character merely to express his or her feelings is seldom enough in cinema. There can be, of course, a negative objective: to prevent something from happening, but this too should be conceived as a result of action (a incident that can be photographed).

3 Can you define what obstacles there might be to this objective? Can you also identify some other character who is a personification of these obstacles? Such a character is the antagonist whose dramatic function is to create conflict with the central figure (though importantly this does not necessarily imply we have less sympathy with the antagonist than with

　　　　　　　　　　　　DRAMATIC CONSTRUCTION

the protagonist). Note that the existence of an antagonist in the story does not mean there is not also conflict *within* the central figure (where, for example, he is being pulled in conflicting directions by certain emotions or beliefs). There is, in fact, conflict within all well-defined protagonists, and many characters who seem tame when it comes to extroverted action will have clearly defined introverted tensions brought into the open at times by the antagonist for the audience to observe. Note too that in the buddy movie there is always some thread of conflict between the twin protagonists, one that typically climaxes somewhere in the third act. But whatever tension develops between these two characters, it will usually take second place to the dramatic conflict in which the twin heroes confront some third antagonistic faction. Their conflict is a subplot (often vaguely comical), a secondary case of character-in-action that runs parallel to the main narrative tension.

4 How does the conflict lead to crisis? What is at stake for the main characters? Is there a confrontation scene? In a well-constructed story the audience is held in expectation of what is called an obligatory scene brought about by a reversal (or, indeed, a series of reversals). Note that the obligatory scene, usually the denouement of a story, classically expresses the theme. It is an expression of the story's central moral, the point expressed as a generalisation as seen in character-in-action. (A good way of defining this moment, in fact many moments in a dramatic narrative, is to ask: 'Who does what with which to whom and why?')

Exposition

Exposition is what we might call dialogue exchange, or the craft of explaining. It provides the audience with information about circumstances, past events and situations, about characters and their relationships, that the audience needs in order to understand and enjoy the story. When exposition is dramatic and well constructed, we no longer think of it as exposition at all.

While I was employed as a contract writer, a junior member of the script department of a British film studio, I heard a phrase used in story conferences to describe inept exposition: 'My uncle, the Duke . . .' It was, presumably, a quote from some deservedly forgotten script that was meant to establish the aristocratic status of the speaker's family, addressed to some secondary character to whom the information was hardly news. Though such dialogue could, in theory, be dramatic (if, for instance, it was addressed to a character who, up to that moment, was ignorant that the Duke had a nephew or that the speaker had an uncle who was actually a peer of the realm), it is a good example of an elementary 'rule' of exposition, indeed about dialogue in general: if the only purpose of dialogue is to provide expository information not to the characters in the scene but to the audience (for example dialogue about events and characters off-screen), it is boring. Why? For the simple reason that information forthcoming through dialogue is dramatic only when it involves exploration of character through tension, when what is revealed produces an on-screen effect in which we, the audience, have some emotional stake, when it produces some reaction in certain characters that promises a further development of the narrative.

The Norwegian playwright Henrik Ibsen, according to many theatre critics, was one of the great masters of dramatic construction of the nineteenth century. His play *The Wild Duck* opens with a scene of exposition not untypical of the way many plays of his era began. It says something of the changes in theatrical fashion and the craft of writing for the stage that the scene – which involves a manservant and a couple of hired waiters in a study, behind the scenes at a dinner party – was obviously quite acceptable technique for exposition of that period. In fact, for many decades the typical opening of a play was an exchange between servants who exchanged gossip about their employers and, in the course of this, gave the audience necessary information about the background of the principal characters before they made their entrances. It has no doubt been a great loss to the novice playwright that dramas cannot be so easily set in the kind of household where the servants are available in supporting roles to perform this ever so useful narrative function.

With due respect to the great Ibsen I suggest you study the scene as an example of very weak craftsmanship by today's standards, and certainly by the standards of the very best contemporary screenwriting. The reason is simple: the two primary characters who appear in this opening scene are not important characters. In fact, they never again appear in the play and have been devised for no other purpose than to provide background to the story and characters we have yet to see. Though they may be said to be foils, they are utterly uninteresting since neither has any real relationship with the main action of the plot, or any particularly revealing relationship with the main characters. And even in this exchange, one that takes place between two figures who are essentially irrelevant to the subsequent drama, there is very little tension or conflict. Nothing is at stake and nothing really happens. The probable result is that the audience is likely to remember very little about what the characters are saying. It's just all talk.

As an antidote to Ibsen, here are the opening lines of a very different piece of writing, one that shows how exposition can be illuminating of essential plot points and also useful in terms of exploring character motivations and feelings.

'You were standing in the doorway of your club?'
    'Yes, officer.'
    It was no good remonstrating with him. Four or five times Maigret had tried to make him say 'inspector'. What did it matter anyway? What did all this matter?

1. From *My Friend Maigret*, translated by Nigel Ryan, Hamish Hamilton, 1956, p. 1.

'A grey sports car stopped for a moment and a man got out, with a flying leap almost, that's what you said, isn't it?'

'Yes, officer.'

'To get into your club he must have passed close to you and even brushed against you. Now there's a luminous neon sign above the door.'

'It's purple, officer.'

'So what?'

'So nothing.'

'Just because your sign is purple you are incapable of recognizing the individual who a moment later tore aside the velvet curtain and emptied his revolver into your barman?'[1]

This seems to me an excellent example of effective exposition. Naturally a somewhat different approach to storytelling is necessary when writing a film script, but Georges Simenon (who produced a series of novels featuring Inspector Maigret) demonstrates here a solid understanding of what we might call 'active exposition', and students of dramatic construction have much to learn from him.

You can see why exposition is dramatic – often quite powerfully so – only where it is presented in the context of a scene that has strong conflict, suspense and action (hence reaction). Your task in establishing exposition is likely to involve the invention of some situation that produces a vigorous clash of wills between characters and requires one or other of those characters to make explanations. When exposition is absolutely necessary (when you have to establish information as a preliminary to certain narrative developments), it is frequently the foil figure who will ask of the protagonist those questions that provoke the necessary information and thus satisfy the audience (albeit, most probably, temporarily). This is, all too often, a technical problem for beginning writers: how to 'feed' the protagonist neatly, economically and through action. As explained, talk for the sake of talk (because the writer needs to convey certain pieces of information to the audience) is the antithesis of drama, whether on stage or screen (though, as you will have by now guessed, much more so on the screen). Thus the trick of inventing a scene with effective exposition is to devise supporting characters who are involved in a dramatic situation where specific questions have to be asked or certain pieces of information offered in order that the tension is (perhaps

DRAMATIC CONSTRUCTION

temporarily) resolved and the audience dramatically satiated.

Occasionally a screenwriter will fall back on the expository device of the flashback, the argument being that it saves the film-maker from having to shoot lengthy scenes that might be driven solely by dialogue. In practice, however, the device of the flash-back, though it may appear to be thoroughly cinematic, can be disappointing. It is, in fact, inherently undramatic. While drama is *action* now and onstage, the flashback may be more *activity* because it shows events that do not have immediate results in the here-and-now.[2] Because a flashback is a description of past (and already resolved) tensions, it often lacks the force of immediate narrative impetus and can all too easily become an interlude that interrupts the flow of the story, even if it has values that, though not so dramatic, are still rewarding in other ways. (The 'remem-brance of things past' often has a reflective and poetic quality that, while lacking suspenseful qualities of plot-laden narrative, can lend much lyric feeling to a film.)

Another point that needs to be made about exposition is related to what we might call the whodunnit, the detective story or private-eye yarn. Such stories tend to be constructed as a sys-tem of unravelling past events about which we, the audience, and often certain characters in the story know nothing. This unravelling pattern might continue all the way to the final scene, as for instance where the detective assembles all the suspects to deliver an interminable and barely comprehensible review of all that has gone before, holding back the announcement of the murderer's name in a singularly unnecessary and unconvincing way. Equally silly formulas are the ones where the unmasked vil-lain holds the hero at the end of a pistol while he delivers a dan-gerously long monologue that is supposed to explain everything that went before, or where the Austrian psychologist (speaking in a barely comprehensible accent) carefully explains to the anx-ious crowd sitting before him the psychological malady of the now safely straitjacketed serial killer. When these scenes work, it is not usually because there are in any way credible – we enjoy them only if they are sufficiently ingenious. Having been branded as clichés, such formulas are now generally discredited. But, as always, it is worth remembering that a cliché became a cliché for good reason: it worked when first invented.

2. See 'Activity versus Action' below.

There are a few cases where this kind of exposition is done so well that it works very effectively. The last scene of *The Maltese Falcon* is such a case, a classic example of ravelling and unravelling at the same time. The long dialogue scene in which Sam Spade manipulates all the villains into mutual betrayals is present conflict, tension here-and-now onstage while simultaneously proving to be exposition of all the mayhem that has happened, not only during the story, but even before it began. The film *The Third Man* is another example, though with a slight difference. For the first two thirds of Graham Greene's story the action takes the form of a search into the past, an investigation of the mysterious death of the controversial figure (Harry Lime) who is best friend of the protagonist (Holly Martins) and lover of the girl with whom the protagonist is becoming involved. Then, at what might be considered the end of act two in conventional dramatic structure, comes the climactic revelation: Lime is very much alive. Up until Lime's appearance the story is in effect a whodunnit with Martins investigating the possible murder and the British military policeman (Calloway) and Harry's abandoned girl (Anna) as classic figures of the formula. The revelation creates what Aristotle called a peripeteia, a turning of the tables, a point in the story where certain discoveries produce a reversal of the current narrative situation. This might be an upset in the characters' relationships, like a role reversal, or a situation where something hidden is revealed, something pursued is captured or escapes, or conversely, a secret thing – revealed only to us the audience – remains secret.

In *The Third Man*, following the peripeteia that Harry is still alive, the narrative becomes a drive toward future events through both direct suspense and character conflict. It is no longer an unravelling of the past but now cause-to-effect momentum towards events in the present. In this sense the story becomes simpler: all secondary and supporting roles are dropped from the action as it now centres on the tensions between the four principals. No more mystery, nothing but the hero caught in the middle between his devotion to his old friend, his moral repugnance over the racket that has brought him into reluctant collaboration with the authorities (and against his friend) and his unrequited feelings for the girl that his friend has betrayed.

DRAMATIC CONSTRUCTION

Modernist Trends

Do you agree with any of the following?

1 Plots are old-fashioned. A story with a plot is contrived, artificial and boring.
2 When you start writing a script, just begin at the beginning without trying to plan how it will end. Planning isn't necessary. It's much better to be spontaneous. Improvise as you go along.
3 The most boring thing of all is to be obvious. It's much more interesting to be ambiguous. Leave it to the audience to work out what you mean. Why does everything have to be explained?
4 Ideas and issues are what interest me. That's where I like to start: from an idea. I don't really care much about the characters so much.
5 I think the most interesting theme nowadays is alienation. That's what's true to life because everybody is alienated nowadays. A character that wants to do things, or who has something he wants to achieve is somehow phoney, or corny.
6 I like symbolism. I don't see the point of characters that are realistic. It's much more interesting when they're abstract.
7 I like to play with scenes of fantasy rather than reality. I like dream sequences and flashbacks. It's more interesting when you can play around with time.

Remarks like this are very common from students at CalArts, though they are often expressed in very much more complicated language. Let me say that *all* these comments make sense to me. I really do understand and respect the points of view being expressed here. I also recognise that they, or views of more or less the same kind, represent contemporary approaches to cinema that are very attractive to many students today. I have only one problem: they are not really compatible with the subject I teach here, and it may well be that the student who holds these views will be quite disappointed by the end of this course.

The truth is I cannot help you explore what is often called Modernism in cinema. This is one reason why I keep referring to 'movies' rather than 'cinema'. The craft of storytelling is rather un-Modernist. It's old. Ancient, in fact. And though it is always changing, always in flux and never really fixed, its roots go very far back in time. To the film-maker who feels the time has come when traditional and conventional narrative/dramatic forms need to be subverted, I say to you that my particular background in storytelling will only help you explore the past. The future is for you. Let's now examine some of these remarks more closely.

Plot isn't necessary. It's boring.

Absolutely correct. That is, when an audience becomes aware of the existence of plot contrivance, it is irritating and causes a loss in the 'willing suspension of disbelief' that is so important in storytelling. The best plot is the one you don't notice is there. Plot tends to be recognised only when clumsily constructed, when somehow imposed on the material, and when it doesn't grow out of the character interactions.

Often this remark from beginning film-makers means something rather different – that he or she doesn't have much talent for creating an un-contrived and natural story structure where the narrative sequence of events is rooted in the motives of the characters. Indeed, to achieve this is not easy, and seems to be a skill that comes only with an enormous amount of experience, if it comes at all (often deviated from by the fact that many writers experiment with technique for its own sake). Early attempts at the laborious carpentry of plotting are bound to be clumsy and obvious. The mechanics will creak and the gaps will be obvious. For this reason, it is important to study classic story structure. This is the point of plodding through and analysing your favourite films in the Step Outline form.

Don't bother to plan. Why do you need to know the end of your story before you begin? How can you know the end until you've got there, in fact?

Oddly this is almost the same point. But there may be some mis-understanding, because improvisation and planning are not mutually exclusive.

I suggest that the writer who embarks on a script without a strong feeling of how the climax and resolution of the story will emerge is more than likely to lose his way and end up nowhere in particular. Even if he does improvise entertaining scenes along the way, the effect may be disappointing because there isn't any spine that holds it all together and sustains the tension to the end. My cousin, a successful playwright and screenwriter, dis-agrees. He declares, with admirable arrogance, that the best work is done when he begins at page one, invents as he proceeds, and never revises while he ploughs ahead. The characters and their conflicts take over, dictate their own plot, and abruptly reveal to him the main crisis and denouement as he reaches the third act. What is particularly irritating, of course, is that he can prove his point, as this method works for him.

There is also the question of what we mean by 'knowing'. What level of knowing are we talking about here? Modernist critics have coined the term 'dysnarrative' for the kind of narra-tive structure so elliptical that its connective plotting, even if you dig deeply, remains hidden and disguised. But make a Step Outline of, for example, Alain Resnais's film of Alain Robbe-Grillet's complex script *Last Year at Marienbad*, a work with a kind of anti-narrative structure, and you are likely to find a nar-rative tension that is, in fact, very much present.

Aristotle's phrase 'unity of action' refers to the sense of com-pleteness that is a basic satisfaction in almost every dramatic work. The paradox (as Jean-Luc Godard suggested) is that 'the beginning, the middle and the end' are there even in those cases where they are 'not necessarily in that order'. So if you think you have a great beginning of a story, but the end is weak, the real truth is that you don't yet have the right beginning. (Buster Keaton, when speaking about his silent comedies, once told an interviewer: 'Somebody would come up with an idea. "Here's a

1. From Kevin
Brownlow's *The
Parade's Gone By*
(University of
California Press, 1968),
p. 481.

good start," we'd say. We skip the middle. We never paid any
attention to the middle. We immediately went to the finish. We
worked on the finish and if we got a finish that we're all satisfied with, then we'll go back and work on the middle. For some
reason, the middle always took care of itself.'¹) Though when
inventing a narrative you probably won't have the precise ending worked out in advance (if so, your story is apt to be predictable to both your audience and yourself), you should
always have at the back of your mind a strong instinct of
whether a particular step in the story is moving towards the
ending you have given some thought to, whether the fuse you
might be working with at any one time will become part of the
smouldering chain that leads to the big bang at the end. A
writer should be both conscious and unconscious of structure
while at work. There are some writers who would declare, in
contradiction of my cousin, that they like to work out every
detail of a story beforehand. They prepare a meticulous Step
Outline of not only the sequence of scenes but sometimes the
moves within a scene. They write notes to themselves on the
characters and prepare some key lines of dialogue to be used at
important moments. But frankly, I am equally suspicious of this
method, and suspect the process is more complex.

Though it may suit the temperament of many writers to prepare a scenario as the skeleton on which to build the more solid
flesh of character behaviour, it seems that having done so, they
deliberately 'forget' their preparatory work. While working, all
writers are, in a sense, improvising. If a particular writer likes to
map out the storyline in advance, it is more than likely that as
the characters come alive in his imagination, they will insist on
taking a route that he hadn't quite anticipated. In any powerful
story it often seems that the characters dictate to their creator.
(Read Pirandello's play *Six Characters in Search of an Author* for
a dramatic illustration of this process.) As you develop your
dramatic skills, you will find this an exhilarating and quite mys-
tical phenomenon. A writer's creations will often seem to know
where they are going better than he does himself. Even the
story's climax may come as a surprise to him, though it is usually
a surprise that has been cooking away in the subconscious for
some time. When it does surface (often quite abruptly), the

dramatist discovers that actually it has been present from the beginning.

One hears much talk about the value of improvisation among students of acting, many of whom automatically equate the technique with spontaneity. It is as if any performance based on words written down in advance can never be as 'true' as when improvised. Of course improvisation can be an invaluable instrument of the director (in particular) and of actors, as well as the writer. Improvisation exercises during the rehearsal process are sometimes the only way for a director to deal with the actor who has begun to pay more attention to the delivery of lines than to the impulses and motivations underlying them. Particularly when working with 'poetic' material, it can be important for a director to insist that actors ignore the text completely, improvising a new language of their own in order to get at the character intentions, before they return to the text itself at a later stage. In this sense, improvisation in acting is, up to a point, similar to the process of writing. But the fallacy of assuming that an actor's improvised dialogue can wholly substitute for the work of a director and writer is evident in many improvisational efforts I have seen, where the scenes initially appear to have exhilarating freshness and realism but presently become boring because there seems to be an essential element missing. There is no real point to them, no drama, no structure. They just don't go anywhere.

Between planning and inspiration there is no contradiction. In fact, one can go further: neither is really valuable without the other. Meticulous preparation of outlines, sketched scenarios and notes can even become a handicap and an inhibition unless, through judicious forgetting, they still leave great freedom for spontaneity within the scope and integrity of the central theme. (It has been said that the genius of the human imagination is that as we find use for those apparently forgotten things buried deep on the back shelves of our consciousness, they can be transformed as they are brought back to conscious mind.) Improvisation is truly valuable only when it has its roots in the highly disciplined and often exhausting work that has gone before. In place of such efforts, it is likely to be thin stuff, weak and trivial.

'Clarity' and 'Ambiguity'

2. *Hitchcock*, p. 17.

Obscurity is seldom a virtue. If the point you want to make has any significance, then there is no harm in making it clearly. 'To those who question whether clarity is all that important, I can only say that it is *the* most important quality in the making of a film,' wrote Truffaut.[2] Indeed, failing to make an important point clearly is likely to confuse and irritate the audience.

A problem for many beginning writers is that they underestimate their story's need for expository background. Knowing the information himself, the writer tends to assume that it is all quite obvious, even though, all too often, it isn't. Why does the writer need to explain everything? Because if the audience needs expository information in order to appreciate and understand an important situation or a character, then the author's failure to prepare for this may disastrously weaken his audience's enjoyment of the story as a whole. Clarity is the communication of essentials and the exclusion of the non-essential, no simple matter at all, since it can be tricky to decide what is not really essential and then find a way to reduce emphasis on such things. It can take great ingenuity and considerable insight to isolate what is important (and, therefore, must be retained, even accentuated) in material that is confused or overcomplicated by irrelevancies and banalities.

In ensuring his script is as clear as possible, the inexperienced dramatist often lives in terror of obviousness, believing that to be obvious is not only to be boring, it is to be banal. What this really amounts to is anxiety (frequently justified) due to the fact that he does not actually know how to explain things without being dull. Such anxiety prompts him to believe that certain things are more interesting if left implicit. Thinks the writer: why is it so important that everything is clearly explained? Isn't it much more intriguing if there is some ambiguity?

There is, I sense, a feeling among many who regard themselves as creative artists that there is something rather boring about having to study the craftsmanship necessary for clear communication, and conversely, something much more exciting and 'artistic' about work that isn't very clear, that is ambiguous. Simplicity and clarity are, in the minds of such writers, somehow the same as banal and dull. And it is true, of course, that

DRAMATIC CONSTRUCTION

dull work is often obvious. But the feeling that obscure or confusing exposition is somehow more aesthetically interesting is a terrible trap. Is 'obvious' the same thing as 'clearly stated'? Does the absence of clarity make a story more interesting because it is harder to comprehend? Plainly, I don't think so. Nobody ever got despised by the critics for being blazingly clear in terms of setting up exposition. Such film-makers might be accused of lacking subtlety in their storytelling, but subtlety and clarity are very different things. There is no danger in being obvious if what you are being obvious about is also exciting. Just as the virtues of good journalism are economy and clarity, telling the story as swiftly as possible with minimum waste of effort, the same can be said for scriptwriting and directing.[3]

Incidentally, 'ambiguity' is a term that the novice often uses too loosely. It should not be regarded as the same thing as confusion or obscurity. The word means having two alternative meanings, which can be very interesting in dramatic terms if both meanings are clearly made and wholly valid at the same time. The key to ambiguity in this context is that unanswered questions seem to have more impact when they are clearly posed by a character within the story. Audiences are not so concerned about uncertainty over answers to unclear situations or issues so long as the dramatist has made clear that the ambiguity is deliberate.

Issues as against characters

I have, on occasion, claimed that many of our film students should think less and use their imaginations more. Intelligence is often equated with the capacity to criticise and analyse. But film, in my opinion, is not the best medium for directly stimulating thought. It is too richly loaded with sensory, emotional, and intuitive informational data, while most intellectual issues are best directly explored when abstracted from the complexities and contradictions of human psychology. In this sense, even drama itself – where emotions and sensory impressions are liable to get in the way – may be somewhat incompatible with our rational and intellectual faculties.

A fully rounded character is one that, by definition, cannot be conceived in two-dimensional terms. In comedy, as in some other

3. So concerned was Mackendrick to ensure his students were able to articulate themselves clearly on paper that he reproduced for them in a handout these lines from George Orwell's 1946 essay 'Politics and English Language': '(i) Never use a metaphor, simile or other figure of speech which you are used to seeing in print. (ii) Never use a long word where a short one will do. (iii) If it is possible to cut a word out, always cut it out. (iv) Never use the passive where you can use the active. (v) Never use a foreign phrase, a scientific word or a jargon word if you can think of an everyday English equivalent. (vi) Break any of these rules sooner than say anything outright barbarous.' (Orwell, 'Politics and the English Language', from *The Collected Essays, Journalism and Letters: Volume 4* (Penguin, 1970), p. 169.

dramatic forms, a stereotype is enough to tell the story (indeed, broad comedy often requires that the comic figure is a caricature who cannot feel too much pain and whose emotions are simplified to the point of absurdity). Similarly, a story that concentrates on ideas and issues is also less likely to require characterisation that has real emotional depth. One thinks of George Bernard Shaw, a didact whose plays were felt to be more like verbal debates than human dramas and whose characters were not much more than mouthpieces for his own political and social opinions.

'Alienation'

Some years ago, 'alienation' was immensely fashionable as a theme in the cinema, though today even the word seems to have gone out of fashion. It may, however, still be evident as an attitude among young film-makers (indeed, among all young people) for whom early adulthood is a period of enormous tension, who are understandably disturbed by the world around us, and who feel a considerable helplessness and anxiety as they try to confront it. Alienation, in this sense, may be the desperate attempt to protect oneself from oppressive anxiety. By deliberate distancing of oneself from emotion, one can avoid hurt. Or, at least, this is what psychologists at the tabloid level might argue.

I can offer no comfort. I do confess I feel dispirited as I see solipsistic student projects that deal with the relations between human beings in a way that indicates an alienation from *all* feelings of tenderness, an absence of emotional sensitivity. I believe that film, more than any other medium, is capable of exploring feelings. I think it is built into the very mechanics of the apparatus, the psychology of perception of the moving image with sound (the mental reading in the brain of information coming from the eye). Cinema hits us at gut level – its impact is sensory and physical. Drama has, from its early beginnings, aimed at a catharsis that the ancient Greeks felt would cleanse the human spirit through emotions of pity and terror. Though the ridiculously unabashed emotionalism of early silent film may seem nothing but hilarious today, I cannot but hope that a device which is designed to exploit the phenomena of emotional connections in the way that cinema does will survive the aesthetic of alienation.

DRAMATIC CONSTRUCTION

Of course, stories that deal with alienation (those that deal with highly subjective, introverted and private matters, thoughts and feelings that are not generally communicated to others) are, by their very nature, problematic in dramatic terms. The alienated figure (often a thinly disguised projection of the student writer himself) is either unwilling, or more often unable, to make the positive act of connection through active, and hence dramatic, communication. Therefore the student interested in exploring the theme of alienation must determine how best to make dramatic the non-doing and non-communicating character, a not inconsiderable task.

'Symbolic figures'

Symbolism tends to be more effective in theatre than on the screen. One of the limitations of cinematography is that it can be too real in the sense that it supplies more visual information than we may actually want. Any cinematographic image shows us so much that it is extremely hard to depersonalise it. It signifies a particular and individual creature, not an abstraction like Mankind or Motherhood. It is the very nature of film to be specific and concrete. On the other hand, this is why cinema can make use of something like Surrealism, because the unreality of a Surrealist image is created by the disturbing juxtaposition of incompatible but utterly real elements, something that cinematography can do brilliantly.

A Technique for Having Ideas

There is no technique for having ideas. Having said this, I might describe a theory I heard many years ago, developed by a college professor. A friend of the professor who publishes a magazine called him, asking if he had any suggestions of how to provide some training for the editors and writers of the magazine that could stimulate their capacity 'to have ideas'.

The professor reacted very sensibly. He laughed and told the publisher that there was no such training. The gift for original creativity can perhaps be identified but, he explained, it cannot be taught. Satisfied, the professor gave the subject no more deliberate thought, but then found the problem nagging him. Eventually he returned to the publisher not with any answer, but with some ideas he had developed about the often strange and mysterious process of creativity. He subsequently produced a lecture on the subject that he was invited to give at a number of places, including some of the major advertising agencies who like to create the impression of seriousness for the benefit of their clients. There are, the professor said, the following stages:

1. Collecting Data

Doing research, gathering material. Assembling the mass of raw material that is more or less relevant to the subject about which you are expected to be creative. This is an activity that requires a great deal of effort and energy. It might involve travelling, talking to people and taking copious notes. It can involve study in libraries, a great deal of reading and sometimes the collection of visual references. In many organisations there are librarians and researchers employed for this purpose, but with or without help from trained researchers, it is the creativity seeker who needs to spend time and energy in acquiring experience – direct and personal – of the raw materials.

The activity of collecting data should not be confused with the stages that follow. The characteristic of the good researcher is that he is not only thorough but has an open mind. A good researcher does not make up his mind about the value of the data he is collecting before it has been collected. Inevitably he will have some idea of what may or may not be useful and relevant, but he refrains from the kind of prejudice that might prevent him from discovering useful material just because it does not immediately appear to fit his needs.

It is astonishing to me that, among students at CalArts, so few recognise the value of this data-collecting period. Of course it is the kind of work where one deliberately postpones what every student thinks is the most vital moment: the actual invention of something original. The great temptation at this stage is to grab at a gimmick that catches the imagination and at once leap into the business of writing a script, or even start shooting film.

2. Organising the Data

Tabulating the material collected. Analysing what has been found. Making sense of it all. While collecting data takes energy, curiosity and a mind open to new experiences, this subsequent step is very much more analytic and critical. It takes the kind of intelligence that differentiates, contrasts and categorises, that is able to recognise parallels and similarities.

Does this have anything to do with creativity? You might not think so, but in essence both of these two first stages are the equivalent of life experience. Film students are often criticised because they have learned technical skills but don't have anything to say. It's hardly fair to blame a young man or woman in their late teens or early twenties for inexperience of life. But in truth the problem may not be so much a lack of experience as the inability to investigate and then organise available information absorbed from the experience of others. Illustration of this is offered in the work of men and women who have lived quite sheltered lives but have, through studies of other places, times and people, recreated worlds foreign to their own.

1. See Koestler's *The Act of Creation* (Arkana, 1989; first published 1964), a volume that Mackendrick cited to students. In the opening lines of his book Koestler explains that he is proposing 'a theory of the act of creation – of the conscious and unconscious processes underlying scientific discovery, artistic originality, and comic inspiration. It endeavours to show that all creative activities have a basic pattern in common' (p. 17).

The writer who has spent some time in the collection and subsequent analysis of material is liable to feel ready to start putting it all into a script. But the result can be disappointing if what is really needed is a story, a concept. The data may be at hand, the subject has been explored and represented, but what about the idea? It remains to be found.

3. Incubating the Material

Sleeping on it and waiting. There is, of course, no practical system for assuring that a good idea will come next. Good ideas, feeble ideas, marvellous ideas – they all seem to have life of their own, arriving unannounced. In fact one way to discourage their visit is to be too impatient. It's not so much something you do, it's something that happens. Why then does it seem to happen more to brilliant men and women than to stupid ones? The answer may be because of the two earlier stages. Materials collected and then placed in a frame of reference are stored in memory, and the more that is accumulated the more likely the inspired short-circuit will spark. But it may not be all that accidental. What has been called 'sideways thinking' may be more a kind of relaxed mental state than a deliberate act, one that can be recognised and to some extent cultivated.

Could 'sideways thinking' be another term for what Arthur Koestler calls 'bisociation'? Koestler coined this term to describe a phenomenon he calls the 'Act of Creation'. It's the spark that ignites original concepts, an event that takes place in semi-consciousness or absent-mindedness where the mind is free-associating. Koestler likens it to a sort of mental short-circuit that sparks a connection between two hitherto unconnected frames of reference.[1]

4. Preserving the Spark

If the real ignition of an idea is involuntary (though the result of much investment of nervous energy and hard work), the process that follows is very much dependent on effort and discipline: to ensure that the spark of creativity establishes a level of productivity and efficiency throughout what can be a lengthy period of

DRAMATIC CONSTRUCTION

gestation before the birth of the infant work. There are two mistakes that can be made here. On the one hand there is the individual who has too little patience and humility to wait for the spark and so embraces an idea that has not been incubated long enough. On the other is the individual who has waited, perhaps too passively, for the spark of inspiration, and is subsequently confronted by the inadequacies of his skills, his lack of practical experience (often compounded by the delusion that were he only to start work, his first efforts would be of exceptional quality). Between these two stools many fall, and in many cases the imaginative energy required to keep the spark alive is lost. The proficient hack seizes too soon on an idea that expertly renders immature and superficial ideas. The inspired amateur has a brilliant concept that dies through incompetence of expression.

For many students, the unwelcome news is that the only way to maintain creative talent at the right level is through practice. Lots and lots of practice. Expressive skills ought to become automatic, and only when technique becomes a kind of reflex, responding instantly without inhibition, is the imagination left free to supply continuous energy. This is the energy that fuels inspiration. When that energy runs low, there is the danger of technique taking over and the creator settling for the easier cliché in order to avoid the difficulties a work of true originality entails. Technical competence and craftsmanship have, in recent years, been seen as an alternative to originality. Students must, of course, make up their own minds about this. But it is worth me explaining here and now that if you appreciate the virtues of technical inexperience and incompetence, there is no point whatsoever in you attending any more classes, since you will be less corrupted by craft if you rent your own equipment and misuse it without the distractions of your teacher's instruction, however earnest.

Slogans for the Screenwriter's Wall

Movies SHOW . . . and then TELL. A true movie is likely to be 60 to 80 per cent comprehensible if the dialogue is in a foreign language.

PROPS are the director's key to the design of 'incidental business': unspoken suggestions for behaviour that can prevent 'Theatricality'.

A character in isolation is hard to make dramatic. Drama usually involves CONFLICT. If the conflict is internal, then the dramatist needs to personify it through the clash with other individuals.

Self-pity in a character does not evoke sympathy.

BEWARE OF SYMPATHY between characters. That is the END of drama.

BEWARE OF FLASHBACKS, DREAM SEQUENCES and VISIONS. In narrative/dramatic material these tend to weaken the dramatic tension. They are more suited to 'lyric' material.

Screenplays are not written, they are REWRITTEN and REWRITTEN and REWRITTEN.

Screenplays come in three sizes: LONG, TOO LONG and MUCH TOO LONG.

Student films come in three sizes: Too Long, Much Too Long and Very Much Too Long.

Student films come in three sizes:
~ TOO LONG
~ MUCH TOO LONG
~ VERY MUCH TOO LONG

(AND IN VIDEOTAPE IT'S WORSE)

Movies SHOW
... and then TELL !

A true movie is likely to be 60% to 80% comprehensible if the dialogue is in a foreign language.

If it can be cut out, then CUT IT OUT. Everything non-essential that you can eliminate strengthens what's left.

Exposition is BORING unless it is in the context of some present dramatic tension or crisis. So start with an action that creates tension, then provide the exposition in terms of the present developments.

Screenplays aren't written
They're RE-WRITTEN
and– RE-WRITTEN
and – RE-WRITTEN
and – RE-WRITTEN

The start of your story is usually the consequence of some BACK-STORY, i.e. the impetus for progression in your narrative is likely to be rooted in previous events – often rehearsals of what will happen in your plot.

What is happening NOW is not as exciting as what may or may not HAPPEN NEXT

Coincidence may mean exposition is in the wrong place, i.e. if you establish the too-convenient circumstances before they become dramatically necessary, then we feel no sense of coincidence. Use coincidence to get characters into trouble, not out of trouble.

PASSIVITY is a capital crime in drama.

A character who is dramatically interesting is intelligent enough to Think Ahead. He or she has not only thought out present intentions, but has foreseen reactions and possible obstacles. Intelligent characters anticipate and have counter-moves pre-pared.

NARRATIVE DRIVE: the end of a scene should include a clear pointer as to what the next scene is going to be.

Ambiguity does not mean lack of clarity. Ambiguity may be intriguing when it consists of alternative meanings, each of them clear.

'Comedy is hard' (last words of Edmund Kean). Comedy plays best in the master-shot. Comic structure is simply dramatic struc-ture but MORE SO: neater, shorter, faster. Don't attempt comedy until you are really expert in structuring dramatic material.

The role of the ANTAGONIST may have more to do with the structure of the plot than the character of the PROTAGONIST. When you are stuck for a third act, think through your situations from the point of view of whichever characters OPPOSE the protagonist's will.

PROTAGONIST: the central figure in the story, the character 'through whose eyes' we see the events.

ANTAGONIST: the character or group of figures who represent opposition to the goals of the protagonist.

DRAMATIC IRONY: a situation where one or more of the characters on the screen is ignorant of the circumstances known to us in the audience.

If you've got a Beginning, but you don't yet have an end, then you're mistaken. You don't have the right Beginning.

In movies, what is SAID may make little impression – unless it comes as a comment or explanation of what we have seen happening.

What is happening NOW is apt to be less dramatically interesting than what may or may not HAPPEN NEXT.

What happens just before the END of your story defines the CENTRAL THEME, the SPINE of the plot, the POINT OF VIEW and the best POINT OF ATTACK.

Make sure you've chosen the correct point of attack. Common flaw: tension begins to grip too late. Perhaps the story has to start at a later point and earlier action should be 'fed in' during later sequences.

What happens at the end may often be both a surprise to the audience and the author, and at the same time, in retrospect, absolutely inevitable.

Character progression: when you've thought out what kind of character your protagonist will be at the end, start him or her as the opposite kind of person at the beginning, e.g. Oedipus who starts out arrogant and ends up humiliated, Hamlet who is indecisive at the start and ends up heroic.

ACTION speaks louder than words.

Most stories with a strong plot are built on the tension of CAUSE AND EFFECT. Each incident is like a domino that topples forward to collide with the next in a sequence which holds the audience in a grip of anticipation. 'So, what happens next?' Each scene presents a small crisis that as it plays out produces a new uncertainty.

DRAMA IS ANTICIPATION MINGLED WITH UNCERTAINTY.

A SHOOTING SCRIPT IS NOT A SCREENPLAY. The beginning screenwriter should be discouraged from trying to invent stories in screenplay format.

A FOIL CHARACTER is a figure invented to ask the questions to which the audience wants answers (asking the question may be more important than getting the answer).

NEGATIVE ACTION (something not happening) needs to be dramatised in positive action terms. You show something starting to happen which then is stopped.

TWO ELEMENTS OF SUSPENSE ARE HALF AS SUSPENSEFUL AS ONE.

CONFRONTATION SCENE is the obligatory scene that the audience feels it has been promised and the absence of which may reasonably be disappointing.

What you leave out is as important as what you leave in.

Screenplays are STRUCTURE, STRUCTURE, STRUCTURE.

Never cast for physical attributes.

Aristotle's 'unity of action' means that ONE dramatic tension should dominate. All others should be subordinate to it.

Every character is important.

Exercises for the Student of Dramatic Construction

'Narrative' is a term that implies things being in sequence: one situation followed by a subsequent (and presumably different, but related) situation. The word 'dramatic' implies doing or being done to, an action or reaction. Narrative/dramatic structure (a story) therefore depends on the connections of cause-and-effect. A consequence of the first incident or situation is that a new (and often very different) situation will arise. Simple as this is to explain, it is frequently difficult for the student film-maker to grasp in practice. And practice is what it seems to take.

Of the three basic elements of a film story (plot, theme and character), plot is in many ways the least important. A story's plot is the sequential ordering of connected events and incidents (usually in the form of cause-and-effect) that sustains the narrative momentum. But in the end, when a good story is over, it is seldom the plot that sticks in our memory – it is the situations and the characters, and sometimes what we call the theme. Not too long ago it was argued that conventional narrative structures (stories with plots) were dead, that it was, apparently, no longer either necessary or desirable to make films of this type. Though this is a rather Modernist reaction, it does raise useful questions. Is plot in itself rewarding? If the most intelligent among contemporary audiences have become bored by emphasis on plot, is it because the tidal wave of second-and third-rate entertainments seen on the screen and television are nothing but plot, full of characters who are no more than figures manipulated by the strings of stories far from being either credible or interesting, or with themes worth considering? And so on. It is clear, however, that without the underpinning of a solid plot, the other elements can sometimes fail to hold the attention of popular audiences.

I suspect it is probably not possible to teach the capacity to create vivid characters and deal with resonant and meaningful themes. These are talents a writer is born with and that no teacher can supply. Plotting, on the other hand, is a matter of craft. It is a knack developed by lots of practice, and in such matters a good instructor can provide guidance. Important to understand is that plot is apt to be the aspect of a story that emerges at a quite secondary stage of the creative process. Let me rephrase this: of course plot is important, it just is not the most promising place at which to begin. Character and situation seem to be the most fruitful thing to dream up first. They are, of course, the same thing, for a character is not a static thing. A character, inseparable from action, is revealed through transactions with other characters, rarely in isolation.

When teaching the Dramatic Construction course, I have tried to describe a system that was used for many years in the script departments of major studios. It was a method used most frequently only after a draft screenplay had already been completed, but before a revised draft was authorised. It is a system I wholeheartedly recommend to you. The writer takes upwards of a hundred blank postcards, writing on each of them the minimum number of words that describe a step in the narrative (for example, the important character interactions in a scene). All that is needed is a phrase to signify in the simplest possible way the action that is taking place. The size of a postcard means there is no room for anything but the most concrete and specific narrative steps (remember: who does what with which to whom and why?), meaning every scene has to be noted down in its most elementary fashion. This is the point of the exercise. Each card will represent something like a minute of screen time and a page of the screenplay. And, if the lettering is large and the words few, one is able to stand back from the notice board where these cards are pinned up and see an entire Step Outline (described below) laid out.

In this form there is, all too obviously, nothing but the bare bones of the story. This is really the point, because within this scaffolding it will often become all too evident what structural flaws exist. Though best done in a small team you can use the method on your own. Just the doing of it may prompt you to see with some unexpected clarity certain problems you felt were there, but couldn't quite put your finger on. The eye is able to scan the complete board, moving swiftly backwards and forwards to see how the fuses of the story are set, and identify any dead wood that needs to be hacked away. You might be able to see how certain fuses can be planted much earlier in the story and how exposition can be brought in later. Perhaps certain narrative elements have to start at a later point and the action found detailed on earlier cards fed into later sequences. You will be able to see where the tension does or doesn't hold, where the pace quickens or the suspense is relaxed, where the major climaxes come and the peripeteias are due.

One should be prepared for major shocks at this juncture. If there is something seriously wrong with a project, an experienced storyteller can often diagnose it at this point. It is typical of the producer, the director and actor that they have strong instincts about what is wrong and what doesn't work, but often don't know how it can be put right. Using the postcard system means that problems will be more visible than they have been before. The most common flaw of a story is that there is superfluous action that can be eliminated in order to accelerate the momentum of the narrative, scenes that are either wholly unnecessary or that often can be topped and tailed. Go through your script and test each incident and character to see if it can be removed from the story without damaging the whole. The 'rule' here is that anything that can be cut should be, because when everything non-essential is eliminated, what remains is greatly strengthened.

To help you develop your skills at plotting, the Step Outline form is well worth studying. A Step Outline is a working document, often prepared at an interim stage in a screenplay's development, meant to be read only by people who are already involved with a project. It can function as the rough sketch made when writers and producers are confronting the problems of adapting a novel, a play or property that is not yet organised as screen material. It can also be made at a stage when drastic reconstruction and revisions have to be made to an early draft of a screenplay. What it is not, however, is the form in which the story idea is first put down. In the context of a Dramatic

Construction class we shall make use of the Step Outline form to analyse completed films. By doing so we will retrace the history of some of our favourite stories and uncover the skeletons under the skin and flesh of these completed works.

So what exactly is a Step Outline? It is a brief analysis of plot structure of an already existing feature film, a bare synopsis of the steps of a story, a tool with which to dismantle and expose the dramatic narrative structure and mechanisms at work. It is a list of the basic steps in the progression of a film narrative as one scene (meaning an episode that often has its own internal structure, minor crisis and peripeteia) moves to the next. It is nothing but plot mechanics, the bones of the narrative stripped of flesh and nerve, and should be as short as possible while still containing everything essential to the structure of the story. Length will vary according to how dense the plot in question is. An outline may be only three or four pages in length, or it may take up to fifty pages if it is important to explain a complex plot.

It is useful to set down the steps in numbered paragraphs. These usually represent scenes, a unit of dramatic action. One is apt to think of a scene as being an event that takes place in a single geographical location, but a more useful way is to consider it as an incident or confrontation that contains within it the action/objective dialectic of narrative progression (the dramatic event) as seen in the larger shape of the story as a whole. A scene is a section of a narrative in which there is one clearly defined purpose and intention, the space occupied by a single predominant episode of dramatic tension, though contained within the scene might be a series of smaller steps or story beats. The idea is that each character is likely to have not only a central objective to his or her behaviour but also minor and incidental activities that are necessary to achieve en route to this main objective.

Analogies with literature are not always accurate, but you might think of the way a writer breaks up a book into chapters, a chapter into paragraphs, paragraphs into sentences, sentences into clauses or phrases, each having individual structure and meaning. Thus a story beat might be a sequence of several lines of dialogue or certain actions prompted by a single identifiable intention. It might even be something as simple as the articulation of discrete feelings and thoughts. When a story is looked at in this fashion, you have to be very clear in your analysis of what actively occurs in every scene (especially if it takes place in more than one location) and your story as a whole. You have to recognise where the story has just come from and how every particular step affects what may, or may not, happen next.

In this respect a Step Outline is not just a list of scenes – it is a chain of events. As you number the scenes, keep in mind that each should read as a progressive move, a step in a cause-and-effect chain. Think, for instance, of beginning each new paragraph with the unwritten phrase, 'So the consequence of this is . . .' This should help you recognise the need for the drive that gives continuous energy and tension to a story. After each paragraph of a Step Outline the reader should know why he is still sitting here, wondering and waiting for what happens next. Remember: 'anticipation mingled with uncertainty'. Both factors are necessary. The anticipation is our sense of expectancy about what has just happened and how it is likely to produce a new event we suspect is likely to follow. The uncertainty is our sense that even though we have an idea as to what will happen next, we cannot be sure of precisely how it will turn out. We anticipate but are still ready for surprises. The task of the storyteller is thus often the invention of a structure along the principle of Chinese boxes. A situation is created where our curiosity is whetted by the desire to uncover or disclose a solution, or to unravel a knot of tension, but when the discovery is made or the knot unravelled, it shows only another box, another hiding place.

In order to concentrate on plot structure, I suggest you provide at the start of an outline a list of the story's principal (and important subsidiary) characters alongside a couple of lines describing their age and relationships to each other. (Don't bother about physical appearance unless it is significant to the story and the action. Some years ago, a student produced an outline of *Bad Day at Black Rock*. It had been a number of years since I had seen the film, and I was puzzled by the feeling that something was missing. Then I realised that the synopsis did not mention that the central figure is a war veteran who has only one arm. Since this small detail is quite central not only to the character but the plot too, it was a curious omission.) When writing about the principals be sure to emphasise their interrelationships only in so far as this defines their motivations and hence actions. This might mean putting down something about their past history, information that provides the character with a purpose and dramatic intention in their present action.

An outline contains no unnecessary descriptions written for atmospheric purposes. It will also generally ignore aesthetic qualities of the work. *Hamlet*, for example, has a plot that, when read in the Step Outline form, is not all that interesting compared with the extraordinary depth and resonance of the true genius of the work expressed through its poetic language. The outline is concerned only with action, which means there should be no explicit explanation of character or motive, no intrusion of the writer's opinion. Inevitably, because an outline concentrates on plot, it has no space for exploration of nuances of meaning and provides little comment on the story's theme or the characterisation developing within that structure. However, when writing a Step Outline, a good writer can, in the minimum of words, set down the beats of a story that will describe the character-in-action with utmost clarity and that will in turn *imply* character and theme.

A Step Outline need not be tedious to read. Though it is a working document, it should be interesting and exciting. The need for economy and simplicity does not mean it should be merely a list of incidents and events full of abbreviations and disconnected phrases. It should have its own narrative drive and momentum. Expert journalists are apt to have this knack, the ability to set down information that has force and clarity in its emphasis on cause-and-effect momentum. Be sure to write in sentences with subjects, verbs and objects. This has the advantage of disciplining you to write in the language of action and reaction rather than static conditions and ongoing, continuous activities that do not involve much tension and that tend to be overly descriptive and explanatory. It has been interesting for me to appreciate that from the very grammar of the sentence structure in which an outline is written, I can sense whether or not the student has got the hang of cinematic narrative progression.

It is a good idea to pick for your first Step Outline a film you find interesting and dramatically rewarding. At the same time do not forget that some of the films particularly exciting to students are very difficult to vivisect in this way. The Step Outline, as we have said, strongly emphasises plot. When a film has a very strong and obvious plot structure it can be relatively easy to put into outline form. But plot is in some ways the least interesting aspect in many superb films. Contemporary cinema is apt to depend on values that are much more subtle (even impossible) to communicate in an outline. So I advise you to start with a film that has a single and strong narrative line. Watch the whole film through. On the second viewing make notes on each scene. These initial notes can be very cryptic: a list of the characters, sometimes a key dialogue phrase, no more. Once you have memorised (internalised) the sequence of story events, you are ready to start on the outline proper. The real task at this point is to eliminate everything that is not a step or move in the narrative. The great temptation is to interpret, to write in a way that communicates the particular qualities of the film. But remember that the purpose of the Step Outline, as distinct from most other forms in which a film story can be written, is to reduce the plot mechanism to its bare bones, to strip it of all its other values.

My first attempts at teaching a workshop on dramatic structure were not a success. Not, at any rate, in my opinion, though even with all the mistakes I made, I myself learned a great deal (probably more than the students did). I started off by inviting students to write their ideas in the form of a Step Outline because it was my impression that novice writers find plot structure very hard, particularly the kind of plotting that builds. A strong story is likely to have a rising line in its tension. Though it may from time to time be relaxed, the tension of the dramatic conflict is likely to become more powerful towards the final sequences, up to the final crises that precede the resolution of significant tensions and conflicts.

Yet when the students submitted their outlines, few of them had a good ending. Belatedly, I began to realise why: I had made the mistake of inviting them to begin with the plot. I should have known it was wrong to suggest they start their inventive work by thinking in the pattern of the Step Outline, because in my own professional experience as a writer it was clear that an outline is never written in the early stages of the process by which a story is initiated. If an outline is done at all it is likely to be the work of someone who is boiling down a story that is already in a more elaborate and richer form, for example a story editor or a director analysing the plot structure of an existing script that requires structural work.

The problem with using the outline form as a blueprint for an original story idea is that though it may provide an idea of the structure, it is a skeleton without flesh and blood. It is a dead thing. Plot in itself (when divorced from character and theme) is lifeless material, mechanical narrative with no creative vitality. So use the Step Outline (which is, in the context of narrative structure, a purely analytical approach) for study purposes only. Use it as an instrument for dismantling, vivisecting and exploring the structure and engine of an *already existing* dramatic structure. As my workshop ran into these problems, I realised I had to make an agonising reappraisal. I confessed my error and explained that I had made a mistake in suggesting the Step Outline as suitable for exploring story ideas. Instead, I suggested that a story is best investigated in terms of character.

Though it has been said that writing is acting in your head, few students of film-making have experience of acting, least of all improvisational acting. Yet I know of no better way to develop a sense of character than this kind of exercise, the practice of make-believe that involves pretending to be an imagined character. Inhibitions against this practice are many. To start with, students who have no experience of public performance are shy. There is no cure for shyness except the brutal experience of making a fool of yourself. Some consolation may be offered to you: the fact is that people who are instinctively shy are, paradoxically, often the best actors when they have learned to overcome their inhibitions. Conversely, it is the personality so lacking in shyness that he is without self-consciousness who may find it is impossible to be anyone but himself.

The same is true for writing. The dramatic writer ought to have an ear for dialogue, an ability to hear inside his head the speech rhythms and intonations of his characters, in just the same way a good mimic does. It is one more reason why a screenwriter is at an advantage if he has at least the imagination of an actor, even if he does not have the technique necessary for performance. When I realised that the exploration of character was probably the best way to start work on a story, I intuitively felt that the best way to do this might be to improvise the voice of these characters, writing in first-person singular. I have been looking into the process of exploring character motivations through the writing of monologues, an exercise many students have found to be very useful. The rules of the game are these:

1. When you find you have a good premise for a story, an opening situation, but then discover that the story bogs down and doesn't seem to provide a good third act, lay aside the plot. Ignore the problem of narrative for the moment and concentrate on the characters.
2. In particular, think about the antagonist. Sometimes it is easy to identify this figure, on other occasions quite difficult. Your first idea may not be the correct one. (Who, for example, is the antagonist in *Oedipus Rex*?) The best clue to the antagonist is that he/she is the figure who personifies the obstacle to the purposes of the hero/heroine.
3. Now imagine yourself in the role of this antagonist. Begin to write an interior monologue in the first person, an account of the story as seen through the eyes of this antagonist. Don't worry too much about the sequence of events, just improvise freely on how the antagonist would describe, if he were writing in some private diary, all his thoughts, secret impulses and self-justifications for whatever he does, or wants to do. Invent whatever back-story is necessary to explain the antagonist's attitudes and behaviour.
4. When writing, try to remain more or less consistent with the actions, situations and characters you have established, or have already envisaged. Though you (as antagonist) will be writing mostly about your relationship with your story's protagonist, you may find that to make your behaviour believable, you have to elaborate on matters of which the protagonist is ignorant. Conversely, in your role as antagonist, you will almost certainly be ignorant of situations that are known to the protagonist (and even to yourself as author). Through this split-mind process, you should find that you are inventing opportunities for dramatic irony when you return to the task of constructing the plot.
5. Write all this in retrospect, as if you were recapitulating the

DRAMATIC CONSTRUCTION

events of a story as you look back on it from the end. Even if your first person character happens to be dead, begin with some equivalent of, 'Now that it's all over . . .' Curiously, you may discover that if you write this exercise before you have worked out the main dramatic crisis of the story (before you know how the tale will end), the antagonist will begin to take over the story and will start to dictate the action him/herself (not necessary a bad thing).

6. Often the monologue will bog down. When it does, try switching to another role. Lay aside the unfinished monologue, along with your plot, and start over, writing another account of the same story as seen through the eyes of one of the other figures. This process may have to be repeated three, four or even five times until you have brought to life several of the principal characters involved in the action.

7. When the process is working well, there seems to come an abrupt moment when you find you have what you need. At this point, return once more to the task of writing a script in narrative form. You may find, incidentally, that some quite new point of attack has emerged, that your first attempt at plotting actually began at the wrong place in the story. And as you now start to write in the much richer and more colourful form of either a screenplay or a dialogue treatment, you can use as dialogue some of the lines that you invented for the monologues. Lines that were conceived as private inner thoughts can now be directed at other characters.

By improvising in this way, while constantly thinking of the plot beats, in particular from the point of view of the protagonist of a story, you are forced into the invention of situations and incidents that are the raw material of narrative structure. It is also a demonstration of how a good story works from the point of view of any of its primary characters (and sometimes, even the minor ones too). This is a process easier to demonstrate than to describe, and as an illustration, here are two monologues I have written in this manner: Johnny Friendly (the antagonist in *On the Waterfront*) and Harry Lime (played by Orson Welles in *The Third Man*). Your own monologues might be much longer than these. Do not worry about this. You are advised to write, as a first draft, as much as you feel is necessary, before perhaps trimming and polishing during the rewriting process.

Johnny Friendly

Like I told them, I'll remember every damn one of these bastards. I won't forget. That little weasel, Pop Doyle, the one that pushed me off the gang plank into the mud, I'll take care of him. They all thought that was funny. Well, they'll be laughing outa the other side of their mouths by the time I get through with them.

I can wait. Right now the heat's on and I may have to watch my step. Might have to get out of town for a while, too. Florida, maybe. I got good connections and some things going for me in the docks down there. It's not like here, of course, because up here we really got it all sewed up tight. I mean we had it all sewed up till that dumb little ex-tanker turned cheese-eater on me.

After all I did for the little bastard. Jeezus! I found that little jerk when he was nuthin'! Really nuthin'! I got him fixed up with a trainer an' we brought him on real good. Just because we wouldn't give him a shot at the title, you think that's what got him sore? He wasn't ready for it. We wasn't ready for it! We woulda given him a chance later when we got the right odds. I'm tellin' ya, I loved that kid. I loved him like he was a son. And what does he do to me?

Not just to me either. Because all the rest of them are gonna be in trouble. Oh, sure, the Crime Commission is gonna put on a big show how they cleaned up the rackets, but that'll blow over and that's when the Mob will move in and take over. I know the guys that'll do it. Same guys that I had to go up against when I made my move.

Everybody knows that story. Three guys with shivs and I had to hold my hand over my throat to keep from bleeding to death. But I still took care of them.

You gotta let them know you're tough. You don't last around here if you don't. All the same, I don't like it when you gotta waste a guy. Shouldn't be necessary. You just lean on 'em a little. That's what I told those goons when they had to take care of the Doyle kid. Don't bump him. Not unless you have to. Just lean on him. I guess he must've given them an argument.

I guess the Doyle kid was a friend of Malloy. Okay, so maybe we made a mistake using him to get the Doyle kid up on the roof. Yeah. Maybe that was a mistake.

DRAMATIC CONSTRUCTION

Harry Lime

I've decided I'll risk it. It's a small cafe on a corner of one of the badly bombed out old squares. I used to meet Anna there. It's got a back entrance as well as a front and it's near to several of the manholes down into the sewer system I know by heart. The message I've sent back to Holly is that he should be there at about ten o'clock, so there won't be many people about. Vienna goes to bed early these days and I'll have a chance to reconnoitre to see that he's come alone. If it is a trap, I should be able to get away fast.

There is a risk, of course. It could be a trap. Popescu is convinced that Holly has betrayed us to Calloway. He was here an hour ago, in a panic because both Kurtz and Winkel were arrested today. I've been expecting it, of course, because ever since Calloway dug up my coffin and found Harbin's body, he's known that I'm alive. And, in any event, Holly probably told him he'd met with me.

The real question is how much the police have told Holly. If it's a trap, like Popescu says, then Holly is working for the police. That's hard to believe. Ridiculous, of course, but the truth is that I'm fond of him. He's been useful in the past and in these circumstances might be even more useful. Popescu has panicked, and if I have to get across the borders to the West, that's where Holly could be valuable.

I don't think Popescu is right: I don't believe Holly would let Calloway use him. Why should he? What kind of pressure would they put on him? A reward of some kind? That's not like Holly. I've been thinking about him. He's really a very trusting soul, as unsophisticated as the dumb characters in those pulp Westerns he writes. I've never been able to finish any of his books, but they have helped me understand how his mind works. An extraordinary capacity for sentimental loyalty. It used to astonish me even when we were at school together.

On occasion, I admit that I've had an occasional twinge of conscience about the way I used to take advantage of Holly. It was just too easy. The truth is, of course, that he has a desperate need for hero-worship. He always needed me more than I needed him, so I don't see how I can blame myself. I've never really needed anyone. In a way one envies people like Anna and

Holly with their simple-minded faith. Typical of Holly, that thing he said in the Prater. 'You used to believe in God.' Very comforting it must be to be so sure there is some benevolent Almighty up there, looking down on us all, keeping score of our good deeds and our bad, deciding who goes to Heaven and who to Hell. Right now it's hard to believe in Heaven, and all too easy to believe in Hell. All you have to do is keep your eyes open and look around.

Calloway is the real danger. My only real worry is that Holly seems to have been seeing too much of him. Two bits of bad luck, neither of which could have been foreseen. The first was that Holly arrived in time for my funeral, and Calloway latched on to him. I got the report from Kurtz and Winkel who saw them leave together. The other was that Holly saw me outside of Anna's apartment. A disaster, of course, but Holly's expression when that light went on still makes me laugh. It was almost worth it.

Holly must have gone straight to the police. I didn't expect that. He meant no harm, I'm sure. From what I can gather, the only reason he was still in Vienna is that he had got it into his head that I'd been murdered. He was playing hero in one of his paperback thrillers, the amateur detective that pursues the villains who have killed his best friend. A comedy, but also highly inconvenient and, as it has turned out, very dangerous.

The fake accident was not nearly as well worked out as I would have liked. I had used Anna to get a message to Harbin to come and see me at the apartment that night. Harbin was scared, of course, because the police had been grilling him. We were nervous because Harbin was our source at the hospital for our penicillin supplies. We were paying him more than enough, but he was scared and was trying to pull out. The real danger was that Calloway might make a deal with him. But as I've said, there was no need to kill him. That was Popescu.

I called in Kurtz and Winkel at once. They were both in a hysterical state of terror. It took an hour to calm them down. Neither of them was in any real danger because they were not there when Harbin died. I had to explain to them that I was the only one who had direct contact with Harbin, and I was the one that the police would be after as soon as Harbin was reported missing. We had to dispose of the corpse. And I had somehow to disappear. Put like that it was too obvious what we had to do. My driver was the only other person we needed in order to stage my tragic end, with Winkel just happening to be passing by so that Harbin's corpse could be identified as mine.

Under the pressure of the inquest, the burial and so on, I actually forgot all about Holly. I suppose, if I had thought of it in time, I could have got Kurtz to send him a wire, telling him that I was dead. But I forgot until it was too late. Poor, pathetic Holly arrived just in time to attend my funeral, and then couldn't be persuaded to go home.

Should I go to meet him or not? Will I be walking into a trap? How does one calculate the odds? Though it's true that Holly could be a real help to me in wrapping up all the business here so that I collect all the money that we've been making – enough for both Holly and I to live the rest of our lives on – the truth is that I could cut my losses and get out on my own. I'm just not sure. Oddly, the real reason I've decided to take the risk is that I'm curious. Is Holly double-crossing me or not? I need to know.

Needless to say, this last monologue wouldn't make nearly as good a film as the one that Graham Greene and Carol Reed devised. Why? One reason, I think, is that though Harry Lime may function in the story as the activator of most of the plot, he's actually less interesting as a character than Holly Martins (played by Joseph Cotten). Though he has certain complexities – he is obviously torn between feelings of affection and friendship for his old long-time friend and his own desperate self-interest – Lime is not really at the centre of the main theme of Greene's story.

It is important to understand that choice of a story's point of view very often determines the theme. It is not infrequent that a writer will make an early draft of his story with one protagonist, then later rework it from the point of view of another. Graham Greene, who wrote *The Third Man*, was interested in the theme of loss of innocence, and in this context Lime is to a great degree a character who, because he is cynical from the start, has no character progression. Martins, on the other hand, is the very personification of the theme of loss of innocence. Through what can be interpreted either as feelings of jealousy over Anna, or feelings of moral duty under the persuasion of Calloway and his experience in the children's hospital, Holly Martins betrays the friend who used to be his hero. At the character level and in terms of theme, this is a much better story.

I can offer only a few practical pieces of advice when it comes to the actual writing of your story.

Remember that scripts are not so much written as rewritten and rewritten and rewritten (Mark Twain's rule for writing: 'Apply seat of pants to chair'). During a period of nearly ten years when I was under contract to a British studio, first as a contract screenwriter, then later as a writer/director, a pattern emerged. Every screenplay that finally became a film was rewritten a minimum of five and a maximum of seven times. There was no explicit rule about this, nobody could explain why it became standard practice – it just worked out that way. Another noticeable pattern was that many subjects did not even reach screenplay form at all and were scrapped after the first draft (while a script that required too many re-writes was usually abandoned after the seventh draft). So plunge ahead regardless. Don't wait to get it right, just get it written.

'Art-with-a-capital-A' may be a little different from drama in some respects. Drama, or to put it in more vulgar terms, the craft of inventing stories, invokes the invention of characters. A character, we say, is the personification of a point of view. Stories usually involve some kind of conflict (points of view that are in opposition), and to create a really convincing and plausible villain, the writer has to 'find the villain' within his or her own nature. The villain (antagonist) is the personification of what the hero is up against and because of this he or she is often much more important to the structure of a good story than the protagonist. (Think of your favourite films: don't you remember the villain over the hero in many of them?) So if you are one of those film-makers who find yourself utterly out of all sympathy with public sensibilities, there is one tactic available to you: personify what you find obnoxious. Make the public itself into a character and work at making him or her into a convincing antagonist who can represent those views that are in conflict with the values you find important. (One other thing to note: a contemporary story, in these days when we seem somewhat uncomfortable about 'heroism', may well be more dependent on the defeat of the antagonist than on the victory of the protagonist.)

A number of years ago I attended some meetings in London where psychologists were experimenting with a therapeutic process called 'psychodrama'. A typical example would be difficulties in communication between, say, a daughter and her mother. The psychologist would begin by inviting the patient (the daughter) to act out an argument with someone playing the role of the mother. (On occasion, a professional would be recruited to help with these improvisations.) This in itself was often helpful to the patient. Just the opportunity to act out, in the presence of some sympathetic onlookers, the pain of the unhappy relationship would bring some relief of tension. But it was the next stage that was extraordinary. When some progress had been made in this game of make-believe aggression, the psychologist would ask that the daughter and the 'mother' switch roles. Results varied. For some patients, the challenge was impossible. But in other cases the game was sensational in its effect, creating theatrical moments of incredible impact.

It was the memory of this experience that prompted me to create an exercise that I have found useful when working with students who are encountering problems with formulating original story ideas. The first step is often easy. The student invents an effective first-act situation, a premise to a potential drama, one involving a protagonist conceived in some convincing situation. For most students the difficulty lies up ahead. As soon as this situation has been presented, students' stories often begin to lose narrative momentum. Tension slackens and there is no feeling of a build toward the kind of crisis that will provide a coherent third act. The solution, which has proved effective in many cases, is to ask the author temporarily to play the game of role reversal by improvising a new version of the story as it might be seen from the point of view of the antagonist, a figure with whom it is not so easy for the author to identify, but who, when identified, proves to be the crucial missing element. (This is a technique that can also be applied equally effectively to existing stories and films.)

Remember too that the chain of linked happenings that constitutes a story is usually anchored at the end. This can be a problem for the writer without experience. As you begin, think ahead, for the end is what matters (though the King of Hearts, from *Alice in Wonderland*, may have been seriously oversimplifying when he advised 'Begin at the beginning, and go on till you come to the end: then stop'). Another quote from *Alice* makes more sense: 'How do I know what I mean until I've heard what I want to say?' This, if you think about it, means that you may recognise what the beginning of a story needs to be only when you have stumbled upon the end.

According to story editors, those individuals looking for fresh young talent for the entertainment industry, the most common weakness in scripts submitted to them is that 'they have no third act'. Important to realise is that a weakness in the third act is not just a weakness of the end of the screenplay, it is a fundamental weakness of the whole work. A beginning is the start of a structure that is completed at the end. As such, a premise that is interesting but doesn't go anywhere is not a dramatically viable premise. Perhaps there is another way to put it: a situation that seems promising but lacks the momentum to keep going all the way to the end may be a premise not yet explored to its full potential.

Having a sense of how everything is going to work out at a story's culmination does not, of course, mean you have to know the end precisely, only that you have a strong guiding instinct. It might be suggested that you start with the end and work back. This is useful, but only up to a point. Only when a story has been well structured does one recognise that the ultimate crisis and resolution were not only somehow implicit in the initial premise all along, they were inherent in the opening scenes. In this sense, dramatic tension depends more on the *how* of the events than the *why*. By the time the obligatory scene and peripeteias arrive at the end of the story, we have in some sense been anticipating and preparing for them for some time ('Of course! How else could it have ended!'), even though we take some pleasure in the way the storytelling has been engineered so that we are still, to a certain extent, taken off-guard.

If you really have absolutely no instinct of where you are going, then maybe you are not yet ready to decide on the point

DRAMATIC CONSTRUCTION

at which to start. This is something demonstrated by the experience of writers who have discovered that, in writing a novel, they have to sweat through many pages before they arrive at the situation that turns out to be the beginning of the story they actually want to tell. The material that gets thrown away is never lost, however, for it either reappears, perhaps as back-story to the final story, or forms an essential rehearsal of the character relationships and situations that give depth and dimension to the emerging story.

When writing a scene, ask yourself: what element of the back-story might have been a rehearsal for this moment? Stanislavsky always urged that the actor concentrate on three questions concerning the past, present and future of character-in-action: 'Where have I come from?', 'What am I doing here?' and 'What is it that I mean to achieve?' This is the point of back-story. In order to determine what a character's motives are you have to know what has happened to him or her up till this moment. What we do now, and how we react to the things and people around us, is affected by what has been done to us, or by what we ourselves have done, on some previous occasion. (This is similar to the world of the director when he is on the film set. In preparation for the task of putting a scene on screen, he must be able to imagine, with absolute clarity and solidity, the world of the whole story at hand, a universe of which the scene he is currently working at is merely a small and perhaps relatively unimportant part.)

An interesting example of this is Graham Greene's work on *The Third Man*. Greene felt that his first draft had to be written not in screenplay form but as a short novel.[1] From some experiences of my own as a director working with writers on wholly original material I can support his view that a screenplay is, for many authors, not the best format in which to explore the beginnings of a story. A more literary form frequently allows the imaginative writer more freedom to explore, often apparently at random, the subtleties and complexities of potentially rich character relationships, moods, and those editorial thoughts and comments that will perhaps never make it into the screenplay. Early drafts are freer in structure. It is in rewrites that this structure is boiled down into the stark economy of a tightly structured screenplay.

[1]. See 'When Not to Write a Shooting Script'.

Importantly, back-story is at its most effective when it is present action, in the sense that it is something seen now and on-screen as some kind of recapitulation of earlier events. The point of attack in a gripping narrative may be the moment when an incident ignites a fuse that, through twists and turns, will smoulder along the trail that leads to the detonation of the last act. But effective narrative leads us in both directions, to what went before as well as what will, or will not, happen next. The taxi-cab sequence in *On the Waterfront* is dramatically dense for this reason. The key material is about something in the past: the night when Terry was forced to throw a fight so the mobsters could make money on him. On one level his dialogue is simply exposition of character, an explanation of why he calls himself a 'bum'. In dramatic terms, however, the real here-and-now action is the effect on Charley. Because of this story of past betrayal he knows he cannot now persuade Terry against testifying to the Crime Commission, and since Charley is responsible for ensuring that Terry won't testify, his own life is now in danger. Thus what is a recapitulation of the past is also the key element in present action.

When watching a scene, especially an obligatory scene, there are several points to note for study purposes.

1. Analyse the action. Each character will always certainly come to the confrontation with quite specific aims, the clash of which is likely to lead to a peripeteia of some kind. Ask yourself: what are the aims of the main characters? Break down the scene into its moves. Is there a peripeteia? How is it prepared, and how is it detonated?
2. What are the themes of the scene and in turn, most probably, the story as a whole? The conflict of an obligatory scene is often rooted not only in what the characters are doing (character-in-action) but also in the themes that each might personify. Mark those spoken lines where certain ideas expressed by the characters prove a particular point or perhaps enunciate a general truth and where the characters make us, the audience, ascribe certain moral (or amoral) qualities to them.

3. Aristotle uses terms like *diction* and *melody*. Study the scene for characteristic language (as expressed in a particular way by the actors) that illustrates personality. As you have marked the moves or the beats of the scene, so also distinguish the variety of contrasting emotions and mood changes in the character-action that might not be immediately apparent in the text, but which might be articulated by the actors. These are the unexpected colours of a performance, and exploring them is a good way to encourage freshness and vitality in the actor. Through phrasing and intonation, the pitch of the voice and the timing of the lines, good actors are able to communicate with far more subtlety and feeling. As contrasted with silent cinema (which inevitably has more of a two-dimensional and primative quality to it), this is one of the most important elements of sound films.

4. Drama is at its most effective when there is foreshadowing of the events ahead. Look for the moment in the story when it becomes absolutely clear that the final resolution is about to be played out, and consider which characters will be involved. Note exactly what the resolution means in terms of conflict and role reversals. At the same time, take time to look back at the story as a whole, and find those incidents that have irrevocably brought the characters to this climatic moment.

There are many exercises that the student of dramatic construction can undertake, but I have found that some of the most effective are born of very simple ideas.

Construct obstacles for the following:
1 A pretty young stenographer in Minnesota has weak lungs and wants a heavy winter coat
2 A lawyer is running for the legislature
3 A schoolteacher wants to accept a good position in a distant town
4 Two men want to marry the same girl (the girl is the protagonist)
5 A group of miners demands a wage increase
6 A fifteen-year-old girl has learned a serious piece of scandal about someone she idolises (state her objective as well as her obstacle)

7 A fifteen-year-old boy is determined to enter the Navy

8 A young wife wants her husband to be proud of her

9 A factory owner wants to replace an incompetent foreman

10 A doctor wants to spare a patient the knowledge that she has borne an idiot child

For the following protagonists, find a clear, dynamic objective, and a way to make these objectives appealing to an audience of (a) businessmen, (b) farmers, (c) university students, and (d) church members:

1 Shakespeare

2 A man who inherits a farm (and likes farming)

3 A pioneer in the American Midwest

4 The mother of a soldier killed in the war

5 A woman who married five old men (all living, none divorced)

6 St Augustine

7 Al Capone

8 The daughter of a moderately rich elderly widow

9 A woman whose husband lets her know she bores him

10 A man of mediocre ability who had a great ancestor

Follow these stories through, and write down what the obligatory scene of each could be.

1 The attractive but prudish protagonist constantly reprimands two delightful old friends of her father for taking a drink. She becomes engaged to a fine, lively young man, the proprietor of a tavern.

2 Two women are close friends. One of them discovers that her husband is ruining the husband of the other and forcing him into bankruptcy.

3 One of the guests at a dinner party, a newcomer to the town, is particularly jumpy. Another guest seems to recall meeting him before. Still another finds that he makes her nervous.

4 After a hard day at the office, Jack plans to lounge with the papers all evening. He does not know that his wife has asked her parents to dinner.

5 A woman in love with her husband does not know him to be a criminal.

Follow these stories through, this time using the 'Once upon a time . . .' format.

1 Start with the ending of a crime story. Regard the murdered individual as the objective, the murder as the obstacle. Find a protagonist and plan a course of action.

2 Start with a news story: a prize fighter discovered that his wife, a former chorus girl, was being unfaithful with his manager. In the divorce court he asked for custody of their son on the grounds that his wife was unfit to rear the boy. Find protagonist, objective, and course of action.

3 Starting with a character of your acquaintance, find or invent an objective that would place him in clearer harmony with his universe. Assume he recognises the need for this objective, or for a substitute he thinks he needs. Explain what might stand in his way and let these constitute the obstacles. Plan a course of action in which he gets the objective, another where he fails to get it.

When Not to Write a Shooting Script

Film-making is one continuous process. The stages overlap. Though usually done by different people in the professional world, the many technical jobs involved in producing a film merge into each other, and when a good film materialises it is a unity: the parts are so welded together that no one really knows who did what. The members of a film crew should feel like the man a friend of mine met some weeks ago. 'Sandy Mackendrick?' the man said. 'I know him. He worked on two of my films.' I had indeed worked on two films with him: he was the stand-by carpenter, and is a first-class carpenter because he knew that the films were his as much as anybody else's.

A script is never the sole domain of either writer or director, and only when both are true collaborators will the resulting film function as well as it possibly can. Even though the final form of a screenplay is not a set of mimeographed pages but a finished film, the director's role should never be considered as starting during casting sessions or once he walks onto the set, nor even once the scripting process has been completed. Rather, it must be rooted in the very origins of the first dramatic conception. Screenwriting is a reductive process, a gradual condensing and tightening of the structure found in an original work. It is a procedure during which the director will, for example, spend time with the writer, indicating to him how the ideas contained within his dialogue can be made more economically by action and incident through the use of cinematic language, something often exploited most efficiently at the editing bench.

Important to understand here is that one of the writer's jobs is to be the connection between two other personalities: the director speaking the film 'language' and the performer discovering the role. In fact, among screenwriters I have worked with a few of the

DRAMATIC CONSTRUCTION

most talented are former actors. The great strength of the writer who has a good understanding of acting is an ear for playable dialogue, because words always need to be more effective in the mouth of the actor than on the page. But more important than this is that even before they invent any dialogue, many writers act out the physical behaviour of their characters in their imagination. By doing so, non-verbal actions (as well as any dialogue deemed absolutely necessary) as written on the page emerge as a direct expression of impulses, feelings and thoughts. In this sense, the screenplay becomes a point of departure for the interpretive actor from which he has to work backwards so as to retrace the writer's imaginative ideas and impulses that originally gave birth to the scene. Writing, it is said, is acting in your head.

In a sense, writing, acting, directing and editing are all performing skills. The competent director follows the same process as the actor: he goes back to the creative origins that the writer has supplied, collaborating with the actor in rediscovery of the characters and situations that were originally images and voices in the mind of the writer. And the editor, who is presented with very tangible visible and audible records of these images and voices must capture all over again the evolved and still evolving make-believe. One of the best editors I ever worked with was a former actor. I used to watch him as he sat at the editing bench, running the unedited footage over and over again. While he did this you could see on his face that he was absorbing the actions and words of the actors, instinctively acting along with their performances until he found the precise frame where the actor was, essentially, telling him to make the cut. A good editor will even rediscover magical elements of the footage that the writer, actor and director didn't know they had put there.

I have never directed a film on which I did not myself function as close collaborator of the writer or writers. In the majority of instances I assisted in the construction of the story and also helped write drafts of dialogue, or for various reasons spent time rewriting dialogue during the shooting when the screenwriter was not available. I have, in fact, never made a film in which the dialogue did not require some degree of editing either at the shooting stage or in the post-production period. But this is no more than a natural part of the group process of film-making.

1. In his 1954 essay 'A Film Director and His Public', Mackendrick wrote: 'Whether he likes it or not (and as a rule he does not like it much) the man who wants to express himself on celluloid is part of a group. If individual and personal self-expression is what he wants, he is in the wrong business. Even in the early stages of writing a film script this still applies.'

In the ideal situation (seldom, if ever experienced), the collaboration of a writer and director would start at the very inception of the subject and involve the writer being present throughout, an observer of the rehearsals who could not only edit his own text, but make suggestions to the director and actor on the interpretation of the scene.

As such, I have asked and taken screen credit for only those screenplays on which, at a quite early stage, I worked alone on a complete version of a full draft of the film. In fact the films of mine that seemed most satisfactory to me were usually developed in this way. As a writer (not an *auteur* but an honest-to-God word-merchant), while preparing a script that another director was to work on, I would make the necessary mental effort to think of that other future director even though I was pretty sure it would actually be me. It was quite helpful at some point to call in a new screenwriter who was, as inevitably happens, quite critical of this draft and would insist on rewriting substantially. With this newcomer on the scene I would be forced out of the role of the original author, required to look objectively and critically at my own initial efforts. Since I'd had the privilege of selecting this new writer and had chosen him to supply the talent, skills and insights I felt I lacked, this was not too difficult. I could easily divorce myself from too passionate an attachment to the original draft.

Many film students seem to be intoxicated with the idea of the *auteur* in the cinema, the idea that a commercial feature film can be regarded as the work of a single individual in the way that a painting, a novel or even a musical might be. Though this is a very misleading concept, it appears that few students are enthusiastic in their attempts to collaborate.[1] It is actually my impression that students generally have no real desire to be screenwriters at all. At least, not *just* screenwriters. Those students who come to CalArts interested in narrative/dramatic work often have in mind the goal of being directors, not writers. Moreover, the beginning film-maker is very apt to harbour (unrealistically, I would suggest) the immensely attractive fantasy of being what is called in the industry a 'hyphenate' – a screenwriter/director – without having been subjected to the painful experiences of studying these two crafts separately.

DRAMATIC CONSTRUCTION

The overwhelming temptation of many students when faced with problems of dramatic construction in the scripting stage is to dodge the real challenges by fantasising about the much more pleasurable (and indeed easier) problems involved in actually shooting the film. As such, the particular passion of many students is to work, from the start, on their own stories in shooting-script form (those containing precise shot, framing, and editing details, including the staging of actors and camera angles) before putting their ideas on paper as either a screenplay (dialogue with basic expository explanations), or even a treatment (the bare bones: plot and essential action of a story). Do not fall for any of this. Get your screenplay right as a story before you let yourself off the hook by indulging in the delights of being a director.

Every year I try to persuade students that at the early stages of devising a story for the screen, even the dialogue-based screenplay format can be a mistake. I regularly fail in this effort. Let me explain my bias. It is common practice that in the early stages, your story is in some other form. It might be a novel or a short story, it might even be a series of newspaper articles (for example *On the Waterfront*). On occasion, what might be required is an adaptation of a play written for the stage, though many writers will tell you that when this is so the task of writing a coherent screen version is particularly difficult. It may even be necessary to throw the original theatrical script away and start again from scratch. In such circumstances, a writer may find that before embarking on a screenplay full of dialogue it is better first to prepare a sketch in the form of a story treatment. Written in prose form, a good treatment might be as long as the intended screenplay, though will always be more literary in form, even reading like a short novel. It can reveal very clearly the potential of a story with as yet undeveloped dramatic structure or characterisations, and can be a very useful overview of problems that will have to be faced at a subsequent point of the process. Moreover, starting in prose means focusing on two crucial elements of screenwriting. First, the final work will inevitably contain less dialogue. Second, the themes of the story are more likely to rise to the surface of your mind as you write.

2. *The Third Man and The Fallen Idol* (Vintage, 2001; first published 1954), pp. 9–10.

The treatment form offers real opportunities for the writer to express himself directly to readers, much as a novelist does. Not such a rigorously disciplined and restrictive form as the screenplay, it allows him real freedom and more scope. The best case made for this kind of literary original as a precursor to material for a film has been made by Graham Greene, a novelist who has worked successfully in cinema. In the preface to the published version of his original prose draft for *The Third Man*, Greene describes how he worked out the original story with the director (Carol Reed) during months of close and intimate collaboration, always thinking of the story only in cinematic terms. The written story, he insisted, was never intended to be published. It was nothing more than background material for a film.

To me it is almost impossible to write a film play without first writing a story. Even a film depends on more than plot; it depends on a certain measure of characterisation, on mood and atmosphere; and these seem to me almost impossible to capture for the first time in the dull shorthand of a script. One can reproduce an effect caught in another medium, but one cannot make the first act of creation in script form. One must have the sense of more material than one needs to draw on. *The Third Man,* therefore, though never intended for publication, had to start as a story before those apparently interminable transformations from one to another.[2]

Let me use my personal experience to explain why, as a starting point, a treatment is preferable to a first draft screenplay. I learned much of what I know as a contract writer at a British film studio, hired on a year-to-year basis as a member of staff and given assignments as they arose. This usually meant working on a project that had already been given approval for development, whereupon a writer was given six weeks to produce a new draft of a script the producers insisted needed more work. Sometimes this was at the request of the director who had recently been hired and had ideas for specific changes, or because of casting issues (perhaps a star would not commit to the venture until assured that certain changes were made).

Remember that postcard on my wall? 'Screenplays are not written, they are rewritten and rewritten and rewritten.' The result of this is that today, the credits for a screenplay are rarely

DRAMATIC CONSTRUCTION

given to a single writer. When, after a number of years, I graduated to the position of director, I began working on projects the studio assigned to me. Quite soon I yearned to be the initiator of my own work. When this was the case, I realised it was wiser to begin my original ideas in a loosely structured treatment form. Why? Just as few directors relish the idea of writing a script for somebody else to direct, many writers are not enthusiastic about writing a screenplay based on somebody else's carefully plotted treatment of a story idea. Writers prefer to work on their own ideas and generally find it harder to get enthusiastic about characters and situations that are not of their own invention.

Through experience of writing revised versions of other people's screenplays I learned how important it is for the writer to make the subject his own, but at the same time knew that a director can often persuade a good writer to work as his collaborator if he offers him a project in a form that is, to a great degree, not yet frozen in its fully dialogued form. A treatment written by a would-be director might give strong indications as to the ideas behind the plot and even contain details of the story itself, but leaves the hired screenwriter with much difficult and demanding work still to do. If it is understood, as I believe is proper, that the director is not expecting a screenplay credit (which means the writer will have a chance to get the coveted solo screen credit), many writers will seize the chance to take over a story in such an inchoate form and successfully make it their own. The director has thus achieved his aim of fashioning the structure of the subject in its earliest form and then handing the story over to a writer who can bring his own ideas and vision to the project. When this works the ideal situation is that both writer and director believe that everything effective in the completed film was their own contribution. (One thing to note here is that at a later stage, through camera coverage and editing, a director who knows his craft can essentially rewrite without altering a single word. Providing there is sufficient coverage of a scene, it is usually possible to edit the footage so it even plays against the spoken text, emphasising subtext instead. Curiously, when the director manages this trick successfully, the screenwriter may be hardly aware of how it has been achieved.)

3. *Poetics* (Dover, 1997), pp. 13–14.

A writer who seems over-eager to indicate just how exciting, in cinematic terms, a scene will be is apt to alienate a director reading his screenplay. As it is put down on the written page, a good script does not concern itself with technical matters. Eager to show his competence as a director (instead of a screenwriter), the student is liable to introduce into his writing technical jargon that is meant to demonstrate his acquaintance with problems of production (the simplest example being specific shots and camera moves). I urge you to avoid this, for these things are not your business. While the impulse of a good director will be to scratch it all out, it also clearly indicates to the producer that you are a bumbling amateur. In addition, a concern with technical issues is usually a distraction from the much more important challenge of storytelling. The screenplay of an experienced writer wastes few words on qualities that, in the completed film, will be the contribution of the cinematographer, art director, costume designer, or any other member of the production team. Directors, rightly or wrongly, regard it as their prerogative to contribute these kinds of details. The experienced screenwriter understands that atmosphere and tone is not his responsibility, that his only (and vital) function is to provide the dramatic tensions, incidents, actions, reactions and situations (as well as, of course, the dialogue). Incidentally, the first person to make this point was a man writing on the subject of drama a couple of thousand years ago: Aristotle. In *Poetics* he writes that 'The Spectacle has, indeed, an emotional attraction of its own, but, of all the parts, it is the least artistic, and connected least with the art of poetry. For the power of Tragedy, we may be sure, is felt even apart from representation and actors. Besides, the production of spectacular effects depends more on the art of the stage machinist than on that of the poet.'[3]

Let me briefly tell you about a screenplay I had the pleasure of working on some years ago. I was collaborating with a screenwriter for whom I developed a great deal of respect. We spent months together in story conferences during which he improvised scenes. Then, when I went off to explore locations and work with a production designer, this writer went off to do the job that is essentially solitary: the final act of writing. When I read his completed screenplay, what astonished me was my discovery that the writing was, in a sense, already a shooting script, even if it never once gave explicit details of framing, shots or editing. Each time the writer began a new sentence, I could see a new camera set-up in my mind. An example might be something like: 'The young man picks up the few chips he has left, gulps at his drink, and moves to the table, where he hesitates, looking back.' Here I saw a master-shot, framing the man in the foreground from behind. Then: 'Belatedly, he has noticed the mirror on the wall behind his chair and is struck with an unpleasant realisation.' Perhaps a shot from his point of view, with the back of his chair seen reflected in the mirror. Finally: 'But the couple who have cheated him are already gone.' A long-shot, framed as a tableau of the situation, showing the card table and the man standing by his chair. This kind of writing has a vitality and pace that makes it highly satisfying and exciting for a director to read. To be candid, it is exactly the kind of energy I find lacking in most student scripts, which are often too wordy and literary. In effect, when writing his script, the inexperienced writer often yearns for those qualities legitimate in the most expressive literary industry form (the treatment), but that should play no part in a screenplay.

Professional screenplays have a quality in common with good journalism: they use the minimum number of words to communicate the maximum information. A good screenplay must be not only easy to read, it should be easy to read fast. It is true that a script is only the blueprint for a completed film and should bear to it the relationship that an architect's plans have to the final building, the construction of which is to be done by someone else. But a screenplay, a piece of writing that deals with things emotional, should itself be a pleasure to read. The shorthand style required of you should never be so dull that it fails to spark in the reader the feelings that the finished film itself is meant to inspire.

Preoccupation with dialogue may be at the root of another common mistake in the work of beginning scriptwriters. Sensing that the dialogue may lack emotional impact, in an attempt to provide atmosphere and mood the writer might describe in some detail the physique of the leading characters, even though at this early stage the screenplay really is nothing more than a document designed to assist the packagers of this potential film (studio executives, producers, directors, stars, agents). All these people will much prefer to make their own mental picture of the leading role as played by whichever actor they fancy in the part. From the writer's point of view it is therefore a mistake to write with a specific actor in mind. This is particularly true if you are harbouring a secret (or not so secret) ambition to direct yourself. Nothing so annoys a producer as the effort of a writer to show that he is really a director. And most intelligent actors will tell you they prefer a role that is a character in its own right, rather than one apparently tailor-made for them. (At a time when Alec Guinness had established for himself a reputation, there were many scripts sent to him by agents who described them as being 'perfect Alec Guinness roles.' Alec made it a principle of refusing even to read them, on the grounds that if he was the only actor who could play the role it couldn't be a role that was worth playing.)

There is an even more important reason why a screenwriter should never think in terms of a particular actor. All of us, inevitably, are liable to fall into the trap of believing that because we can *describe* our intended meanings, we have already *created* the desired effect. When you write with an actor in mind, you are liable to feel that having created an identifiable image on the page, you have also created a well-defined character as he or she will appear on the screen. But this is rarely so. Drama is *doing* and *making*, and characterisation in film is not nearly so concerned with appearances and physique as it is with motives and temperament. It matters not one bit what your character looks like if he or she cannot be characterised through his or her actions as laid down in the story beats. (This is, incidentally, exactly the same problem many students of directing encounter. Like writing and acting, directing is much more of an imaginative and intuitive activity than an intellectual one. The great trap is that, when the director explains to the actors the effect he hopes to achieve, he feels at least halfway to having achieved it. But the opposite is usually the case: what you have done is skip the really hard work and substituted for it the much easier pleasure.)

For the sake of those producers who have limited ability to imagine an actor's delivery of a line, many writers will add adverbs in to the dialogue passages ('angrily', 'quietly'). But producers and directors heartily dislike this. It is not only another unwarranted attempt by the writer to influence the direction, but like the description of the actor's physique it is often an indication that the screenwriter is relying on the actor to give emotional impact to the words, and is dodging his real task: to create feeling and emotion in the language itself. Simply, the good screenwriter recognises that interpretation of this kind on the page is an indulgence by someone who has failed to make his words, or the context in which they are played, interesting and dramatic of themselves. The legitimate use of the adverb instruction is only when the intonation, or the reading of the line, may be a contradiction of the words as written, as in: '(coldly) How nice!' But even here it is better left out wherever it is clearly implicit to the intelligent reader.

Once Upon a Time . . .

One hopes that there are still some mothers and fathers who tell bedtime stories to their children. In the long-lost days before television, it was something every parent did. It would be depressing if television had destroyed that ritual of infancy for ever.

One hopes, indeed, that storytelling is still alive not only because of its value to listeners. The gifts of the raconteur, the verbal storyteller face to face with his audience, are of immense value to anyone with ambitions to work in the narrative/dramatic media, cinema or theatre. As soon as passages are read aloud and performed, certain important questions are immediately brought to the surface of the storyteller's mind. 'To whom am I addressing this tale? And to what purpose?' I am, frankly, a little uneasy every time I confront the fact that such skills (and also such questions) do not come nearly so easily to CalArts students as I recall they did to young people of my generation. This is one reason why I feel that students of dramatic construction should get as much experience of acting as possible, something that can help develop that essential component of the writer's imagination: an ear for dialogue.

The face-to-face experience involved in the art of the raconteur is invaluable to an understanding of what a story is. Writing a story down on paper logically ought to involve the same processes as reciting it out loud to an audience, but it doesn't. Storytelling is, plain and simple, a performing art. Essential is the sense of tension between storyteller and listener, an understanding on the part of the writer of when tension is holding up and when it has slackened, of the build towards a crisis and the curious feeling of satisfaction when a promised climax is delivered. The solitary author who is communicating with an imaginary reader is all too apt to fall into the kind of self-indulgence

DRAMATIC CONSTRUCTION

that comes from assuming his reader is as interested in the subject as the writer is. The raconteur will discover soon enough that his listeners are likely to be less patient and less interested than he is, that their attention spans are inevitably shorter than he expected.

Storytelling is the knack of swiftly seizing the imagination of the audience and never letting it go. Digressions and elaborations are permissible, but only when the audience is already hooked by the promise of some satisfaction to come. The tension to that hook may be slackened now and again, but the line must be snapped tight at any moment when the dramatist senses the danger of losing his catch. This is why I confess that, in the past, I found it enormously useful during pre-production of a film to select someone whose instincts I respected and, rather than giving them the screenplay to read, tell the story out loud to them, even if only in synopsis. By doing this I could get a palpable sense of just where the momentum was sagging, where the action could be telescoped, and how the climaxes should be timed.

For a listener to attend with genuine interest and appreciation is to provide a powerful control over a performer. Feedback of any kind tells the storyteller where there is a need for more exposition or (more often) where there should be less. The raconteur will instinctively find himself learning where suspense is strong enough to provide opportunities for expansion, elaboration and restructuring, or where there is a need to accelerate the pace by simplifying and skipping over the inessentials to get to the point faster. Even if the listener is silent there emerges invaluable feedback. In fact, the right kind of attention from listeners is almost always silent, as they will hopefully be so taken with the story being told that they will, at every step of the way, want to know what happens next.

Dramatic structure is, you might say, the craft of keeping an audience excited, of avoiding boredom in your listeners. In fact, I find it useful to think of the audience as the enemy, to try to tell the story while always remembering that the audience has somewhere better to go and something better to do. Assume that as a storyteller you have to keep your audience buttonholed at all times by curiosity, expectation and some kind of suspense. With this in mind, I advise you to examine a few of the stock phrases which the traditional bedtime story uses. As material for illustration, I'll use one fairy tale (*Cinderella*), one dramatic classic (*Hamlet*), and one classic film (*Bicycle Thieves*).

'Once upon a time . . .'

The genre (e.g. Western, spy thriller, historical epic, ghost story). The place and time period, the closed world of the story, the social and/or ideological values in the subject, the conventions belonging to the often imaginary setting.

'there lived a . . .'

The protagonist. The central figure in the story, the character through whose eyes we see the events. Sometimes, but not necessarily, the hero. Implied in the choice of the protagonist is often the point of view that the dramatist wants us to take.

'who . . .'

The action of the protagonist. We use the word 'action' in the sense of what the character want and does, the will or purpose of the character.

'but . . .'

The obstacle, whatever or whoever stands in opposition to the action, the goals of the protagonist. This is often personified in the role of the antagonist (villain). In contemporary drama it is a character (or group of figures) who represents opposition to the goals of the protagonist. Note that if there is to be dramatic tension, a passive or weak protagonist is apt to call for a strong antagonist.

'so one day it happened that . . .'

The 'Point of Attack' (the initiating incident or the premise). This is the moment at which the action starts. In nineteenth-century plays it was common that the dramatic tension didn't really start to grip until somewhere near the end of the first act, and all that went before was exposition (establishing the back-story). But in tightly knit contemporary story structures it is often preferable to begin the story with some dramatic event and only then retrace its origins through exposition, since exposition is more dramatic as soon as there is something at stake.

'so then, as a result of which . . .'

Narrative progression. Most stories that have a strong plot are built on the tension of cause-and-effect. Each incident is like a domino that topples forwards to collide with the next in a sequence that holds the audience in the grip of anticipation. The pattern is likely to be that each scene presents a small crisis that, as it is resolved, produces a new uncertainty (defined in the classic phrase 'anticipation mingled with uncertainty', almost a definition of drama in itself).

'But meanwhile . . .'

Simultaneous development: subplot. The tumbling domino can set off a second trail of collisions. Some complication in the plot.

'so that unbeknownst to . . .'

Dramatic irony, a common and indeed almost essential ingredient in strong story structure.

'until the time came that . . .'

A confrontation scene. There may be several such scenes throughout a suspenseful story, but in stories that provide the simple but intricate satisfactions that popular audiences desire, dramatic structure is often a graph of rising and falling tensions. The progressive high points are the crises, separated by relaxations of tension. Early scenes, often after the initial hook of the premise, are generally less suspenseful than later ones. Conflict or tension starts off as not being so strong, but progressively the oscillations on the graph grow more extreme with the big show-downs usually taking place near the end. Note that a story can quickly become monotonous if tension is constant. During relaxation in tension the basic suspense is still present – latent but still present. The return to the central plot inevitably gains an additional impact because of a temporary respite (the example often quoted from Shakespeare is the farcical interlude in *Macbeth* with the porter that follows the murder of Duncan and precedes the discovery of the crime).

'when suddenly – to the surprise of . . .'

A peripeteia, the Greek term for a turn of the wheel, used by Aristotle to describe the unexpected shift in relationships, often a form of role reversal that produces a resolution of the drama. It is likely to require a strong element of dramatic irony.

'so it turned out that . . .'

The resolution, the denouement, literally the unknotting of all of the tensions in the story.

'and for ever after . . . '

Closure, the sense of having come full circle. It need not, obviously, be in the form of a happy ending, but it should provide some level of satisfaction. Classically, the end may be surprising, though in retrospect, it is recognised to be inevitable (it is what 'had to happen').

Consider how these stock phrases can be applied to the three wildly different stories of *Cinderella*, *Hamlet* and *Bicycle Thieves*. Observe how, in each case, the period and the location determine the tone: folk-fairy tale in *Cinderella*, high tragedy and epic poetry in *Hamlet*, neo-realist documentary in *Bicycle Thieves*.

'Once upon a time . . . '

Cinderella: The place is vaguely Germanic, a country of small kingdoms, princes and townsfolk. The time is the Middle Ages. But it is also a realm of fantasy in which there are good fairies and magic spells. Characters are simplistic. The stuff of fables, folk stories and childhood. The tone is also of nineteenth-century moral tales.

Hamlet: The locality is Denmark, the castle of Elsinore. The period is the sixteenth century, a time of violence, of wars and murders, and rival claims to thrones. Again the values are feudal, with emphasis on revenge motivations.

Bicycle Thieves: The city of Rome as it was in the aftermath of the Second World War. A period of great poverty, but also a time of communities struggling to re-establish human values. The city is rife with disillusion, petty crime and the black market. The tone is of a desperate search for decency and dignity after the years of fascism (hence a political dimension).

'there lived a . . .'

Cinderella: A motherless girl, ill-treated by stepsisters.
Hamlet: A Prince, in mourning for father recently dead.
Bicycle Thieves: A working-class unemployed bill-poster.

'who . . .'

Cinderella: Is forced by her two stepsisters to slave in the kitchen in soot-stained clothes.
Hamlet: Is unhappy because his father has died and his mother has married his uncle, the dead king's brother, very soon after.
Bicycle Thieves: Is desperate to get a job to support his young wife and their little boy.

Observe how each character is equipped with the dynamics of character-in-action, a built-in interior struggle.

Cinderella: Dreams of romance and escape from the mistreatment by her stepsisters.
Hamlet: Torn apart by his feelings of indecision and inadequacy, contrasting with the heroism of his warlike father.
Bicycle Thieves: Struggles to maintain his dignity and job which is the basis of his self-respect, as well as the respect of his wife and son.

Note also that the protagonists, as well as the antagonists, and even other characters with whom the central figure is involved in some kind of dramatic conflict, can be seen as personifications of the story's themes.

'but . . . '

Cinderella: Cinderella is left at home by the fire and her stepsisters live in luxury.

Hamlet: Hamlet mourns his dead father, hates his uncle, and is tortured by the ambivalence of feelings for the Queen (his mother). He also is tormented to the point of suicidal despair by his low self-esteem, his inability to take heroic action.

Bicycle Thieves: The bill-poster, who has recently pawned his bicycle, waits amongst the other unemployed standing in line every day for the chance of a government job while his wife and children wait at home.

Thus are established the elements of struggle, the circumstances of the characters who personify the forces that stand in the way of the protagonist's desires or intentions. In effect, the protagonist sets the story in motion, and through interactions with foils will illustrate the story's root-idea and theme.

'so one day it happened that . . . '

Cinderella: Learns of the ball that is to be given by the Prince who is in search of a bride. Cinderella is not invited. Antagonists: the Ugly Sisters and the rest of the snobbish townsfolk.

Hamlet: Is brought by his companions to confront his father's Ghost. He is told of the murder but has no proof and is not sure that his fears are not the result of his neurotic paranoia. Antagonists: his uncle Claudius (the 'villain') and Hamlet's own insecurities.

Bicycle Thieves: A job offer is announced on the condition that the applicant has to provide his own bicycle. But his bicycle, which he has redeemed from the pawnbrokers, is stolen from him. Antagonists: the callousness, disillusion and cynicism of the period, the sense of hopelessness in the struggle for human dignity.

'so then, as a result of which . . . '

Cinderella: With the help of the magic wrought by her Fairy Godmother, Cinderella goes incognito to the ball, but she forgets the condition that she has to leave at midnight and loses her slipper. (Note the element of dramatic irony created by Cinderella's disguise.)

Hamlet: The play-within-a-play exposes the guilt of Claudius, Hamlet's uncle. But Hamlet kills Polonius by mistake and Claudius uses this as a pretext for sending Hamlet to England while also arranging to have him killed. Claudius's conspiracy misfires when Hamlet returns to Denmark, and again Claudius plots to have him killed by poison during the duel.

Bicycle Thieves: In a desperate search for the stolen bicycle, the bill-poster and his small son explore Rome, going to the police, the trade unions, the church, finally finding the old man who can identify the thief, but losing him again. During this the relationship of the father and the son (the story's real theme) is further developed.

'But meanwhile . . .' and 'so that unbeknownst to . . . '

Cinderella: The Prince and the Ugly Stepsisters have no idea that Cinderella is the mysterious beauty at the ball.

Hamlet: Hamlet knows nothing of the plot to have him killed when he lands in England.

Bicycle Thieves: The son is sent away in order that he should not see his father abandon his dignity as he attempts to steal, just as he has been stolen from.

'when suddenly – to the surprise of . . .'

Cinderella: Obligatory scene and peripeteia. Cinderella is revealed to the Prince as the girl at the ball with the glass slipper. The Ugly Sisters lose out, the tables are turned, and the Prince weds Cinderella.

Hamlet: Claudius is killed by Hamlet while Hamlet's mother accidentally drinks the poison. Hamlet himself perishes. For Hamlet it is also a peripeteia of character as he finally expresses himself in violent action.

Bicycle Thieves: The bill-poster, wholly disillusioned in his search for social justice, turns thief and fails even in this. The small boy, witness of the failure of his father's attempt at crime, takes his father's hand even as the crowd reviles them both.

The point of this somewhat absurd comparison between a great Elizabethan classic, a childish fairy story, and a well-known Italian film is to underline how basic the nature of the psychological phenomenon we call a story seems to be. Effective stories grip us, whether at a superficial level or in a profound and significant way, a feeling perhaps easier to recognise than to explain.

Based on the terminology above, you might experiment with an improvisational game that needs a group of three or more players. Player One begins 'Once upon a time there was . . .', thus inventing the time and place (the genre) and the protagonist. Player Two accepts these and invents the problem and/or the back-story that defines the motivations of the protagonist. Player Three then continues, supplying the figure of an antagonist ('But . . .') that provides conflict. Player Four now has to devise the initial point of attack, some incident or event that triggers a narrative that will create suspense, expectations, and the potential for plot developments.

At this stage, those players who are catching on to the knack of dramatic structure will already be thinking ahead: the possibilities of peripeteias, some kind of reversal of character relations, a twist to the original premise. Needless to say, this game is very unlikely to produce a work of real creative quality since such a thing must spring from more private, personal and, hopefully, more profound intuitions. But it can sharpen your understanding of the storyteller's craft. Note that though part of the fun is to present to your neighbour a challenging problem, you should also play fair, meaning you should yourself have in mind at all times a potential structure. And remember that it is not really the final product that matters – this is an exercise in the process of swift and fertile invention.

I am not certain the game works when you are given a lengthy period of time to think. It should probably have a rigid structure

DRAMATIC CONSTRUCTION

within which you should be as impromptu and as spontaneous as possible. Invention, it has been said (by William Archer), is apt to be 'memory in disguise', and invention is often at its most fertile when it comes directly from unconscious associations. The unconscious works at high speed, while writing is sufficiently deliberate to allow internal censors to work and inhibit spontaneity (after all, talented raconteurs generally perform best when under the pressure of an audience).

The two great virtues in the game are tension and surprise. The storyteller manipulates an audience that is hopefully always impatient. 'So what happens next?' is the question an audience quite understandably wants to be constantly asking itself (and the storyteller). If 'what happens next' has been foreseeable, tension will inevitably drop. Narrative momentum hopes to keep its audience off-balance at all times, either through suspense, anxiety, or fear of the next event.

Activity versus Action

Cinema is based on the illusion of continuous movement, an illusion that takes place in the brain, rather than the eye. What the eye actually sees is a very rapid sequence of projected images, each of which is entirely static, while the brain reads these as a continuous flowing movement. There are two different kinds of movement: activity and action.

When examining a completed script, the student should be able to take each and every scene in that story and ask: 'What actually happens in this scene?' Such a question implies completion of some action, so that by the end of the scene the relationships between characters have in some way been altered and some new situation has resulted. There is often, in many student film scripts, a failure to distinguish between the two concepts of activity and action. At its simplest it is the grammatical distinction between the imperfect and the perfect tense. An activity is present when someone is said to be in the continuous process of doing something ('he is writing the script'). It deals with ongoing situations that have no beginning, middle or end. Action, on the other hand, is inherently dramatic, and makes up the entire completed activity ('he wrote the script'), implying that the thing being done may produce an effect that so alters the present circumstances it, in turn, produces a new result, thus provoking another, often contrary counter-action. (Compare this to the theatre where action is apt to be less a physical activity than a confrontation between characters, where the story progresses because of conflicts of personalities and verbal exchanges.) As it is used by teachers of drama, an actor's action is defined by his or her purpose in the scene: it is what he or she intends to do.

Thus an action, as film-makers use the term in a narrative/

dramatic sense, implies the intention of making something happen and accomplishing a result. This is a concept that can be seen in the simplest and most basic of cinematic structures: animated cartoons. Animation remains one of the most direct forms of cinematic storytelling that exists. To understand this you really ought to examine a good cartoon frame by frame, something I did long before I became a fully fledged member of the movie industry. What I learned from it was not just the principles of animation, but also those of dramatic construction and film grammar.

One of the first exercises required of the student of animation is to draw a cartoon figure of a man walking. I make no apologies for using childish comic drawings as illustrations of the principles of narrative/dramatic structures. The value of caricatures is that they exaggerate and simplify some of the so-called principles with which we are concerned in this course, principles we are apt to take for granted.

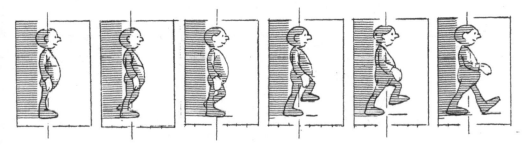

When these, or similar drawings, are put under the camera, photographed, and then projected, the result may indeed be continuous and smooth motion, a flowing progression. But it may look a little too smooth – it has no momentum and does not really look like walking. The body appears to float along and there is no sense of weight. These images represent merely an activity with no real force of action or energy. But then this is not really what walking is. It is merely a sequence of phased images of a couple of steps, a cycle that can be repeated. The animator has intentionally tried to space the drawings out at equal intervals so the movement will flow and seem smooth.

Your instructor demonstrates what walking really is. It is rather more complicated than you may at first realise. He starts to make a step by leaning forward and throwing himself off balance, toppling in the direction he intends to go. As the centre of gravity tilts, the head begins to fall forwards and also downwards, dropping a little in height. During this he lifts one foot, thrusts it forward so it meets the impact of the ground, and checks the fall. With this impact the forward momentum is checked and there is a reverse thrust, upward and back. The head lifts again, bobbing upward and back. The centre of gravity is tilted back a little. Forward movement of this kind is a rather complex process and not all that smooth. The tilt of the body changes and the head bobs up and down on every step. But this kind of walk has real energy. It is an action, and at every point when your instructor's foot makes impact with the ground, his energy is used against the force of gravity. The step is a contrary force that kicks back from the falling movement, upwards and backwards. It is the alternating thrusts of the two contrasted forces that provides weight, energy and momentum, and that give life to the movement.

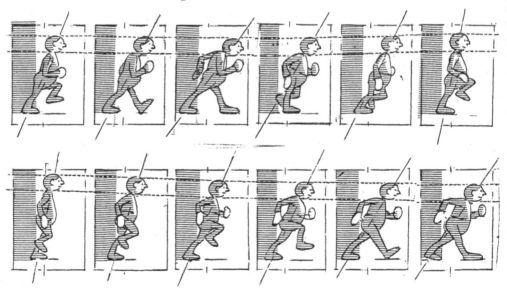

What you have here is an illustration of Isaac Newton's principle, 'To every action there is an equal and opposite reaction.' It is presented here in terms of cartoons that are apt to exaggerate such things. But I invite you to consider it in another

DRAMATIC CONSTRUCTION

context: the dynamics of drama, for we find a similar kind of dynamism in an effective dramatic narrative. A story that truly excites has momentum and drive ('What happens next?'), the progression of which is more than ongoing activity – it is action, movement with purpose that is confronted by certain obstacles (whether physical or not). In a sense, it is similar to the mechanics of the internal combustion engine. In an effective story, each scene will have its own build: it is a mini-drama in itself. Tension is increased and pressure builds (much as the piston in the cylinder will compress the gas), then comes the flashpoint, the explosion that drives the piston in a contrary direction. The audience should know when a story is reaching its climax, for it should be clear when certain tensions have been (or are about to be) resolved or relaxed, even though there may be yet more uncertainties and important dramatic structures that remain unresolved. Note that it is usual to resolve secondary tensions before primary ones, and that an ability to pinpoint primary tensions between characters is likely to lead to the definition of a story's central theme(s).

Returning to the example of animated cartoons, compare the versions here of a man walking through a door. Here is the smooth movement. The figure progresses in the direction of the door in a sequence of equally spaced phases. It is movement, not action.

The more experienced animator will take the principle of dynamics a little further by splitting the activity into a number of different stages.

The figure starts out essentially static. In the first frame he turns to look at the door (he is 'making a take' at it, as a comedian might say), a gesture that is not only a turn of the head but a slight recoil. Then he prepares for the action. This may be an elaborate 'wind-up' akin to the gestures of a baseball pitcher. The second frame is nothing but a blur, the smear of movement indicating that the figure is vanishing through the door at a speed too fast for us to see. In the third frame, the doormat is lifted from the floor by the rush of air. Unlike the little man its movement is slow, it twirls gracefully and settles to earth again in a heap on the threshold. Note that the overall timing may be no shorter than the three equally spaced images above. But the difference is that the movement – the real action – takes place in a split second. We show more of the preparation that anticipates the event, then more of the reaction, the after-effects.

You may wonder why this is relevant to dramatic construction. Again, I offer this as a simplistic caricature of a principle that applies as much to animated cartoons as it does to the complex and subtle problems you will encounter in your work when writing stories. To explain, let me give you this one-liner:

What is happening now is apt to be less dramatically interesting than what may – or may not – be about to happen.

In its essence, drama is tension. It is the interaction of two contradictory forces: our expectations of what might

DRAMATIC CONSTRUCTION

happen next and the uncertainty of the outcome. In dynamic terms, this means that as a film-maker (a writer and director), you should spend just as much time (if not more) emphasising and exploring the preparations and after-effects of an event as you do the actual happening itself. The practised cartoonist is much less interested in the actual moment of action than in the before and after. He caricatures the gathering of energy that precedes the explosive act (the wind-up), while the action itself is often barely visible or is even off-screen. But its reverberations are exhaustively explored.

Theorists of dramatic structure point out that drama is the art of preparing crises. A series of interesting incidents or events may indeed be as entertaining as a complete narrative. But real drama is created by the continuous and very real involvement of the audience as its emotions are engaged both in advance of a crisis and then in the repercussions of what they have just witnessed. Every dramatic writer knows this, or soon learns it. To reiterate an important point: screenwriting has been called the task of exploring not action, but reaction.

Dramatic Irony

1. *Hitchcock*, p. 73.

The director Alfred Hitchcock was once asked if he had a formula for creating dramatic stories. Hitch gave an answer that is
simplistic to the point of being a cartoon image. He said:

> Let us suppose that there is a bomb underneath this table between
> us. Nothing happens, and then all of a sudden, 'Boom!' There is an
> explosion. The public is *surprised*, but prior to this surprise, it has
> seen an absolutely ordinary scene, of no special consequence. Now,
> let us take a *suspense* situation. The bomb is underneath the table
> and the public *knows* it . . . In these conditions this same innocuous
> conversation becomes fascinating because the public is participating
> in the scene. The audience is longing to warn the characters on the
> screen: 'You shouldn't be talking about such trivial matters. There's a
> bomb beneath you and it's about to explode!'[1]

Hitch's image, like almost all strongly structured dramas,
makes use of what we call dramatic irony. The *American
Heritage Dictionary* defines irony as 'The use of words to convey the opposite of their literal meaning.' Dramatic irony is
defined as 'The dramatic effect achieved by leading an audience
to understand an incongruity between a situation and the
accompanying speeches, while the characters in the play remain
unaware of the incongruity.' Simply put, in any situation where
we, the audience, are aware of significant circumstances of
which one or more of the characters on stage or screen are
unaware, there is an element of dramatic irony.

The classic example of this is a scene from Sheridan's play *The
School for Scandal*. Sir Peter Teazle has married a very attractive
and high-spirited wife much younger than himself and, though
in truth both of them love each other dearly, they are always
quarrelling. But neither is aware of the other's real feelings. Sir

Peter has a half-brother, Joseph Surface, who is a devious and malicious character. Feigning sympathy and friendship with Sir Peter, Joseph is really trying to seduce Lady Teazle, who is sufficiently exasperated by her husband to be open to his advances. The scene takes place when Lady Teazle keeps an assignation with Joseph in his private rooms. Joseph has started his attempt to seduce Lady Teazle when a servant appears to announce that Sir Peter has arrived and is on his way upstairs. Joseph has time to hide Sir Peter's wife behind a screen in the corner of the room before Sir Peter enters.

The scene, which you should look at in detail, is quite complex, involving several other characters and a situation in which Joseph, in order to prevent them from exposing the woman behind the screen, has to pretend he has been entertaining another woman, obviously for immoral purposes. The incongruities are elaborate. We, the audience, are held in a state of comic tension while we wait for the inevitable moment when the screen collapses and all is revealed. One of the ironies, of course, is that in the course of the dialogue between Sir Peter and Joseph, Lady Teazle learns of her husband's real feelings about her, feelings that drastically alter her attitude to both men.

It occurs to me that the device of dramatic irony is so standard a formula of dramatic construction that, in truth, it is quite rare to find any really well-structured story that does not make use of it. Think of the stories you have encountered where we, the audience, are aware of circumstances of which one or more of the onstage characters are ignorant and are thus kept in a state of 'anticipation mingled with uncertainty' as we wait for some turn of events (peripeteia) in which the suspenseful situation is resolved. Can you think of any dramatic work that does not make use of this structure, however indirectly? It seems to me that as students' projects are offered to me, it is the absence of clearly structured dramatic irony (especially in visual terms) that is their weakness.

There is a sense in which the most basic elements of film grammar have potential for dramatic irony. The standard pattern of editing starts with a master-shot, the angle within which all dramatic elements are visible. It is an objective God's-eye-view that makes the audience aware of the situation as a whole. It allows us to locate ourselves spatially within the shot, to see exactly where the characters are in relation to each other and their environment, and to observe these interactions from the outside. The master-shot is often followed by closer angles, for example close-ups of individual characters. A close-up, depending on a number of factors, invites us to concentrate on the thoughts and feelings of one particular character. A reverse angle that follows a close-up will often seem to be the point of view of the preceding close-up character. This choice of screen sizes and pattern of shot juxtapositions encourage audiences to switch from His viewpoint of Her to Her viewpoint of Him, and then, in the master-shot, to the audience's viewpoint of the two of them, of their interactions.

Consider the scene in Sheridan's play. A film version would almost certainly be covered in a master-shot that shows most of the room, Joseph and his visitors, while the hidden Lady Teazle would perhaps be visible to us, but to no one else. Then there would be closer shots, including cutaways to the reaction of Lady Teazle listening behind the screen. Even in a scene where dramatic irony is not so obviously staged, one can see the principle at work. The camera set-ups and editing might be designed to reveal private thoughts and feelings of one of the characters, of which everyone else is ignorant.

As you explore some of the great classics of stage and screen, you will see that most have a 'bomb under the table'. The first scene of *Oedipus Rex* shows the young King swearing an oath that he will investigate the murder of the man who was previously King of Thebes, husband of Jocasta to whom Oedpius is now married. The audiences for whom this great play was first performed were well aware of the irony here, for the murderer that Oedipus has sworn to find and punish is Oedipus himself. Not until the story's final confrontations will he be forced to recognise the awful truth, though the bomb has been ticking away all throughout the play. Eventually Tiresias spells it out for him in full: Oedipus has killed his own father and committed incest with his mother. Likewise, the very first scene of *Hamlet* sets the fuse for the bomb: the Ghost has been seen on the castle battlements. A couple of scenes later Hamlet is told by the Ghost that the present King, Claudius, murdered Hamlet's father.

DRAMATIC CONSTRUCTION

Hamlet's dilemma is that he has no real proof of the crime and is disturbed that the Ghost might be a figment of his own paranoid state of anxiety and indecision. The trap of the play-within-a-play solves that issue, but a new obstacle arises when Hamlet mistakenly kills Polonius.

In a farcical film I directed, *The Ladykillers*, the comedy is based entirely on ironies. We are certain that the figure who follows Mrs Wilberforce back from the police station is up to no good, but the little old lady has no suspicions about Professor Marcus. Nor does she realise that the five men apparently rehearsing a string quintet in her upstairs room are, in fact, criminals planning a dastardly robbery. And when she does find out, she is innocent of the fact that they are trying to decide which of them will do her in.

Hitchcock's example is, of course, a perfect example of dramatic irony. With a bomb under the table, the tension may or may not be present in the mind of one of the characters in the scene. But it is certainly in *our* minds, and this is what is important. Well aware of the danger that awaits them, we are apprehensive about whether the characters on screen will become aware of it too. If you extend Hitchcock's illustration in its caricature form, you have an encapsulation of several of the classic elements found in dramatic structures.

EXPOSITION   *DRAMATIC IRONY*

SUSPENSE

DISCLOSURE

REACTION/ACTION

PERIPETY

　　　　　　　　　　DRAMATIC CONSTRUCTION

William Archer Revisited

1. *Play-Making, A Manual of Crafts-manship* (originally published by Small, Maynard and Co., 1912; all citations in Mackendrick's notes refer to the Dover reprint, 1960). Archer (1856–1924) was a noted journalist and drama critic whose translation of Ibsen's *Pillars of Society* was the first of the Norwegian play-wright's works to be produced in England. See *William Archer* by C. Archer (Yale University Press, 1931) and *William Archer* by Peter Whitebrook (Methuen, 1993).

William Archer was a British drama critic and playwright whose book *Play-Making* was published in 1912.[1] Archer was a friend of playwright George Bernard Shaw. He had met GBS in the reading room of the British Museum and, explaining to Shaw that he felt he was quite good at inventing plots, admitted that he lacked talent in writing dialogue. Shaw, already with an established reputation for debate, was supremely confident in his skill for lively dialogue, and suggested they collaborate. Thus it was that William Archer supplied the skeleton of the dramatic structure of Shaw's first play.[2] Though Shaw went on to write many plays, while Archer on his own produced only a series of deservedly forgotten melodramas, the two remained close friends all their lives. To speak personally, Archer's book on dramatic structure is the best text I know on the subject of dramatic construction.

Having said that, I do understand why some people find *Play-Making* hard-going. The examples Archer uses to illustrate his ideas are from playwrights of the late nineteenth century. While he does also cite Wilde, Shaw and Ibsen, Archer generally deals with writers who seem very dated today. In addition to this, students argue that because the book is so old, Archer's theories must be out of date. Dramatic style has changed a great deal since 1912, not only in content, but also in form. One relevant question, then, is whether Archer's commentary applies, for instance, to more modern forms of theatrical writing (the plays of Beckett and Ionesco, for example), and, of course, to cinema, a medium that was in its absolute infancy when Archer wrote his book.

It is perhaps understandable that a film student of today finds it hard to translate the concepts Archer is writing about to

2. In 1884 Archer and Shaw started collabo-ration on *The Way to a Woman's Heart*, the title of which was later changed to *Rhinegold*. See Michael Holroyd's *Bernard Shaw, Volume One: The Search for Love* (Chatto and Windus, 1988), pp. 274–7. See also Shaw's foreword to Archer's volume *Three Plays* (Constable and Company, 1927).

3. John Howard
Lawson's *Theory and
Technique of
Playwriting and
Screenwriting* (G. P.
Putnam's Sons, 1949).

4. It is interesting to
note that even in 1912
Archer himself felt he
had to qualify his
reasons for writing
Play-Making. 'Having
admitted that there are
no rules for dramatic
composition, and that
the quest of such rules
is apt to result either in
pedantry or quackery,
why should I myself set
forth upon so fruitless
and foolhardy an enter-
prise? It is precisely
because I am alive to its
dangers that I have
some hope of avoiding
them. Rules there are
none; but it does not
follow that some of the
thousands who are fas-
cinated by the art of the
playwright may not
profit by having their
attention called, in a
plain and practical way,
to some of its problems
and possibilities' (p. 5).

5. Archer, *Play-Making*,
p. 3.

cinematic equivalents when *Play-making* is full of examples
from playwrights seldom read or performed today, for example
Pinero, Galsworthy and Somerset Maugham. (Worth noting is
that John Howard Lawson, writing in the 1940s, picked up a
great deal from Archer and expanded his ideas as they apply to
cinema.[3]) Linked to this is the fact that there is, among contemporary students, something of a reaction against the notion of
'rules' when it comes to dramatic writing in both cinema and
theatre.[4]

But though style in any medium of expression is constantly
developing, new forms are invariably organically rooted in earlier
forms, even when there is an obvious rejection of past formulas
that have become too rigid, too stereotypical, and too stale to
have fresh meaning. A real understanding of the 'progress' of the
evolving nature of cultural forms has to be an exploration of the
present and possible future as they relate to past forms from
which they have developed, and continue to develop. As such,
many of Archer's comments seem to me common sense and
easily translatable to contemporary writing, and it should not
be too difficult for any reasonably intelligent film student to find
a modern film that can be used to illustrate almost every point
that Archer is making. All it takes is a little effort. (After all, the
challenge of any textbook is to provoke the student into this
kind of study that has relevance to his or her own experience
and work.) With these notes, therefore, I have tried to supple-
ment the examples that Archer uses with some instances of contemporary films.

On the question of 'rules' of dramatic construction, Archer
himself warns:

There are no rules for writing a play. It is easy, indeed, to lay down
negative recommendations – to instruct the beginner how *not* to do
it. But most of these 'don'ts' are rather obvious; and those which are
not obvious are apt to be questionable . . . There are no absolute
rules, in fact, except such as are dictated by the plainest common
sense. Aristotle himself did not so much dogmatise as analyse, clas-
sify, and generalize from, the practise of Attic dramatists. He said,
'you had better' rather than 'you must.'[5]

The furthest Archer will go is claiming that:

DRAMATIC CONSTRUCTION

One thing is certain, and must be emphasised from the outset: namely, that if any part of the dramatist's art can be taught, it is only a comparatively mechanical and formal part – the art of structure. One may learn how to tell a story in good dramatic form: how to develop and marshal it in such a way as best to seize and retain the interest of a theatrical audience. But no teaching or study can enable a man to choose or invent a good story, and much less to do that which alone lends dignity to dramatic story-telling – to observe and portray human character.[6]

6. Archer, *Play-making*, p. 7.

To be honest, I'm not sure even this isn't overstating the case. I would rather say that it is possible to examine how certain dramatists have constructed material in a way that at times has seized the interest of the audience. If they have also succeeded in seizing and retaining *your* interest, you should take a closer look at just how they did this. Though drama cannot be taught as such, it can most definitely be learned the way most skills are learned: by examination of others whose work you admire.

On Choosing a Theme

The theme of a story is usually established only in the final climax during the obligatory scene where the confrontations dramatise the point of the narrative. This is the part of the story the audience has been waiting for and that the author is obliged to deliver. It is also where character, plot and theme are most clearly integrated. This confrontation is likely to be a high point in the mechanics of the action, where principal characters are placed in situations designed to reveal their most significant qualities, their moral weaknesses or strengths, their sympathetic or unsympathetic traits, their true feelings about others. Such showdowns also serve to demonstrate the author's underlying preoccupations, those themes that give unity and meaning to the story. Without characters, a theme is an abstract and generalised statement of conflict or tension – it describes rather than dramatises. What the student needs to learn, therefore, is how to convey the theme of his story through the creation of characters who interact within the scenes he creates, and not just imbue a single character (the protagonist) with that theme. Archer writes: '"Theme" may mean either of two things: either the sub-

7. Archer, *Play-making*, p. 11.

8. Ibid., p. 11.

9. '[M]en do not act in order to represent character, but qualities of character emerge as a result of their actions' (Aristotle's *Poetics*, translated by N. G. L. Hammond, Museum Tusculanum Press, 2000, p. 18).

ject of a play, or its story. The former is, perhaps, its proper and most convenient sense.'[7]

Archer suggests that a conscious and deliberate decision about theme is seldom fruitful as a starting point. If you set out to devise a story in order to illustrate some moral or political issue, the chances are you will find the resulting situations and characters two-dimensional, and the plotting contrived and predictable. You will end up creating puppets who have no real vitality and that you will be forced to manipulate yourself, rather than leaving them to the forces that arise from interactions with other characters. As Archer writes:

[O]ught a theme, in its abstract form, be the first germ of a play? Ought the dramatist to say, 'Go to, I will write a play on temperance or woman's suffrage, or on capital and labour,' and then cast about for a story to illustrate his theme? This is a possible, but not a promising method of procedure. A story made to the order of a moral concept is always apt to advertise its origin, to the detriment of its illusive quality.[8]

I think Archer is right in suggesting that theme is an abstraction of the story, its moral, social, political message in a generalised form.

For many writers, one of the basic functions of dramatic writing is to present to the world those ideas, attitudes and emotions that express his concerns, even if they are heavily masked, dressed up in new costumes and with names changed to protect the innocent. As you start to devise a story, there is often a strong urge to create both plot and characters that represent a theme that interests you. The best way of doing this is to personify elements of that theme by splitting your soul and creating different characters from these little pieces. Students are often urged to write about things drawn from their own experience (it has been said that invention is often memory in disguise). This means a story's protagonist is inevitably an element of the author's personality, a result of the splitting of the writer's psyche so he can – in his mind and on the page – play more than one role.

In fact, it should be understood that *every* character in a story, being a creation of its inventor, is to some extent the author speaking in disguise. It is not only the hero but the entire complex of active interrelated figures who are projections of his mind.[9] The writer plays God, taking up a position not of one single point of

DRAMATIC CONSTRUCTION

view but rather rapidly shifting points of view that looks at different characters at different moments, until finally he and his audience see everything from every angle. Dramatic invention is apt to be a game of psychodrama of this kind, the challenge of which can be severe: it requires the writer to step outside of his more comfortable identity and see himself as others do, requiring a certain psychological maturity that may not come easily to the young and inexperienced.

The theme of everything you write (even, in many cases, of something you are doing only for the money) is tied to your own point of view, your attitude to life and sex and religion, your personal social, ethical and political outlook. A theme is so integrally part of a writer's temperament that it will automatically colour his approach to the whole world. In effect, the work of a conscious and competent writer will inevitably be constructed upon certain meaningful ideas and beliefs. If the writer feels strongly about something, it will be yelling at him from his dreams. A good story is not one that a writer contrives – it takes on a kind of energy of its own that has the writer in its grip and forces him to come to certain previously unforeseen conclusions.

For this reason, I advise students not to worry about looking for a theme. In a sense, theme is something that chooses you, and (it is pointed out by many critics) is seldom consciously recognised by an author who finds expression for it. Indeed, if the author knows in advance what he really means to say, he might not say it so well. Connected to this is the idea that the 'message' (whether it be political, social or otherwise) of a story does not necessarily have to be explicit at any point. Sometimes it is (for example in *On the Waterfront*, when Terry is talking to his brother in the taxi cab), but much more frequently a theme is something left to the audience to feel at an intuitive and emotional level. A good writer will let his audience pick and choose their own themes and 'messages' from the story he is telling.

Graham Greene is a writer who cannot help but bring into everything he produces the themes that haunt him: the struggle between belief and disbelief, guilt and betrayal. Alexander Korda and Carol Reed, producer and director of *The Third Man*, came to Greene with nothing except the proposition that a

10. See Graham Greene's 'Preface' to the published novella version of *The Third Man* (Vintage, 2001; first published 1950), p. 9.

11. At the American Film Institute in 1977, after being asked about securing the rights to a novel already owned by a studio, Mackendrick explained that because the original source would almost certainly prove to be impossible to obtain, the best thing was to 'find out what attracted you to the story. Try to find out the essential theme and forget everything else. Try to place the theme in another context with other situations and characters. Many of the best directors really only make one story over and over again, they find new circumstances into which to set their original theme or fable, and the story is rediscovered in new contexts. So try to discover what it is that turns you on, the thing that makes your hair stand on end. Do you remember A. E. Housman's description of the definition of poetry? "It is that which if you recite to the mirror in the morning your bristles will stand when you shave."'

film be made against the background of Vienna just after the Second World War, a city occupied by the four Allied Powers, divided into zones and plagued by black-market racketeering. But the theme of *The Third Man* is not necessarily found in this historical and geographical point of departure. For that we should look to the fragment of a story situation Greene had jotted down in a notebook long before: the idea of passing in a busy London street an old friend whose funeral had been attended months ago, a scene that is not in the finished film but which, combined with the Vienna setting, furnished the basic plot mechanism.[10]

Let me give you another example, this time from my own experience. Prior to working on *The Man in the White Suit*, I spent considerable time trying to find a story on a theme that quite disturbed me: the political and social responsibility of the scientists who developed nuclear fission without regard for the purposes to which their invention might be put. Perhaps because all my efforts were too specifically directed in one place, and because, quite understandably, my producers thought the topic was too disturbing to be acceptable popular box-office entertainment, I got nowhere with it. Then I read an unproduced play by a cousin of mine. It had a different theme as its central story: it was about the gradually dawning consciousness of the daughter of a manufacturer of textiles under the tutelage of a sardonic and sceptical young man who is in love with her.

A quite secondary character was another young man, an inventor, who had devised a liquid for treating fabric that enormously increased its durability. Transferring my theme of 'the responsibility of the scientist' to the situation that was not much more than a subplot of the original play, I devised a story in which the original hero was subordinated (and later entirely eliminated) in favour of a new protagonist and a good many new characters. In effect, I borrowed from the play not much more than the situation of a fabric that was on the one hand a boon to the public and consumers, on the other a threat to certain sections of the textile industry. Centring on this situation I found that by analogy I could explore the theme that would have been rather too controversial and tendentious if I had tried to deal with it directly.[11]

Myth, according to anthropologists, is a magical working out of the conflicts felt by a society. Claude Lévi-Strauss has argued that the social purpose of the earliest forms of religion, mythic rituals and magic ceremonials was to provide communities with a means of 'resolving contradictions' within their society. And in a recent article on the decline of the Western, sociologist Will Wright has written that 'All stories are one means by which societies explain themselves to themselves.'[12] According to psychoanalysts and psychotherapists, a 'personal' myth may have a similar function. Like some dreams, it may be an effort by the creative subconscious to send to the author a message (theme) in the form of a parable. What evidence is there to support this? The best that I can offer is another highly personal example related to a film I directed some years ago, one I was intimately involved with from its conception.

The Ladykillers, written by William Rose, was in fact a dream. Bill woke up one night with the idea complete in his head. He had dreamed of a gang of criminals who commit a successful robbery while living in a little house belonging to a sweetly innocent little old lady. Belatedly, she discovers their crime. A highly moral and simple-minded soul, she insists they all go to the police and give themselves up. Gradually the five men realise that they will have to kill her. But villainous as they are, they cannot bring themselves to murder such a benign and helpless figure. So, quarrelling over which of them should do the deed, they one by one kill each other, leaving the little old lady with the money. The story amused all of us who worked with Bill at the studio where we were under contract. But it was only several weeks later that I began to realise it could serve as the basis for a film script. I went to Bill and we agreed on the project.

Work on the screenplay involved much argument between the two of us, but curiously enough there was never any departure from the simple basic structure of the idea that had come from Bill Rose's unconscious imagination. The fable remained, though a great deal more invention was necessary to develop the deliberately grotesque figures of the criminals, a quintet of rascally types who were dedicated to villainy but not quite wicked enough to take the inevitable step necessary to avoid their own ruin. Bill once declared that the moral of the story was: 'In the

12. 'The sun sinks slowly on the western', *New Society*, 6 May 1976, an article which Mackendrick reproduced in its entirety for his students. Mackendrick was also impressed with Wright's book *Six Guns and Society: A Structural Study of the Western* (University of California Press, 1977), writing a lengthy précis of the book that included Wright's analysis of the three basic formulae of the Western: the 'Classical' Formula (pp. 48–9 of the book), the 'Vengeance' Formula (p. 69) and the 'Professional' Formula (p. 113).

Worst of All Men there is a Little Bit of Good that can Destroy Them.'

As director I worked daily with Bill and the associate producer, though the screenplay was essentially the work of Bill Rose alone. As a fine writer often does, he used his collaborators only as a kind of sounding board. We were his audience during the long sessions of improvisation during which the story was worked out in considerable detail. But one of my most satisfying discoveries was one I did not make until the film had been completed and exhibited. Bill and I were both expatriates in Britain. Though we were both American-born, because my family was Scots I was sent to Scotland to be educated, while Bill volunteered to join the Canadian forces during the Second World War and then, having married an English girl, decided to remain in Britain after the war. With such backgrounds both of us see Britain in a slightly different way than do the British.

The fable of *The Ladykillers* is a comic and ironic joke about the condition of post-war England. After the war, the country was going through a kind of quiet, typically British but nevertheless historically fundamental revolution. Though few people were prepared to face up to it, the great days of the Empire were gone for ever. British society was shattered with the same kind of conflicts appearing in many other countries: an impoverished and disillusioned upper class, a brutalised working class, juvenile delinquency among the Mods and Rockers, an influx of foreign and potentially criminal elements, and a collapse of 'intellectual' leadership. All of these threatened the stability of the national character.

Though at no time did Bill Rose or I ever spell this out, look at the characters in the film. The Major (played by Cecil Parker), a conman, is a caricature of the decadent military ruling class. One Round (Danny Green) is the oafish representative of the British masses. Harry (Peter Sellers) is the spiv, the worthless younger generation. Louis (Herbert Lom) is the dangerously unassimilated foreigner. They are a composite cartoon of Britain's corruption. The tiny figure of Mrs Wilberforce (Wilberforce was the name of the nineteenth-century idealist who called for the abolition of slavery) is plainly a much diminished Britannia. Her house is in a cul-de-sac. Shabby and cluttered with memories of the days when Britain's navy ruled the world and captains gallantly stayed on the bridge as their ship went down, her house is structurally unsound. Dwarfed by the grim landscape of railway yards and screaming express trains, it is Edwardian England, an anachronism in the contemporary world. Bill Rose's sentimental hope for the country that he and I saw through fond but sceptical eyes was that it might still, against all logic, survive its enemies. A theme, a message of sorts, one that I felt very attached to. But one that it took quite some time for me to consciously recognise and appreciate.

It is worth noting that a theme is often stated as a couple of abstract nouns set in opposition.

The theme of *Romeo and Juliet* is youthful love crossed by ancestral hate; the theme of *Othello* is jealousy; the theme of *Le Tartuffe* is hypocrisy.[13]

13. Archer, *Play-Making*, p. 11.

Translate this to some films we know. The theme of *On the Waterfront* is one man's battle for personal ethics, his struggle to stand up for his rights against the corruption of racketeering unions and the moral apathy of fellow dockers. The theme of *The Hustler* is Being a Winner or a Loser. The theme of *Citizen Kane* is What Shall it Profit a Man if He Gain the Whole World But Loses the Innocence of Childhood (Rosebud and the security of parental love). The theme of *Bicycle Thieves* is the Search for Social Justice and the Values that a Father can Teach his Child. The theme of *The Third Man* is Disillusion of Hero-Worship, sentimental boyhood loyalty versus social responsibility.

To Archer's warning against starting with a 'moral concept', I would add something else. Though it is the aspect of a story that students generally need to think about least when starting a project, it should be remembered that it is the absence of a powerful and reverberating theme that distinguishes forgettable commercial entertainment from something more interesting. A story with a theme that is trivial, unexplored or not clearly identified in the action may be enjoyable while it lasts. But it is not going to linger in your memory very long. Such a narrative is not about anything that deeply concerns the author, and if the author doesn't care it is unlikely that the audience will either.

Dramatic and Non-dramatic

14. Ferdinand Brunetière (1849–1906), French critic and professor.

15. Archer, *Play-Making*, p. 19.

16. Ibid., pp. 24–5.

William Archer is a lot less dogmatic on the subject of the definition of drama than many earlier critics and theorists, though he does spend time debating the propositions of other 'authorities' on the subject. One of these is Ferdinand Brunetière.[14]

'The Theatre in general', said that critic, 'is nothing but the place for the development of the human will, attacking the obstacles opposed to it by destiny, fortune, or circumstances.' And again: 'Drama is the representation of the will of men in conflict with the mysterious powers or natural forces which limit and belittle us; it is one of us thrown living upon the stage, there to struggle against fatality, against social law, against one of his fellow-mortals, against himself, if need be, against the ambitions, the interests, the prejudices, the folly, the malevolence of those who surround him.'[15]

Brunetière's definition seems to work well enough for most stories, but at its simplest it is advice to look for conflict in a story, for the kind of struggle that takes place between a hero and the circumstances that sooner or later he has to confront. Archer, however, tries to take a more practical approach for playwrights, and suggests that:

[T]he essence of drama is *crisis*. A play is a more or less rapidly developing crisis in destiny or circumstance, and a dramatic scene is a crisis within a crisis, clearly furthering the ultimate event. The drama may be called the art of crises, as fiction is the art of gradual developments .

[. . .] But, manifestly, it is not every crisis that is dramatic. A serious illness, a lawsuit, a bankruptcy, even an ordinary prosaic marriage, may be a crisis in a man's life, without being necessarily, or even probably, material for drama. How, then, do we distinguish a dramatic from a non-dramatic crisis? Generally, I think, by the fact that it develops, or can be made naturally to develop, through a series of minor crises, involving more or less emotional excitement, and, if possible, the vivid manifestation of character.[16]

Brunetière, when he is talking about the 'will of man' in conflict, is obviously thinking in terms of Aristotle. Most early drama deals with heroic protagonists, someone who sets the struggle in motion. Implied is that the protagonist is active (after all, the word 'drama' is derived from the Greek work for 'doing').

We live, however, in times that are less 'heroic'. In many contemporary dramas, whether in theatre or cinema, the central figure does not have (or does not seem to have) much positive will. This does not contradict the principles Archer is discussing, it only inverts the protagonist's relationship with the situation that surrounds him. As the protagonist becomes less active and more passive, less certain of his positive purposes, so it is 'the ambitions, the interests, the prejudices, the folly, the malevolence of those who surround him' that take on a more active character. A common compromise is achieved when the protagonist appears passive, inactive, uncertain and undecided for the first three quarters of the piece. Then, in the final confrontation, he or she is forced into a definitive commitment, a positive action.

We can turn to our usual examples. In *On the Waterfront*, the punch-drunk ex-fighter that Brando plays is torn between his commitment to his brother and the corrupt union racketeers on the one side, and the pressure from the priest and the girl on the other. It takes the murder of his brother to force him into a positive act, testifying against the racketeers and then confronting the dockers and Johnny Friendly. In *The Hustler*, Paul Newman is torn between George C. Scott's view of life and that which he shares with the girl, until her suicide provokes him into the final confrontation with the gambler, and with himself. In *The Third Man*, Holly Martins tries to maintain his loyalty to Harry Lime until the evidence supplied by the British military major and the predicament of the girl force him to betray, and finally shoot, his oldest friend.

More complex is the kind of story where the completely passive, undecided, and purposeless central figure does *not* have any final change of heart. There is always a danger that a story with a conclusion that does not seem to resolve anything, and that lacks a peripeteia towards the final crises, will feel unsatisfactory. 'Unsophisticated' audiences often resent this lack of resolution, while avant-garde types admire it as innovation because it manages to avoid the obvious. My personal view is that when the inversion of the classic principles do work for me (as they do, for instance, in a film like Antonioni's *L'Avventura* and Beckett's play *Waiting for Godot*), it is only because the same old prin-

17. Archer, *Play-making*, p. 20.

ciples that Aristotle and Archer, among others, have debated are rediscovered in fresh and unexpected patterns.

Where is the tension in Beckett's work? If it is expectation of the arrival of the mysterious Godot then it is never resolved, as Godot never arrives. But an intuitive audience member senses very quickly that Godot isn't going to appear (actually you only have to consult the cast list). The tension is something quite different. Who is this Godot meant to be, and what does he represent? As one would expect, this 'crisis' is resolved near the very end when the characters come at long last to the realisation that Godot will not be coming. At this moment, the audience is given a strange but somewhat satisfying answer to the main tension of the work: the identity of Godot. And though *L'Avventura* has an extremely elliptical structure, there is certainly a plot, even if it is left to implication. The story is not really about the search for the girl who has vanished from the island. Rather, the tension centres around the heroine's uncertainty about the character of the man who may, or may not, have been the cause of the strange disappearance. When, in the final scenes, Monica Vitti's character finally has to face the disillusioning truth about the kind of man she has fallen in love with, then – if only indirectly and still ambiguously – the history of his previous mistress comes to a conclusion.

As William Archer suggests, there can be highly dramatic plays (and films, of course) where conflict is not so immediately visible. Archer gives *Oedipus Rex* and Shakespeare's *Othello* as examples.

Even the *Oedipus* of Sophocles, though it may at first sight seem a typical instance of a struggle against Destiny, does not really come under the definition. Oedipus, in fact, does not struggle at all. His struggles, in so far as the word can be applied to his misguided efforts to escape the toils of fate, are all things of the past; in the actual course of the tragedy he simply writhes under one revelation after another of bygone error and unwitting crime . . .

There is no struggle, no conflict between [Othello] and Iago. It is Iago alone who exerts any will; neither Othello nor Desdemona makes the smallest fight. From the moment Iago sets his machinations to work, they are like people sliding down an ice-slope to an inevitable abyss.[17]

DRAMATIC CONSTRUCTION

In an attempt to define what drama is, Archer arrives at a view so sensible that one wonders why his predecessors didn't think of it:

18. Archer, *Play-making*, p. 125.

19. Ibid. p. 148

A great part of the secret of dramatic architecture lies in the one word 'tension'. To engender, maintain, suspect, heighten and resolve a state of tension – that is the main object of the dramatist's craft.[18]

The Obligatory Scene

Archer has a chapter in his book on a term that was invented by Francisque Sarcey: the *scène à faire* or obligatory scene:

An obligatory scene is one which the audience (more or less clearly and consciously) foresees and desires, and the absence of which it may with reason resent.[19]

As a definition, this is not of much value. But in the course of studying Archer, it does seem to help us arrive at the key to the meaning of drama. In a single phrase (one that Archer cites from Sarcey): 'anticipation mingled with uncertainty'. This implies that the dramatic conflict inherent in a work may or may not be up there on the stage or screen, just so long as it sets up a tension in us, an event between our ears, a stretching forward of the audience's mind in some as yet unresolved expectation. Obligatory scenes are hard to analyse, if only because the definition is so general it is hardly a definition at all.

As a writer, however, one gets a very strong sense of the feel of such a scene. There is a kind of charge of dramatic energy that is released at such a moment in the story, a sense of having come at last to the point of the whole thing. (In this respect, I should confess to my own quite brutally impatient method of studying screenplays. First, I thumb through the first ten pages. From these, I expect to get an idea of the genre, the environment of the story, as well as an introduction to principal characters, a hint of theme and the hook – the industry's word for the initial fuse of the plot. Next, I turn to the end and then five or ten pages back. Here, I expect to find the obligatory scene, the resolution of the conflicts that were hinted at in the first ten pages. If both of these have intrigued me, then I know the whole script may be worth my time to read.)

Again to our modern examples. In *On the Waterfront*, look at the scene in the bar following the death of Terry's brother, where the priest persuades him that the only effective way to revenge himself against the racketeers in the crooked union is to testify to the Crime Commission. Another possible obligatory scene is when Terry has done just this, and decides to confront Johnny Friendly in front of the dockers who still regard Terry as a stool pigeon. In *The Hustler*, the final match between Fast Eddie and Minnesota Fats (Jackie Gleason) is really a confrontation between Fast Eddie and Bert Gordon (George C. Scott) over Sarah, not pool at all, and is a good example of a *scène à faire*. And finally, in *Bicycle Thieves*, look at the episode when the father sends his son away while he attempts, with pitiful lack of success, to turn thief himself. It is the final act of a desperate man, something we, the audience, have throughout the film suspected he might attempt.

Plausibility and Willing Suspension of Disbelief

It would seem a paradox that the cinema is said to be, in one sense, the most real of all media, but that it is also an enormously effective medium for the unreal, the fantastic and the dream-like. The problem for the film-maker is that he must establish a tone in his work that so captivates audiences that they are not simply willing but in fact eager to believe in the unbelievable. This is a crucial element of the practice of dramatic construction and film-making. The task, in a sense, is technical, for it involves the craft of exposition and the ingenious manipulation of audience expectations. How does one persuade an audience to put aside its normally critical approach to subject matter and willingly collaborate with the storyteller in accepting as logical what is plainly incredible, nonsensical and/or absurd? The phrase 'willing suspension of disbelief' comes to mind. Consider: how is the technique of achieving a 'willing sense of disbelief' different from 'creating a sense of belief'?

Aristotle defined the plausible as that which is possible in the eyes of common opinion. By this definition, plausibility quickly and quietly conforms to the stylistic conventions of a cinematic genre, those 'laws' to which audiences (or at least those full of regular filmgoers) have generally been conditioned and feel comfortable with. In this sense, anything is potentially acceptable once the tone of a film has been adequately established. With comedy, for example, it is acceptable that a character possess a single official vice and that all the misadventure that inevitably befalls him should be the direct consequence of that vice. Moreover, it is rare that we do not sense the genre of a film and its emotional tone and atmosphere within a few moments of it beginning. Just think of the standard opening of a fairy tale: 'Once Upon A Time . . .' The words are the established signal that the listener is expected to swallow whole the events, incidents and the characters of a particular type of fiction.

There can, naturally, be something of an uncomfortable disorientation when a film director doesn't play by the rules. After all, breaking the rules would be no fun if audiences were not able to understand and accept those rules in the first place. Of course, sometimes a director goes out of his way to play around with the explicit purpose of creating disorientation in his viewers. This is something Alfred Hitchcock does on occasion. It is, for example, a 'rule' of drama that you do not encourage an audience to feel sympathy with a protagonist, and then abruptly kill her off halfway through the story. But this is precisely what Hitchcock does to the character of Janet Leigh, murdered in the shower in *Psycho*. This deliberate shock to conventional story structure gives extra force to a scene of already shocking violence, even if, at the same time, we sense that the unusual and wholly unprepared-for dramatic event exists for a particular purpose. This is surely a clue to the potential problem of producing in your audience a willing suppression of common sense and rational scepticism.

To achieve 'willing suspension of disbelief', the storyteller has to persuade the audience to permit special dispensation for believing in things that are implausible. There are many ways to manage this, most of which seem to depend on devices of dramatic structure that manipulate the audience into the position where they will have some greater satisfaction in accepting the thing that is incredible, rather than the thing that is natural or logical. In effect, the audience is bribed. How?

First, delay the introduction of whatever it is that might be regarded as incredible, irrational, absurd, wholly unlikely and contrived. Begin by establishing the plausibility of circumstances within which the irrational element will make its appearance.

Second, whet audience curiosity. Plant hints that are fragments of exposition to come. The audience is usually way ahead of you anyway – they will guess what is coming, even if they sense that it is going to be incredible, irrational or absurd. Modern audiences have seen such huge quantities of conventionally structured entertainment that most of them are highly sophisticated in picking up clues. This is where the pleasure of

DRAMATIC CONSTRUCTION

'willing suspension of disbelief' may lie, as the audience is able to congratulate itself on guessing what the game is to be and on preparing for whatever it is that will be disclosed as incredible, irrational and absurd. In this fashion, the audience becomes a co-conspirator.

Third, introduce characters into the story who are plainly unbelievers, as this develops tension between belief and disbelief. If your audience has reasonable grounds to find your premise unbelievable, create an onstage character who gives early expression to their scepticism. Disbelief is now personified in the action. A key character in a ghost story is the figure playing the part of the cynic, the one who declares, 'There's no such thing as a ghost.' Needless to say, however much the audience might agree with him, this produces a mischievous desire to see the unbeliever discomfited (savaged by a ghost), especially if the director has taken care to give him a pompous, narrow-minded and unsympathetic personality.

Fourth, as an elaboration or extension of this process, it is often effective to devise a domino effect in the exposition. Choose a point of attack in the construction where there are already some characters secretly aware of the 'thing-that-is-unbelievable' but who conceal this knowledge. Set up a conflict with a protagonist who through these knowing characters comes very gradually to the point of confronting the unbelievable. This will set him or her in conflict with a larger circle of secondary sceptics who are as disbelieving as the protagonist was at the earlier stages.

Fifth, introduce disappointments. It is effective to create a situation in which, having loaded the dice against the sceptic, he is then proved correct (for the moment at least). This should produce in the audience an increase in the perverse desire to believe in the unbelievable.

Them!, a 1954 American science-fiction film, is absolute and unashamed hokum. It is simple-minded to the point of absurdity, and nobody is likely to regard it as a work of serious cinema. It is also, at another level, a classic. If there had been an attempt to treat its subject matter with any subtlety, the result would have been a certain disaster. But *Them!* is worth some study, I suggest, because it demonstrates how our 'disbelief' can be easily 'suspended' with some degree of 'willingness'. One of the easiest ways to learn the carpentry of solid, simple plot mechanisms of any kind of cinema is by the careful dismantling and re-assembly of a piece of nonsense like *Them!*

The characters in the film are figures out of a cartoon. We are not supposed to take them seriously for a moment. Like the personages in a Medieval Morality play they are not people, rather personifications of ideas-of-people outlined in quite broad strokes of near-caricature. Couldn't they have made it more real and less corny? Yes, but it would probably have been a mistake because there is no time wasted when you are dealing with figures so quickly recognisable to even the dumbest member of the audience. The plot can move at express-engine speed and we are given no time to question the plausibility of the story.

It just so happens that the first victims of the Strange Phenomenon are a family in which the father is an FBI man on holiday. This conveniently brings the Authorities into the case with no time wasted. The World Famous Scientist arrives with his Attractive Daughter (providing the love interest) who happens to be another scientist, which means she can be easily integrated into the exposition. Note that these all-too-convenient circumstances are boldly established right at the start, before there is even a chance for the audience to question them. Once swallowed, the rest is that much easier to digest. (Two thousand years ago Aristotle explained that when something is unlikely and unbelievable, let it happen off stage.) At regular intervals throughout, the World Famous Scientist lectures the Authorities and provide them (and us) with scientific explanations and moral homilies. This is all picture-book stuff, but at the same time classic exposition because the lectures are directly relevant to the immediate action. Information is supplied because something has to be *done*. First, the crisis is demonstrated. Then, the exposition is supplied.

In a deliberate but very effective tease, the audience is manipulated into the position of being two or three steps ahead of *Them!*'s poor dumb hero, who plays foil to the exposition. We are then promised escalation of the frankly incredible situations and, step-by-step, we get them. The basic element of this fantasy, the Thing on Which We Must Suspend Disbelief (giant ants produced by an atomic bomb test) is the single impossibly fantastic element to the story. All other elements of implausibility are merely unlikely. A rule of the genre seems to be that we are allowed only one major Incredible Thing. Given this, everything else will, surprisingly enough, seem to be logical (if still wholly improbable). Two elements of suspense are apt to be half as suspenseful as one, and several examples of things incredible, magical, fantastic, or even just plain nonsensical, are not nearly as satisfying as a single impossibility from which all others flow. Given this one Incredible Thing, everything else in the story should actually be logical, even over-logical. This is what produces tension: because all of the associated circumstances are strictly rational, we the audience cannot reject the nonsensical elements without rejecting everything else.

This 'rule' may be a reflection of the point often noted by doctors who study psychotic behaviour. They say that the most thoroughly deranged people are those who act in an utterly logical way, except that this logic is based on one insane premise. The madman behaves in a way that would be totally acceptable and realistic if he really were Napoleon. By extension, it is sound practice when devising an incredible story to do a great deal of research on all other associated aspects of the situation. *Them!* actually devotes quite a lot of footage to earnestly real, and entirely accurate, explanations of how ant colonies function. Everything except the initial premise is logical and real. A comparison can be found in the paintings of René Magritte and Salvador Dalí (and even Tenniel's illustrations to *Alice in Wonderland*). While the techniques of these artists are naturalistic, even meticulous in their representational realism, their subjects are a long way from reality.

Density and Subplots in *Sweet Smell of Success*

Recently, a story-editor at one of the studios commented that a common weakness of scripts submitted was the absence of a subplot. I hadn't heard the term 'subplot' for some time. In classic theatrical convention it is common to have subordinate figures who develop stories that are in some degree distinct from the main theme, though they are interwoven into the central subject matter. A good many Shakespearean plays are constructed in this fashion. There is also, of course, the kind of story that deals with a group of characters. We have studied *Stagecoach*, but there are a host of other examples. The epic disaster films like *Airport* and all those television mini-series rely on the pattern of a number of parallel plot-lines.

The extreme case, indeed, may be the television series of the type that has become a formula, where a number of established characters have more or less constant and unchanging relationships, and new and separate plot-lines are developed every week. Each episode contains new plot elements, a new premise and a new resolution, while the main characters and the basic themes (if there really is anything worthy of being called a theme in such television stories) are unchanging. And, because they are never really resolved, each situation can continue for as long as the invention of writers and the interest of the public can be maintained. Though common in television, group stories seem to have died as a form of the cinema these days. They used to be much more common, and if I have a prejudice against them, it is probably because the English studio at which I got some early training was addicted to the kind of stories that had multiple protagonists (the Ealing comedies *Passport to Pimlico* and *Whisky Galore!* for example).

I have never been sure why writers and directors of that era

were so happy with this formula. I think they believed it provided the opportunity for not only more variety of characters but also a lively pacing that could be achieved by intercutting the progression of the subplots. After one film of this kind I began to dislike the structure because I felt it weakened the drive of the narrative rather than strengthened it. *All* of the characters essentially became cameo roles that couldn't be developed in any depth, and the multiplicity of minor tensions was apt to reduce the tension of the main theme. This is why I am not sure if the comment of the story-editor about subplots is really sound. Or at least, I think there is a danger of it being misunderstood by students. I suspect, however, that the story-editor was really complaining of something a little different: a

Mackendrick directs Tony Curtis on *Sweet Smell of Success* (1957).

1. See Sam Kashner's article 'A Movie Marked Danger' (*Vanity Fair*, April 2000) which details the production of *Sweet Smell of Success*.

2. Clifford Odets (1906–63), American dramatist. While at New York's Group Theatre in the 1930s he wrote the plays *Waiting for Lefty, Awake and Sing!* and *Golden Boy*, today regarded as classics of pre-war American drama. Odets, a prolific Hollywood screenwriter in the 1940s, wrote several unproduced screenplays and did uncredited work on various scripts, including a first draft of Frank Capra's *It's a Wonderful Life* (1946). He also directed two films based on his own scripts: *None But the Lonely Heart* (1944) and *The Story on Page One* (1959).

certain thinness of subject, a limited range of themes, a lack of density in the dramatic structure (to say nothing of the fact that, when planning a project that is as short as student projects usually have to be for economic reasons, there is rarely space for subplots).

Students often confuse length with substance. A work that is lengthy is thought to be more serious, more like a proper feature. I have heard complaints from students that a film of only ten or fifteen minutes cannot adequately deal with characters, themes and plots of substance. Personally, I do not believe this and can state a very good reason why it is a better test of students' craft to produce scenes that are only three to five minutes in length rather than a full-length film. A feature of about two hours is usually made up of something like twenty-five scenes, each averaging perhaps five minutes. Key scenes may be a bit longer, but are seldom more than ten minutes. The structure of the entire work, if you are studying a classic dramatic film, is likely to have the traditional elements of plot, characterisation and theme combined in exposition, crises, and the gradual build to the obligatory scene near the end.

What is intriguing, however, is that the structure of the story is apt to be reflected in every scene, each of which serves almost as a microcosm of the structure of the whole. I believe this is why, from the study of one of the significantly shorter scenes within the whole, it is not difficult to evaluate the ability of a director and writer to demonstrate the skills needed to produce a full-length work. Simply, if you do not have the ability to control the dramatic structure of a scene of five to ten minutes, it is doubtful whether you can structure a whole film effectively. Moreover, if a project is meant to demonstrate to possible employers in the industry that the writer/director has the skills necessary for more ambitious tasks, then ten to fifteen minutes is quite enough. Potential employers are likely to be very busy people. Many of them will sample the beginning of a film but cut it off when they have seen enough, missing the obligatory material of the story that is usually near the end.

In the context of density in screenplay writing, let me speak here of *Sweet Smell of Success*, a film I directed in 1957 for the Hecht-Hill-Lancaster Company.[1] Written by Clifford Odets[2] from a first-draft script by Ernest Lehman,[3] it starred Burt Lancaster and Tony Curtis. It is a film I have mixed feelings about today, and I am writing about it here to illustrate some problems in the structuring of a screenplay, not because I mean to claim that it is an important work. It isn't. Among other things, the film was a big flop at the box office, though the reasons for this are perhaps rather complicated. It was much too costly, chiefly because it was made under rather chaotic circumstances: Odets had so badly underestimated the time he would need for revisions of Lehman's script that I had to start shooting while he was still working on scenes to come, and on a couple of occasions filming had to be halted.

Moreover, most of the critics in the popular press (with considerable justification) resented the savagely unflattering picture that the film presented of their profession, or at least of that subsection of it: the New York gossip columnists and their associates, the press agents. At the time *Sweet Smell of Success* was made, a number of people assumed that the character Burt Lancaster plays (J. J. Hunsecker) was based on the famous Broadway gossip columnist Walter Winchell.[4] For obvious reasons, since the story presents both the columnist and his profession in an unflattering light, the producers denied this. But it should be stated that Ernest Lehman (who also wrote the original story upon which the script was based) had once worked in the offices of a Broadway press agent who was a close associate of Winchell. Winchell had also been the subject of a series of exposé newspaper articles that do bear some vague resemblance to incidents in the story.

There were other problems to deal with. The production department had used Lehman's draft for its scheduling and budgeting, so to say the film went over schedule is not really accurate because there never really was a schedule or a definitive budget. I am ashamed to admit that from the point of view of the director, chaos can have some advantages. It forces him to think fast and improvise, seizing on unforeseen opportunities. There is the exhilaration at the fact that the whole elaborate superstructure of executives – whose job it is to look over the shoulder of the director – are at his mercy, because nobody else knows what is going on. On the other hand, it is a wholly disastrous way to

3. Ernest Lehman (b.1915) scripted *The King and I, North by Northwest, West Side Story, The Sound of Music, Who's Afraid of Virginia Woolf* and *Hello Dolly!* Lehman's original script was based on his fifty-four-page novelette entitled *Sweet Smell of Success*, published in a collection of his short fiction in 1957 (reprinted in 2000 by The Overlook Press).

4. Walter Winchell (1897–1972), legendary American columnist and radio broadcaster. See Neal Gabler's *Winchell: Gossip, Power and the Culture of Celebrity* (Vintage, 1994).

make films and, in view of the fact that *Sweet Smell of Success* was not a success at the box office, it did not necessarily help the careers of a number of people who worked on it.

What's more, up to that point Tony Curtis had played only relatively sympathetic parts, and the audience that went to see him, assuming he was the hero of the story, were first dismayed and then angered as it slowly emerged that this nice young man was a monster of cynicism and corruption, more contemptible even than the sinister figure of Hunsecker. There were also some commentators who saw the whole subject matter of the film as an attack on the 'American Way of Life' and the 'success ethos'. Looking back, I cannot say I am surprised at its poor reception. What is a bit more unexpected is that since its release the film has been appearing in art-house cinemas and festivals, and has developed, as they say, a 'cult following', for which much credit must be given to the gutter-poetry quality of Odets's melodramatic lines.

Though in a number of ways *Sweet Smell of Success* does seem ludicrously hammy and theatrical, of course we knew this at the time. It was also clear that it was intrinsic to the genre that the characters and performances should be exaggerated, verging on the grotesque. And while I cannot recommend the film for student study on aesthetic grounds, there is one aspect of it that may be of value for analysis: the writing process, the way that one scriptwriter (Odets) went about the job of rewriting the work of another (Lehman). I have chosen here to look carefully at the film because I was present at the stages when it was being written by these two very experienced writers, and participation in this process taught me a great deal, particularly about the subject we are discussing here: story structure, not only as applied to the script as a whole but crucially also within individual scenes. Corny as the film is (and it is a quite shameless piece of melodrama), it has real vitality throughout because Odets constantly provides glimpses of subsidiary conflicts and tensions.

Clifford Odets was a playwright of some importance in the history of American drama and had been a hero of mine long before I became a film-maker. As a screenwriter, however, he was extremely theatrical. I have to admit I found his dialogue mannered and very artificial, not at all realistic. At the same time, I

DRAMATIC CONSTRUCTION

recognised that not only is the whole plot of *Sweet Smell of Success* somewhat exaggerated, it also deals with an environment and characters who seem to enjoy quite grotesquely colourful forms of speech. (On another level, Damon Runyon's stories of the same environment have a similarly preposterous style.[5]) Clifford sensed, I think, that I was concerned about the problem of style and explained to me: 'My dialogue may seem somewhat overwritten, too wordy, too contrived. Don't let it worry you. You'll find that it works if you don't bother too much about the lines themselves. Play the situations, not the words. And play them fast.' When it came to the highly stylized, almost preposterous, lines the actors had to speak, I found this to be a marvellous piece of advice. Indeed, it reinforced my understanding of dialogue in film: the spoken word is often at its most effective when the actors concentrate not on the words and their literal meaning but on the actions that underlie them, the real intentions and motivations of the characters. A line that reads quite implausibly on the printed page can be quite convincing and effective when spoken in a throwaway or incidental fashion by the actor.

Ernie Lehman and I had become friends during a period when we were both under contract to Hecht-Hill-Lancaster. I had been preparing a project that was cancelled because of casting problems, while Ernie had been assigned as not only the writer of *Sweet Smell of Success* but also as director. He began, however, to have second thoughts about choosing it as his first directing assignment and decided he would be safer if he remained as writer/producer.[6] He asked me if I would like to direct it. I liked the material for several reasons. One was that I had always hankered to make a melodrama, a *film noir* as it has been called, and felt this was a chance to get out of a reputation I had for small, cute British comedies. Another was that, though it was in England, I'd had some experience of the world of tabloid journalism and was both repelled and fascinated by some of its grubbier aspects. A third was that I liked the idea of trying to capture on screen the atmosphere of Manhattan. (It has been done many times since, of course, but *Sweet Smell of Success* was actually one of the first attempts to shoot night scenes on location in the city.) I also appreciated the themes of the story and felt I could

5. Runyon's work served as the basis for the musical *Guys and Dolls*.

6. Lehman's version of the story is different. 'I went on a location-hunting trip, and when I returned, Harold Hecht called me into his office and told me that United Artists had gotten cold feet about the idea of a first-time director directing this picture because they hadn't had such good luck with Burt Lancaster directing *The Kentuckian*, his first and for all I know *only* attempt at directing. I was very upset – and very lucky, because I am sure I couldn't have brought it off at all, not the way Sandy Mackendrick eventually did. I don't know what made me think at that stage of my life that I was capable of directing' (John Brady, *The Craft of the Screenwriter*, Simon and Schuster, 1981, p. 206).

work well with Ernie Lehman, though I did explain to him and the producers that there were certain things about the first draft that worried me a good deal, not least that it wasn't very cinematic. Just about every scene consisted of an exchange of dialogue between two people sitting at a table in a restaurant, at a bar, or in a nightclub. The screenplay was nothing but talk, with little consideration given to physical surroundings and visual atmosphere.

My earliest reaction was that though such an approach was necessary for much of the story, we could at least make an attempt to move it out into the streets. I felt that one of the characteristic aspects of New York, particularly the square mile that constitutes the area between Forty-Second Street and Fifty-Seventh Street (the theatre and nightclub district), is the neurotic energy of the crowded sidewalks. This, I argued, was essential to these characters, people driven by the uglier aspects of ambition and greed. Without it they would seem to be even more unbelievable than they already were. I was enormously lucky to discover that the producers were instantly receptive to this idea, and even before we set down to work on the screenplay, the producers allowed me to take the cameraman (the great James Wong Howe) and the production designer (Edward Carrere) on a reconnaissance trip to New York to explore the locations. It was on this visit to the city that we developed the formula of starting many of the scenes in exteriors, beginning with short passages of dialogue on the claustrophobic Manhattan streets outside the bars, apartment buildings, offices and street corners, before following the characters into the interiors. A complex matter this was, since it meant very careful matching between material shot on night locations in New York and studio-built sets on the sound stages of Goldwyn Studios in Hollywood. I am not at all sure that this effect helped the film to be less theatrical, but do feel it contributed to the inward aggression that helped to make the scenes work. Though the screenplay is immensely talky and theatrical, I think the camera helped disguise this.

In retrospect, I realise I may have been falling into a trap not uncommon in the profession: when a director is uneasy about some aspects of the script but does not know how to resolve them, he will often retreat into concentrating on more technical challenges that allow him to escape from things that are more important. The truth, perhaps, was that I was uncomfortable about characters and situations that I did not really believe in and hoped to conceal these fundamental flaws by the fancy foot-work of visual effects. A common fallacy is that you can make a piece of writing conceived in theatrical terms more cinematic by 'opening it out'. This usually means keeping the same dialogue, but playing the scene against backgrounds of more pictorial interest. Though this may indeed help to provide more atmos-phere, it does not necessarily make the scenes any more interesting.

At this point came a major disaster: Ernie Lehman fell ill. With only a month or so before shooting was due to start, a date that could not be postponed because of contracts to the princi-pal actors, we were faced with the task of finding a new screen-writer to solve a number of the problems we had identified in the script. By enormous good fortune Hecht-Hill-Lancaster had just put Clifford Odets under contract to work on another project and we were able to persuade him to do what, at that juncture, seemed a relatively simple job of story doctoring: polishing the dialogue and making some minor adjustments to the scene struc-ture. We could not have been more wrong. It is, of course, well known that few writers are able to resist the temptation of changing the work of another screenwriter, but none of us realised how much work Clifford found that he had to do. Very little of Ernie's script was left in the end, though the basic themes remain in the film we know today, and with the exception of the final scenes, the plot was substantially as originally conceived. What Clifford did, in effect, was to dismantle the structure of every single sequence in order to rebuild situations and relation-ships into scenes that were more complex and had much greater tension and dramatic energy. Disastrous as this process was from the point of view of the production, the truth is that for me personally it was an experience that taught me a staggering amount. I can make no claims for the completed film, but what I can say is that without this work done by Odets, it would have had none of the vitality you see up on the screen.

It is not easy to explain Clifford's process. It took place mostly in story conferences, daily meetings between three people: Odets, producer Jim Hill and myself. Much of the discussion was lively, aggressive argument in which it seemed that we ripped every scene to shreds, to the point where I was growing increasingly nervous that nothing would be left. But what I slowly began to recognise was that I was being given the privilege of watching the processes of a dramatic intelligence working out the intricacies of character interaction. There was an interesting pattern to Clifford's work on the successive drafts of a scene. During a story conference he would improvise in the way an actor does, sometimes using a tape recorder, more often just talking and making notes. Then he would go off on his own to sketch out a scene that he would come back and read (perform, in fact) for our benefit. His acting, to my mind, was atrocious. Moreover, the scene would usually be horrendously overwritten and much too long. Then he would set about cutting it down quite ruthlessly. Clifford was, in fact, much more drastic in the editing of his own first drafts than any other writer I have working with. In effect, during this process he would reduce the scene to a bare bones of the essential moves of the dramatic action. All that would be left were the key lines that triggered a shift in the story, a peripeteia of some kind.

The scene was still in Clifford's handwriting. Nothing had been typed. At this stage it was my impulse to beg him to have it typed up so we could examine it. But he always managed to frustrate me in this and tried to keep the material flexible as possible as he began to find new problems with it. Often this was because as he improvised the situation by playing it from the point of view of one of the characters, he uncovered previously unnoticed problems related to interrelated characters. Retaining only the essentials of the scene, he would then switch points of view as he improvised the complementary reactions of another figure. Once more the scene would expand and once more Clifford would drastically cut it down again, keeping – at each successive stage – only the essentials from the previous draft, creating a piece of writing with more and more density and sinew.

Naturally this was a time-consuming process. The real reason why many scripts are too long is wittily put in the apology of a correspondent who explained at the end of an extremely discursive letter: 'I'm sorry this is such a long letter. I didn't have time to write a short one.' Dramatic economy, which includes the ability of the writer to cut what at one point he might have considered to be his best work ever, is one of the most important skills a writer can have, learned only through much experience, combined with a ruthless attitude and an utter lack of sentimentality. It takes effort, lots of effort. It means rewriting and rewriting and rewriting – a constant process of distillation. Simply put, I find that many student films are too long simply because not enough effort has been put into the hard work of making them short.

Odets's process was his extraordinary method of building the dramatic mechanisms of a scene. It often required him to produce a number of drafts of dialogue that were progressively dismantled and then cannibalised into subsequent versions. In early drafts the dialogue was heavily weighted in favour of one of the characters who would be permitted lengthy and even cumbersome exposition, quite simple and one-sided explanations of attitude. These were often very near to being overt expressions of internal thought. The next stage might be Clifford's examination of the reactions to such monologues. Much of what he had written would then have to be revised because 'He wouldn't be able to say that because She wouldn't let him get away with it – She'd interrupt him by pointing out that . . .' While working on these easy drafts, Odets was well aware that he was including far too much material, that it would need to be compressed and cut down. But that was the point.

Certain things emerged during this process. A particular line of dialogue that was important or expressive of a significant idea might have to be eliminated from the speech of one of the characters. But it was sometimes possible to retain it by transferring it to one of the other characters (though not necessarily in the same scene). Implausible as a direct statement, it would work fine as an attribution in someone else's mouth. Complex and sophisticated characters are apt to be unwilling, unable or reluctant to explain their feelings and purposes, particularly in situations of conflict. The dramatist often finds it convenient to explain His feelings by rewriting them in the form of Her attributions of feelings and thoughts about Him. Things that He would never admit, or may not even recognise about himself, can be made explicit thanks to Her. ('Methinks she doth protest too much' is a convenient phrase to remember.)

Odets, describing his methods of fashioning a tightly knit and dense script, offered this advice: see that each of the characters arriving in a confrontation scene comes with ammunition (as he used to remark, a character has to have 'a back to his head and money in his pocket'). The climax of many effective plays or screenplays features a scene in which two characters, often the protagonist of the story and an antagonist, confront each other. In Hollywood jargon this is sometimes referred to as the shoot-out, even when the weapons are purely verbal. Intelligent characters (and scenes between characters who have little intelligence are apt to be dull) usually arrive with a number of moves that have been mentally rehearsed in advance. They have thought out not only what they mean to say, but also how it will probably be received.

An argument is, in this sense, like a chess or card game. The instigator (A) is likely to have a fairly clear scheme of opening moves. He will have several gambits in mind and is prepared for the countermoves these may provoke. Similarly, his opponent (B) has foreseen (A)'s intentions and has prepared either defensive tactics or a counter-attack. Thus a confrontation scene between (A) and (B) will often begin with a number of dialogue exchanges that are an exploration of prepared positions, probing for strengths and weaknesses, while also establishing psychological bases. Tension in a scene of this kind clearly arises out of conflict, the clash of wills. The first task of the writer is therefore to be as clear as possible when it comes to the desires of each of the confronting characters. What exactly does (A) want? What obstacles does he expect (B) to raise? How does (A) expect to overcome these obstacles? Through what persuasion? What promise? What threat?

In this respect, once the psychological vying between characters has resulted in, perhaps, one character winning out over the other (albeit temporarily), then come the important expository surprises as certain pieces of information, perhaps unknown to one character, become, in the hands of another, an ace, a trump card. Such dynamics can produce a shift of the dramatic equilibrium, a peripeteia. In an intricately plotted scene there can be more than one such trumping move. Thus it is another of the tasks of the writer to think out just these points where ignorance

DRAMATIC CONSTRUCTION

of some key information leaves one of the characters vulnerable, a move in which the tables can be turned by the other. A character who holds our interest will, during such scenes, often discover something unexpected, some contradiction within his or her own personality, an unforeseen emotional impulse. (Plot moves, however, are only one of the elements in an effective confrontation scene. Indeed, a scene that rests solely on a clash over plot points is likely to be thin stuff. One sees too much of this kind of writing in television stories where characters act aggressively but have no emotional depth or variety of feelings, no potential for shifts of mood, no capacity for character growth.)

The effect of Odets's ideas about density created a depth and conviction to the characters of *Sweet Smell of Success*, greatly enhancing many scenes. As a process it seemed to me rather like the weaving of a fabric that, because of the tensions of multiple interlocking strands, is supremely strong. Clifford would frequently use secondary characters in this way, establishing them as the basis for triangulation, the three-way interplay of characters. I had, as I say, noted that the original screenplay seemed to have a great many scenes that were simple dualogues, interaction between two people. Clifford's instinct seemed always to devise patterns of three, four and five interacting characters. One of his private pleasures was listening to chamber music, especially small string ensembles and quintets. Clifford admired compositions in which the voices of five instruments were thematically interwoven, yet each with a clearly identifiable melodic line contributing to the harmonic pattern. As such, he wanted to make certain scenes in his screenplay follow a similar pattern, where there would be a quintet of voices. There are several instances in the script of *Sweet Smell of Success* where I think Odets was particularly successful in doing this.

In the first story conference between Odets, myself and the producer, Jim Hill, I presented some of the ideas I had already been working on with Ernest Lehman. I had the idea of beginning the film with a sequence I felt would set the general tone of the film: the frantic activity that surrounds the moment when the first edition of a big city newspaper hits the streets (it was finally used as background for the titles). I explained how I could use posters on the side of the delivery trucks and the masthead of the

7. This is the character of Frank D'Angelo in Odets's script.

column itself to set in motion the sequence of scenes that would build slowly to the introduction of the figure of the columnist. I suggested this would be a better start than the ambiguous scene of the suicide that introduced voiceover narration and flashback. (Privately, I have a distaste for these two things, both of which are often a sign of the failure to create scenes in which the exposition is presented in terms of present dramatic action.) I had no need to argue the point, for Odets had already been feeling much the same way. Encouraged, I also made the suggestion that we could establish the profession of Sidney (Tony Curtis's character) visually if we could play a scene not in his home, but rather in an office where the set design and incidental activity could show just how a press agent lives. Perhaps, I said, Sidney could actually have a bedroom attached to his office, something that would indicate his association with the newspaper column and the degree to which he was dependent on his job.

Odets again seized on this. Pursuing the same line, he said he had been thinking about the roles of Sidney's mother and the brother. In Lehman's early draft these two characters appeared in the early scenes but were substantially absent thereafter. Useful, of course, as supporting roles to reveal the background of the protagonist, but without much connection with the rest of the action. Possibly, he thought, there were other more interesting ways to make the same points using characters already established in the script. For example, instead of the character of the mother, Odets proposed that the character of the theatrical agent could be a relative of Sidney's, his mother's brother (such a person would have the right to scold Sidney in much the same fashion as the brother and the mother).[7] The idea of the bedroom/office also prompted Odets to suggest that Sidney has a secretary, Sally, who also sleeps with him on occasion, a sad and slightly squalid relationship that was not only rich in its implications of character, but which meant that scenes now devoted to character exploration could be more explicitly relevant to the plot. (The early scene in Odets's draft with Sidney and Sally in his office where he gives a self-justifying speech is not only an early statement of the story's theme, thus anticipating situations in the climax of the story, it also gives a depth to Sidney's character as it shows us his attitude to his secretary who he treats with such little respect. Thus the character, theme and plot are all functioning at once in the scene.[8])

Clifford promised to work on these ideas. Then he began to focus on the scene he felt needed most work: the introduction, in the Twenty-One Club, of the figure central to the whole subject, J. J. Hunsecker.[9] Lehman's original version contained three characters sitting at the newspaper columnist's table, but very little use was made of them. They were merely extras to the scene, while in Odets's version each of the five characters are continuously in play throughout. For purposes of exposition, Odets had considerably expanded their parts, making them foil figures and effectively providing a compact subplot for them. Like Odets, I felt the scene was not really as powerful as it ought to be, but having no positive suggestions, I had made no complaint. Odets proceeded to give us a demonstration of the way a practised dramaturge, a man with long experience of such difficulties, explores for ideas to solve them.

'I don't understand!' he declared with force. 'This man Hunsecker is a newspaper columnist. I know what that means. What I don't understand is why everybody seems so terrified of him. Why?' Jim Hill protested to Odets, 'Oh, come on, Clifford, he's not just any columnist. Everybody knows how he behaves.' 'No they don't,' said Clifford. 'Some people might know. Maybe you and I know, but most people have no idea. This is a man who treats one of his associates as if he were dirt. But Sidney just sits there and takes it. Why does he need it? Why doesn't he just get up and walk away?' Jim protested again: 'He can't walk away. It's his living.' 'How?' asked Clifford. 'How? Because a Press Agent has to get his clients' names into the paper. That's what they pay him for. And besides that . . .' Jim, in some exasperation, went on to elaborate on the relationship between Sidney and Hunsecker. While he was doing so Odets scribbled notes on his memo pad, then switched his attack. 'But why is everybody else so much in awe of this creature? He insults everybody but nobody talks back to him. I just don't believe in this man.' Once more Hill insisted, 'Don't you understand! This guy Hunsecker is a man who can tell Presidents what to do!' Scribbling again, Clifford said more quietly, 'Oh, sure. But where does it say that? And even if somebody says it, I don't believe it. You've got to *show* me.'

8. See the published script of *Sweet Smell of Success* by Odets and Lehman (Faber and Faber, 1998), pp. 5–11.

9. See James Mangold's piece in the published script, which uses Mackendrick's teachings to analyse this scene.

During all of this I made no comment, as I saw Odets's point clearly. But what had begun to worry me was that, if he was correct (and I felt he was), then there would need to be a lot more expository talk, a lot more of the kind of verbiage I felt was already bogging down the momentum of the story. More exposition, I felt, was bound to weaken the scenes rather than strengthen them. What Clifford had been scribbling down as he talked were Jim Hill's answers that were later worked into the dialogue of the script. Clifford was actually using Jim as a foil, or rather was playing the role of foil himself so that Jim was provoked into improvising the answers to the questions that had not been properly addressed in the first draft script. As for myself, I was indeed correct in my fear that the Twenty-One Club scene would have to be longer and more elaborate. But Clifford's skill meant that as it was transformed from primarily a two-hander into a five-cornered exchange of considerable complexity, the scene became brilliantly tense.

Though I personally was often uneasy about Odets's dialogue, I had nothing but admiration for his skill in scene construction. His adeptness in this kind of dramatic carpentry was quite extraordinary and is something we can all learn from. As I examined Clifford's version of the scene, I realised that its strength was in the ensemble structure he had constructed. It is hardly an exaggeration to say that at any given moment each of the five characters present is involved in some way with every one of the other four. There are, in a sense, twenty-five separate interactions. This, of course, had an immediate effect on the way in which camera coverage is planned, and I had to think very carefully before it was time to rehearse and before it became my task to design the staging. In order to maintain the ensemble feeling before the cameras, with its sense of a continuous flow in interactions, it seemed important to me to design the images so that sometimes five, sometimes three, and sometimes two, figures were in the frame. At the same time, the moves of the actors constantly called attention to the shifting patterns of the axes of their confrontations and interactions.

Before we look at various scenes from the film, here are the characters involved:

Sidney Falco

A press agent, he has a very small list of clients, nightclub owners, band leaders, entertainers of any kind who pay him up to a hundred dollars a week to get their names mentioned in the gossip columns of New York newspapers. Fiercely ambitious, it is Sidney's business to toady up to all of the Broadway columnists. He supplies them with jokes or scandalous titbits, but is also ready to do them any other kind of favour, from supplying them with girls to more devious and malicious chicaneries on their behalf.

J. J. Hunsecker

The most successful of Broadway newspaper columnists. In addition to a daily column in a major newspaper he also has a regular television show. A thoroughly unpleasant character whose sense of his own importance verges on paranoia, Hunsecker has used and continues to use his power over Sidney. The relationship between them is an ugly one, for while Hunsecker takes sadistic pleasure in Sidney's dependence on him, Sidney desperately needs the columnist and conceals his contempt and hatred for the man whose 'sweet smelling success' he covets.

Susan Hunsecker

Younger sister of J. J. She has lived with her brother since the death of their parents and is psychologically and financially dependent upon him. Hunsecker's attitude to her is possessive to a degree that hints at an incestuous obsession. While insisting on his affection for her, Hunsecker has actually managed to drive her to the edge of a nervous breakdown. He sees her interest in any young men as a threat to her dependence on himself and has so far managed to discourage the attentions of anyone who has showed an interest in her. Sidney has been useful in this, since it is essential to Hunsecker that Susan should not realise that her brother is the source of the problems she has with finding a boyfriend. Susan is, however, not nearly as naive as J. J. assumes her to be.

10. From Lehman's script entitled *The Sweet Smell of Success* (pp. 18–25). The unpublished screenplay, marked 'First Draft', is dated 30 March 1956.

Steve Dallas

A jazz guitarist who leads a quintet that plays in Broadway clubs. He is in love with Susan. He is also aware that her pathetic insecurity and low self-esteem is the direct result of her older brother's dominance of the girl. Steve has concealed his own private repugnance of Hunsecker's muckraking newspaper column in the hopes of persuading Susan to leave her brother and marry him. Steve is also well aware of Sidney's activities on behalf of the columnist, though has more difficulty concealing his contempt for the press agent.

Rita

A cigarette girl. She has a child, probably illegitimate, who is in military school. Not quite a whore, she knows that to keep her job at the nightclub she must not reject too vigorously the sexual approaches of influential customers, such as the newspaper columnists. Sidney has helped her in the past and she is grateful enough to go to bed with him on occasion.

Otis Elwell

Another gossip columnist. Cheerfully contemptuous of Sidney and unimpressed by the great J. J., Elwell is nevertheless quite ready to accept Sidney's services as a procurer in return for publishing a slanderous 'blind item' directed at Steve Dallas.

Lieutenant Harry Kello

A New York cop with a reputation for brutality. He is a crony of Hunsecker and supplies the columnist regularly with information about violence and crime in the city. At one time the target of an investigation into the death of a boy who died after being beaten by Kello, the Lieutenant was rescued from dismissal by Hunsecker, who used his influence on Kello's behalf.

Here is the Twenty-One Club scene from Lehman's draft in full and with the original character and place names.[10]

DRAMATIC CONSTRUCTION

INT. ENTRANCE – CLUB FIFTY-SEVEN – NIGHT

A toney club-restaurant. We start on RITA, *a hat check girl with an insolent shape in a provocative black dress, as she steps forward saying:*

> RITA
>
> Sidney . . .?

Then we see Sidney, moving past her toward the dining room without hearing, lost in his own troubles. A captain, GEORGE, *steps in his path, blocks him.*

> GEORGE
> *(coolly)*
>
> Yes, Mr Wallace?

> SIDNEY
>
> What do you mean, 'Yes, Mr Wallace?' I'm going in to his table. I have to see him.

> GEORGE
>
> I'm sorry. I'll have to find out if he . . . wishes to be disturbed.

> SIDNEY
> *(an unbelieving smile)*
>
> George! You're kidding. This is *me* – Sidney.

> GEORGE
> *(who isn't kidding)*
>
> Will you wait here, please.

As George starts away:

> SIDNEY
> *(annoyed)*
>
> Yeah – I'll wait here please.

He takes put a cigarette, lights it. Rita comes up to him.

> RITA
>
> Sidney . . .

SIDNEY
(*without turning*)

Hiya, honey.

RITA

Did you get any of my messages? I've been calling you.

SIDNEY
(*impatiently*)

Sweetie, I've been up to here.

RITA
(*low*)

I'm in trouble, Sidney.

SIDNEY
(*throwing her a glance*)

Again?

RITA
(*shakes her head*)

Not that. It's . . . it's about Otis Elwell.

SIDNEY

That point-killer.
(*he turns away*)

Go ahead. I'm listening.

But with only half an ear, because as Rita talks, he cranes his neck, looking toward the dining room, looking for George.

RITA

Well, last week he told me he was planning to do a column of hat check girls, and would I mind been interviewed, and of course I was thrilled and I said any time at all. So he said how about eleven o'clock in the morning at his apartment . . .

SIDNEY
(*bored*)

Go on.

So I went up there at eleven o'clock in the morning and
it turns out that *Mrs* Elwell is away at Fire Island for
that day and, I mean, after all – eleven o'clock in the
morning. I never dreamt . . . I mean he writes such an
innocent sort of column and he's such a distinguished
looking gentleman and he's not very *young* . . .

(*Sidney throws her a glance*)

I didn't expect . . . *really* . . . eleven o'clock in the morning . . . I was so taken aback I said some terrible things
to him and he got furious and ordered me out of the
apartment and said he was going to have the boss fire
me, and I've been so worried I can hardly think straight.
You think he can do a thing like that, Sidney? You think
he'll make up some kind of a story and have me fired?
He's in there with his wife in the main dining room . . .

Before Sidney has a chance to say anything, George appears.

GEORGE
Mr Hunsecker said it would be all right for you to join
him. Follow me please.

SIDNEY
(*coldly*)
Well, thank you, George.

He starts away.

RITA
But, Sidney . . .

SIDNEY
(*stops, turns*)
Honey – you *worry* too much.

*He goes towards the main dining room, turns right and enters a
small private dining room.*

INT. PRIVATE DINING ROOM

Camera moves with Sidney to a round table where HARVEY

HUNSECKER *is seated with two rather frightened-looking men in evening clothes and a pretty young girl. Hunsecker is in the middle of a monologue as Sidney arrives, and the others are listening, too intently. As Sidney sits down, Hunsecker does not stop talking, nor do the others dare to stop listening.*

> HUNSECKER
> (*harshly*)

. . . But what he *didn't* say is that what you read in *his* column was a *denial* of the *whole thing*! Sure *he* had it a week before I did! But *he* had it *all wrong*. Like he *always* does!

> (*wearily*)

Ah, why do I let these garbage-peddlers bother me? They're nothing but fleas buzzing around a tiger. I waste my strength, my energy, worrying about fleas, there'll be nothing left to fight the dragons with. Hunsecker has to stay healthy. Hunsecker fights the world. And he does it alone. Ask Sidney here. *He* knows. *Don't* you, Sidney? Most press agents are rag dolls. Press them and they say mama. But not Sidney here. Press him and he says Hunsecker. Sidney, say Hunsecker for the young lady.

> (*to one of the men*)

What did you say her name was?

> MAN

Linda Hall

> HUNSECKER
> (*to the girl*)

Movies? Stage? TV?

> MAN
> (*before she can answer*)

Well, actually, Harvey . . .

> HUNSECKER
> (*to Sidney*)

Take her name down, Sidney. Linda Hall.

> GIRL
> (*quickly*)

What for?

SIDNEY *sits tight-lipped, motionless.*

> HUNSECKER
> Take the name down, tootsie.
> > (*to the girl*)
> Do you play gin, honey? Sidney does. Sidney, tell the
> young lady who won seventy-eight dollars from whom
> the other night, at this very table. But he can afford it.
> Look at that two-hundred dollar suit and that thirty
> dollar monogrammed shirt. He must know the right
> people. It's spelled with an 'H'. Right, Sidney?
> > (*turning to the others*)
> A story. True one. Happened last week. Four press
> agents sitting in my outer office waiting to see me, hats
> in hand, hungry for plugs. Suddenly they see a cock-
> roach crawling across the floor toward my office. One
> of the press agents springs to his feet, screams: 'Hey!
> Get in line!'

*The girl and the two men laugh with embarrassment. Sidney
reaches for a glass of water. Quickly, Hunsecker places a cigarette between his own lips and snaps his fingers. Sidney puts the
water down untouched, and lights his cigarette for him.*

> HUNSECKER
> > (*blowing smoke*)
> Doesn't he do that beautifully?

*As Sidney reaches for the glass of water again, Hunsecker drops
the cigarette into it.*

> HUNSECKER
> I smoke too much.
> > (*to the girl*)
> I don't think Sidney likes you, Miss Linda Hall. He
> hasn't taken your name down, as I asked him to.

*The others look at each other nervously, aware of the growing
tension.*

MAN
(*getting to his feet*)
Harvey – I think we're going to have to be running
along now . . .

The girl and the other man quickly rise.

HUNSECKER
If you should run into that dirty paragraph-stealer
during the course of your nocturnal wanderings, feel
perfectly free to tell him exactly what I think of him.

MAN
You bet we will, Harvey.

SECOND MAN
Goodnight, Mr Hunsecker.

GIRL
Goodnight, Mr Hunsecker.

HUNSECKER
(*pointing at her*)
You I like.

She hurries away with her escorts.

But *you* here –
(*he looks at Sidney*)
– are something *else* again. *Sulking*! Like a *child*!

SIDNEY
(*wearily*)
All right, you've had your fun, Harvey. I don't mind.
I'm used to it. But nobody's listening now, so let's not
play games, please –

HUNSECKER
Stop whining, Sidney.

SIDNEY
– I just want to know what happened to the column
tonight.

HUNSECKER
(*looking away*)

Suppose *you* tell *me*.

SIDNEY

The plugs, Harvey. My *stuff*. Where *was* it?

HUNSECKER
(*examining his finger nails*)

The column ran long. I did some judicious pruning.

SIDNEY
(*voice rising*)

I already took the *bows*, Harvey! *This afternoon*!
Robard! Lilly Werner! Sam Weldon! I called Finn
Welbeck on the Coast and told him to expect a
whole paragraph on the *picture*! What am I going to say
to these people? How am I going to explain?

HUNSECKER
(*turning on him*)

Tell them you have a weakness for making promises you
can't keep! Maybe they will *forgive* you this weakness,
Sidney! But not *me*! Not any more! From this date on,
you're out of the column until you keep your promises
to *me*! Unless something is done about Susan and that
sickening boy!

SIDNEY
(*quickly*)

I told you, it's just a summer romance. It'll fade like the
autumn leaves.

HUNSECKER
(*obsessed*)

She smells of love! I can't even go near her any more!
The stink of that lousy dago crooner is all over her like
cheap perfume!

SIDNEY
(*uneasily*)

You're getting yourself all worked up over nothing.

HUNSECKER

Nothing! That's *right*! A *cheap dago nothing* with the
sister of Hunsecker, and *you* sit here talking of summer
romance and autumn leaves and begging for plugs for
your crummy accounts!

SIDNEY

Not begging. Asking. I have a right.

HUNSECKER

Might makes right! The *column* makes right! *I* have the
right, not you! I have the right to tell you I want an *end*
to it! *Finished*! Kaput!

SIDNEY

I'm doing everything I can.

HUNSECKER

It's not enough!

SIDNEY

What do you want me to *do* to him?

HUNSECKER

Harry Kello owes me a favour! I've scratched his back!

SIDNEY
(*frightened*)
No, Harvey! Not Kello!

HUNSECKER

Then use your *imagination*! You seem to have a pretty
good one when it comes to thinking up ways of using
me and the column to get yourself high on the hog!
(*suddenly he covers his face with his hands*)
I don't want to talk about this any more. I've said all
there is be said. No wonder I get sick. No wonder I get
tired . . .

SIDNEY

Look, Harvey –

HUNSECKER
(*uncovers his face, screams*)

No more! Not another word!
> (*He covers his face again, mumbles*)
Go away, Sidney. Please . . . I beg of you . . . go away . . .

As we can see in Lehman's original draft, Sidney is initially refused access to the restaurant by the maître d'. Odets, however, thought that the rejection had to come directly from Hunsecker himself. Lehman also introduces Rita, the cigarette girl, to fill in the time while Hunsecker is consulted by the maître d'. The subplot of Rita is a plant for the idea that Sidney gets later (persuading Rita to sleep with Otis Elwell). The Odets version places this scene earlier in the story.

Lehman has introduced three subsidiary characters at Hunsecker's table: two men and a pretty girl. They are useful as an audience for Hunsecker's monologue, but not much more. We see below how Odets has seized on Lehman's suggestions but has made more use of these foil figures, developing them as characters with a subplot of their own. In Lehman's draft, once Sidney is sitting at the table, it appears he has come to Hunsecker to ask what J. J. is doing to him and why. As a move in the story this is really rather weak as he seems to have prepared no coherent moves of his own. Sidney must surely be shrewd enough to know what Hunsecker's motives are, and would not confront Hunsecker (certainly not publicly) unless he has brought some ammunition himself, which he has done in Odets's version below. First is the bad news that Dallas has proposed to Susan. Second, Sidney has already worked out a method of solving this problem, one he intends to put into effect. He needs only the promise from Hunsecker that he will be rewarded.

Study the excerpt from Odets's version. What he has done is present us with active exposition. The entire subplot of the Senator, the Girl and the Agent is a practical demonstration of the real power of this scandal-sheet columnist Hunsecker, someone seen to be a genuinely dangerous individual. You will see that a page or so of dialogue can be lifted out to form a very brief little mini-drama of its own (Hunsecker's unmasking of the Agent as a procurer, for the Senator, of this would-be actress). It

11. From the published script (pp. 36–51), which differs slightly from the film.

contains a plot, exposition and even a climax within the larger structure of the manipulative and mutual blackmail relationships of the two principals (Hunsecker and the press agent Sidney Falco). Note that this is the only scene in the script where the Senator, the Girl, and Agent appear.

Note too that though in Lehman's draft (as in Odets's too), Hunsecker's insane jealousy at the love affair between Susan and Steve is a plot point, his self-pity and self-indulgence weaken his character as an antagonist. In both the Lehman version and the Odets rewrite, Hunsecker is characterised as paranoid, absurdly vain and egotistical, though in some speeches in Lehman's draft ('I waste my strength, my energy, worrying about fleas, there'll be nothing left to fight the dragons with') he seems to be somewhat childish, altogether unaware of how others react to him. Odets's main criticism of the original scene as written was that no one could take seriously a man so whimperingly weak. In the Odets draft, Hunsecker is no less of an egomaniac but a good deal more shrewd, less self-pitying and complete with a sadistic sense of humour. Note too how in Lehman's version Sidney refers to characters ('Robard! Lilly Werner! Sam Weldon!') we have not met and never will meet. In principle this is weak writing. Character names are valuable to the audience only after they have actually seen the character to whom the names refer. For the same reason, Sidney's frightened reaction at the mention of Harry Kello has little dramatic effect in Lehman's version.

Here is the Twenty-One Club scene from Odets's draft (without details of the camera angles). Unlike in Lehman's version, Sidney has no trouble gaining access to the restaurant.[11]

INT. TWENTY-ONE CLUB – NIGHT

Sidney, entering the club, threads his way through the crowded foyer, coming up to camera near the foot of the staircase. There he meets a Captain who turns to him.

CAPTAIN
How are *you* tonight, Mr Falco?

SIDNEY
(*nodding towards the restaurant*)
Is 'he' inside?

CAPTAIN:

But of course . . .

SIDNEY

Alone or surrounded?

CAPTAIN

A senator, an agent and something – with – long – red – hair.

He pauses. (REVERSE ANGLE) *From Sidney's viewpoint. Shooting through the doorway into the restaurant, we can see the group at the table. (Hunsecker's back is turned to us.) Camera pulls back to include Sidney in foreground. He decides not to go into restaurant and turns away out of shot.*

INT. LOUNGE

Sidney comes round the corner from the foyer and walks through the lounge to the door into the alcove where the phone booths are. Sidney moves briskly past the girl at the switchboard, instructing her:

SIDNEY

Honey, get me Mr Hunsecker.

The girl reaches for a book of phone numbers, then remembers:

OPERATOR

He's right inside, Mr Falco.

SIDNEY
(from inside the booth)

So it isn't long distance.

As the girl, shrugging, puts through the call, camera moves closer to Sidney in the booth. He hears the connection made, speaks at once.

J. J., it's Sidney. Can you come outside for one minute?

Hunsecker's voice, filtered through the sound of the telephone, is sharp and tinny; but the words are now very clear.

Opposite: From *Sweet
Smell of Success*
(1957).

HUNSECKER'S VOICE
Can I come out? No.

SIDNEY
(*tensely*)
I have to talk to you, alone, J. J., that's why.

HUNSECKER'S VOICE
You had something to do for me – you didn't do it.

SIDNEY
Can I come in for a minute?

HUNSECKER'S VOICE
No. You're dead, son – get yourself buried!

*There is a click as Hunsecker hangs up. Sidney, more slowly, also
hangs up. Brooding, he comes out of the booth.*

INT. TWENTY-ONE CLUB. LOUNGE

*Sidney comes out of the door to the phone booths, walks through
the lounge to the hallway. He turns toward the dining room.*

INT. HALLWAY

*Sidney comes to the door into the dining room, camera tracking
with him. Here he pauses, looking towards* HUNSECKER, *who is
seated at a table which is clearly his habitual position. We see
him only in semi-back view, a broad and powerful back. He is
listening to a man who has paused at his table, stooping over
Hunsecker to whisper in his ear. As the columnist listens, his
hands play with an omnipresent pad and pencil which lie on the
dinner table amongst an assortment of envelopes, mimeographed sheets and a telephone. Beyond Hunsecker and the man
talking to him are the Senator, the Agent, and an attractive, if
fatuous Girl.*

HUNSECKER
I'll check it in the morning, Lew – thanks.

*The man leaves; Hunsecker is scribbling a note on the pad.
Meanwhile the Senator whispers something to the Girl, who
giggles softly. Sidney comes across to the table, nervous but*

DENSITY AND SUBPLOTS IN SWEET SMELL OF SUCCESS   145

deliberate. Sidney, without accosting him, stands a few feet from the columnist's elbow and deliberately lights a cigarette. Hunsecker, barely turning his head, sees him. We have heard of Hunsecker as a monster, but he is evidently in a mild phase of his metabolism, for he seems gentle, sad and quiet, as he turns his gaze casually to the Senator, totally ignoring the young man who stands behind him.

HUNSECKER
(softly)

Harvey, I often wish I were deaf and wore a hearing aid . . . with a simply flick of a switch I could shut out the greedy murmur of little men . . .

Sidney shows no reaction to this insult. He steps in closer, an Indian fixity in his face.

SIDNEY

J. J., I need your ear for two minutes . . .

J. J. turns – but not to Sidney. He raises his hand in a small gesture which summons a passing Captain, who steps into picture at Sidney's elbow.

HUNSECKER

Mac! I don't want this man at my table . . .

SIDNEY
(quickly but quietly interrupting)

I have a message from your sister.

The Captain is already there. But now Hunsecker's eyes have switched to Sidney's face. For the briefest of moments, nothing happens. Then Hunsecker, seeming to relax and ignoring the Captain whom he has summoned, turns back to casual conversation with the Senator as if nothing had happened.

HUNSECKER

Forgive me, Harvey. We were interrupted before –

In foreground, Sidney turns to the Captain with a carved smile, indicated that Hunsecker's change of topic is to be interpreted as sanction for Sidney to remain. The Captain, not entirely con-

*vinced, retreats. Sidney finds himself a chair, places it and takes a
seat which is near enough to the table to establish his presence.
During this:*

> SENATOR
> (*who is mildly surprised and faintly embarrassed*)
> Err . . . the Supreme Court story, I was telling you –
> Justice Black.

> HUNSECKER
> (*nodding*)
> Yes, the Justice, that's right. But I think I had it in the
> column.

> SIDNEY
> (*smoothly, casually*)
> Last July, the lead item . . .

*Sidney's interjection is quietly well-mannered. Hunsecker totally
ignores it. The other members of the party are a little astonished
at the interplay. The Girl, in particular, is fascinated; she clearly
admires Sidney's looks. The Senator, noting this, glances at
Sidney, accepting the point.*

> SENATOR
> (*laughing*)
> And I believe that's precisely where I read it, too. You
> see, J. J., where I get my reputation from for being the
> best-informed man in Washington.

> HUNSECKER
> Now don't kid a kidder.

*The Girl looks again towards Sidney. The Senator again sees this,
addresses Sidney pleasantly.*

> SENATOR
> I don't think we caught your name, young man.

> SIDNEY
> Sidney Falco, sir. And, of course, everyone knows and
> admires *you*, Senator Walker.

(*humorously*)
Every four years I get less convinced of that. This young
lady is Miss Linda James.
(*indicates the Girl*)
She's managed by Manny Davis.
(*he indicates the Agent*)
Sidney nods pleasantly to the Girl and the Agent.

SIDNEY
I know Manny Davis.

HUNSECKER
(*quietly*)
Everyone knows Manny Davis . . .
(*as the phone rings on the table*)
. . . except *Mrs* Manny Davis.

Hunsecker is picking up the phone, continuing:

Yes? Go ahead, Billy – shoot . . .

*The Senator, the Agent and the Girl are watching Hunsecker. The
Agent's reaction to Hunsecker's remark is a sickly smile. Hunsecker
repeats aloud a story which is told him over the telephone.*

Uh huh. Sports cars in California are getting smaller and
smaller . . . the other day you were crossing Hollywood
Boulevard and you were hit by one . . . you had to go to
the hospital and have it removed . . .
(*coolly*)
You're not following the column: I had it last week.

SIDNEY
Do you believe in capital punishment, Senator?

SENATOR
(*amused*)
Why?

Sidney glances sidelong at Hunsecker.

SIDNEY
(*pointing to the phone*)

A man has just been sentenced to death . . .

Hunsecker's face hardens; aware of Sidney's impertinence, he does not deign to react directly; he turns toward the Agent.

> HUNSECKER
> Manny, what exactly are the unseen gifts of this lovely young thing that you manage . . .?

The Agent glances uneasily at the Girl beside him.

> AGENT
> Well, she sings a little . . . you know, sings . . .

> GIRL
> *(by rote)*
> Manny's faith in me is simply awe-inspiring, Mr Hunsecker. Actually, I'm still studying, but –

Hunsecker studies the Girl intently.

> HUNSECKER
> What subject?

> GIRL
> Singing, of course . . . straight concert and –

Hunsecker's glance flicks between the Girl and the Senator.

> HUNSECKER
> Why 'of course'? It might, for instance, be politics . . .

The Girl betrays herself with a nervous glance at the Senator beside her. The Senator is unruffled; gravely, he lights a cigar. The Girl laughs.

> GIRL
> Me? I mean 'I'? Are you kidding, Mr Hunsecker? With my Jersey City brains?

Again his glance links the Girl and the Senator.

> HUNSECKER
> The brains may be Jersey City, but the clothes are Trainor-Norell.

The Girl and the Agent are both nervously uneasy. The Senator closely examines the tip of his cigar and, with deliberation, turns toward Sidney.

SENATOR
Are you an actor, Mr Falco?

GIRL
(*supporting the change of subject*)
That's what *I* was thinking. *Are* you, Mr Falco?

Hunsecker, for the first time, half-turns in Sidney's direction, amused.

HUNSECKER
How did you guess it, Miss James?

They all look at Sidney.

GIRL
He's so pretty, that's how.

Sidney bitterly resents the adjective, but contrives to hide the fact; he smiles, gracefully accepting the compliment. Hunsecker (who knows what Sidney feels) is pleased; he turns toward Sidney expansively.

HUNSECKER
Mr Falco, let it be said at once, is a man of forty faces, not one, none too pretty and all deceptive. See that grin? It's the charming street urchin's face. It's part of his 'helpless' act – he throws himself on your mercy. I skip the pleading nervous bit that sometimes blends over into bluster. The moist grateful eye is a favorite face with him – it frequently ties in with the act of boyish candor: he's talking straight from the heart, get it? He's got about half a dozen faces for the ladies, but the real cute one to me is the quick dependable chap – nothing he won't do for you in a pinch. At least, so he says! Tonight Mr Falco, whom I did not invite to sit at this table, is about to show in his last and most pitiful role: pale face with tongue hanging out. In brief, gentlemen and Jersey Lilly, the boy sitting with us is a hungry

DRAMATIC CONSTRUCTION

press agent and fully up on all the tricks of his very
slimy trade!

*Hunsecker has started his speech lightly, but it has built up to
enough cold contempt and feeling to embarrass and intimidate
the others at the table. In conclusion, Hunsecker, his eyes on
Sidney, picks up a cigarette and waits expectantly . . .*

HUNSECKER
(*quietly*)

Match me, Sidney . . .

SIDNEY
(*coolly*)

Not just this minute, J. J. . . .

*A florid man comes up to the table, obviously anxious to catch
Hunsecker's attention. Hunsecker, in the act of lighting his own
cigarette, scarcely looks at the man as he dismisses him:*

HUNSECKER

I know – that loafer of yours opens at the Latin Quarter
next week.

(*more sharply*)

Say goodbye, Lester!

*The florid man retreats. To cover the embarrassment, the
Senator makes a sally in Sidney's direction.*

SENATOR

May I ask a naive question, Mr Falco? Exactly how
does a press agent work . . .?

Sidney doesn't answer.

HUNSECKER

Why don't you answer the man, Sidalee? He's trying to
take you off the hook.

SIDNEY
(*to the Senator*)

You just had a good example of it. A press agent eats a
columnist's dirt and is expected to call it manna.

GIRL

What's manna?

Hunsecker glances spitefully at the Girl.

HUNSECKER

Heaven dust.

The Senator continues to Sidney:

SENATOR

But don't you help columnists by furnishing them with items?

Sidney leans forward, indicating to the Senator some of the items of paper that litter the table in front of Hunsecker; these are both handwritten notes and mimeographed sheets, scraps of assorted items from professional and amateur agents who supply the columnist. Sidney fingers some of them.

SIDNEY

Sure, columnists can't get along without us. Only our good and great friend, J. J., forgets to mention that. We furnish him with items –

Sidney lifts a mimeographed sheet, as an example.

HUNSECKER

What, some cheap, gruesome gags?

SIDNEY
(*to Hunsecker now*)
You print them, don't you?

HUNSECKER

Yes, with your client's names attached. That's the only reason those poor slobs pay you – to see their names in my column all over the world! Now, as I make it out, you're doing *me* a favour!

SIDNEY

I didn't say that, J. J.

HUNSECKER

The day that I can't get along without press agents'

handouts, I'll close up shop, lock, stock and barrel and move to Alaska.

The Agent makes the mistake of trying to agree with Hunsecker.

> AGENT
> (*nodding*)
> Sweep out my igloo, here I come.

Hunsecker vents upon the unfortunate Agent some of the annoyance prompted by Sidney's impertinence.

> HUNSECKER
> (*to the Agent*)
> Look Manny, you rode in here on the Senator's shirt-tails, so shut your mouth!

The Senator doesn't like this treatment of others and his manner and face show it.

> SENATOR
> (*slowly*)
> Now, come J. J., that's a little too harsh. Anyone seems fair game for you tonight.

> HUNSECKER
> (*not as harsh, but –*)
> This man is not for you, Harvey, and you shouldn't be seen with him in public. Because that's another part of the press agent's life – he digs up scandal among prominent men and shovels it thin among the columnists who give him space.

The Senator finds Hunsecker's manner disturbing, but addresses him frontally.

> SENATOR
> There is some allusion here that escapes me . . .

> HUNSECKER
> (*an edge of threat*)
> We're friends, Harvey – we go as far back as when you were a fresh kid congressman, don't we?

SENATOR

Why does everything you say sound like a threat?

Hunsecker leans back, speaking more quietly, enjoying himself.

HUNSECKER

Maybe it's a mannerism – because I don't threaten
friends, Harvey. But why furnish your enemies with
ammunition? You're a family man. Someday, with God
willing, you may wanna be President. Now here you
are, Harvey, out in the open where any hep person
knows that this one . . .

Hunsecker leans into shot pointing directly at the Agent.

. . . is touting *that* one . . .

Hunsecker points to the Girl.

. . . around for *you* . . .

*Now Hunsecker is directly challenging the Senator. He smiles
disarmingly.*

. . . Are we kids or what? . . .

*Hunsecker rises. As he stands up, Sidney follows suit. The Agent,
very nervous, gets to his feet and the Girl does likewise. The
Senator, whose face is sober, also rises from the table.*

HUNSECKER
(*to the Senator, affably*)

Next time you come up, you might join me at my TV
show.

*With Sidney making way for him, Hunsecker walks round the
end of the table to the Senator. The Senator faces Hunsecker
solemnly.*

SENATOR
(*quietly and cautiously*)

Thank you, J. J., for what I consider sound advice.

Hunsecker matches the Senator's solemnity.

HUNSECKER
(*deadpan*)
Go, thou, and sin no more.

There are many things to notice when comparing the two drafts. For example, Sidney's four-line interaction with the maître d' helps establish the characters of the two men and probably of Hunsecker too, while the line 'something – with – long – red – hair' tells us something about the character of the Girl. Sidney's rudeness to the telephone girl is in character, as he is apt to be as impolite to his inferiors as he is flattering to those he needs. (It is also an indication of his anxiousness at meeting J. J.). Sidney's decision that he would rather not speak to Hunsecker in the company of others suggests what later emerges, that Sidney has ammunition for the confrontation to come. As far as the audience goes, hearing Hunsecker on the telephone before seeing him is a tease in delaying the entrance of the chief antagonist of the story.

When the build-up of a confrontation has been this elaborate, it is necessary to deliver some strong conflict immediately. Thus the scene begins with a very direct skirmish between the two men once Sidney starts talking to Hunsecker. Sidney is in danger of being thrown out of the club when he decides to plays his ace (the information concerning Susan). Note, however, that once this card has been played (once a fuse has been lit and a show-down promised), Odets can take an extravagant amount of time before coming to the point (Sidney telling Hunsecker about Susan being engaged), something that comes only several script pages later.

Think also about the joke that Hunsecker tells about sports cars in California. In Lehman's script, Hunsecker tells a joke that is somewhat crude and not all that funny. The incident is not meant as comedy, rather as characterisation: vulgar gags are indeed part of the stock in trade of tabloid columnists. But Odets takes the point a little further, for while the mildly dirty joke is included in his draft for the same purpose, its unfunni-ness is emphasised by the fact that only the sycophantic agent laughs.

Soon after comes a good example of triangulation. Sidney addresses his line 'A man has just been sentenced to death' to the

12. From the published
script, pp. 35–6.

Senator in order to needle Hunsecker in revenge for the fact that earlier Sidney also had been 'sentenced to death'. Note how, throughout the whole scene, a ricochet effect is achieved: a line is delivered to one person, but for the benefit of a third party. This triangulation is what gives density to the interaction.

When Hunsecker does finally start his move (his attack on the Senator), it is with the line 'What exactly are the unseen gifts of this lovely young thing that you manage?' The non-reaction of the Senator is the signal to us that he knows very well where Hunsecker is going. This is marvellous screenwriting, as it offers the director the chance to show through editing and camera angles that the significance of the scene is in what is being implied, not said (specifically in the way the characters avoid eye contact). Inevitably, the Senator's strategy of defence is to change the subject, and he is successful in this because Hunsecker cannot resist the chance to exploit Sidney's humiliation at being called an actor. (All press agents are apt to despise the performers who are their clients.) There follows another good example of the ricochet technique, with Hunsecker's lines about the 'hungry press agent', though directed to the three people sitting opposite him at the table, playing strongly on Sidney's reactions.

When the Senator asks Sidney about his job, it is for expository purposes. The lines explaining the relationship of the press agent and the columnist are elaborations of the things that Jim Hill, as producer, said to Odets during our story conferences. But Odets not only employs the Senator as foil, he also provides the answers through an acrimonious quarrel between Sidney and Hunsecker. Hunsecker's anger at Sidney, based on another totally separate matter, is then switched to a vicious attack on the Agent. These abrupt shifts of emotion are what makes Hunsecker dangerous. However, when at the climax of the scene he moves in for the kill, he is at his most gentle and sincere. Here Odets is finally delivering the promise of a long and slow build-up to the man who 'can tell Presidents what to do'. As Odets explained to me, with his line 'Are we kids or what?' Hunsecker switches back to being humorous and charming because he has 'just tasted blood'.

In scene after scene, Odets helps build density within the script as a whole, for example playing out a short interaction between

Sidney and Jimmy Weldon, one of his clients, just before he enters the Twenty-One Club. Here, an entire drama is created in only two pages (also with camera angles omitted).[12]

EXT. TWENTY-ONE CLUB – NIGHT (DUSK)

Sidney slips through the congestion, but just as he tries to enter the club, Weldon's hand shoots out, neatly ambushing him, pulling him aside into the narrow courtyard. Sidney is instantly resentful of this manhandling, but has to adjust himself, assuming a quick smile for the benefit of Weldon.

> SIDNEY
>
> Jimmy! This *is* a coincidence. I am just going –

> WELDON
> (*overlapping*)
>
> Yeah. A coincidence you should run into the very man you've been ducking all week!
> (*to the girl*)
> This is my press agent, Joan.

Weldon, jibing at Sidney, plays his remarks off the girl, who is amused; Sidney, of course, is not.

> SIDNEY
> (*quickly*)
>
> I tried to reach you twice –

> WELDON
> (*overlapping*)
>
> What do you do for that hundred a week. Fall out of bed?

> SIDNEY
>
> Jimmy, I'm on my way inside right now to talk to Hunsecker. I can promise you –

> WELDON
> (*horsing*)
>
> Joan, call a cop! We'll arrest this kid for larceny!

Sidney flinches, his pride touched.

SIDNEY

Listen, when your band was playing at Roseland –

WELDON

(*cutting in*)

That was two months ago. Take your hand out of my pocket, thief!

The girl tries to quiet Weldon, who has gone from horsing to loud contempt.

THE GIRL

Take it easy, Jimmy dear . . .

WELDON

(*indignantly*)

Why? It's a dirty job, but I pay clean money for it, don't I?

Abruptly Sidney bursts out, giving as good as he has taken.

SIDNEY

No more you don't! What is this – You're showing off for her? They're supposed to hear you in Korea?

WELDON

(*smirking to the girl*)

He's intuitive – he knows he's getting fired!

SIDNEY

If you're funny, James, I'm a pretzel! Drop dead!

Weldon, shepherded by the girl, is already on his way across the sidewalk.

WELDON

It was nice knowing you, Sidney. Not cheap – but nice. Happy unemployment insurance.

Though Weldon is mentioned in Lehman's version, Odets makes much more effective use of the character. When Sidney returns to his office in the second scene of the film, Sally is speaking to a 'Mr Weldon' on the phone. Sidney signals to her that he doesn't want to take the call. By having Weldon actually fire Sidney on the steps of the club just before Sidney is about to confront Hunsecker, dramatic tension is increased as Sidney is now much more desperate. Note also the use of the girl with Weldon who functions as a foil. Weldon's attack on Sidney is more humiliating in front of a witness, and by having Weldon address to her lines that are meant for his press agent, Odets is effectively using her to bounce lines.

One of the elements Odets retained from Lehman's draft is the story of the comedian Herbie Temple and the confidence trick Sidney plays on him. Discovering that the gossip column for next day's edition contains a plug for the comedian, Sidney calls on Herbie and offers to persuade his columnist friend to include an item, even going through the pretence of making a phone call to his office instead of the newspaper. The incident is a complete subplot in itself (seen to pay off in a later encounter with the comedian), and again adds density to the narrative as a whole. Though the scene (along with others in the final film) could be eliminated without serious damage to the main action of the story as a whole, its value is obvious. While the encounter with Herbie does not do much more than further illustrate Sidney's devious methods, it does show him successful in his chicanery and provides some relief from the picture of the young man who is so at the mercy of his co-conspirator, J. J. Hunsecker.

Cutting Dialogue

When I started out working in a London studio I wasn't very good at writing dialogue. Because of this I had to devise methods of communicating my ideas through visual means, something that got me a break just when the film industry in Britain was expanding, and very quickly (absurdly, if you must know) won me the reputation of being very good at cutting dialogue.

My first job in the film industry was as a very junior contract writer in the script department of a British studio. Screenwriters with established reputations were at that time hired by the studios on a freelance basis for individually negotiated deals. These were usually renewable on the option of the studios with six weeks allocated to each draft. The studios might ask for two or three drafts, with the final one a fairly close collaboration between the screenwriter and the director. But it was always understood that the studio was free to assign a new writer at any point in the process. Contract writers, who had a lower status, were on regular salaries and were expected to work on any subject assigned to them. The contract writer, in this sense, was much more of a hack. He didn't get a screen credit and was likely to be given the task of doing draft rewrites of other scenes, bits of carpentry proposed by either the producer or the director. The whole thing was, for me, marvellously good experience, and one of the things I find regrettable about the film industry today is that this sort of training ground for beginning writers no longer exists.

I have a story to tell of an early experience. I do so with slight embarrassment, since it probably does me little credit, but it does at least illustrate a point. Shortly after I had been put under contract, the studio started developing a story that was meant as a musical of sorts. The storyline was unremarkable, dealing with the marital problems of a very young couple.[1] To work on these scenes, the producer had hired a well-known British playwright. One scene involved a situation with the young wife who, while shopping, runs into a man with whom she had had an affair before she met her husband. Reminding her that she had left something (a pair of skates, as I recall) in his apartment, he takes her back there and, with practised charm, makes an attempt to seduce her. Being rejected, he accepts the situation with grace.

It was not a scene of any great originality, and possibly because of this the writer put a great deal of effort into making it as fresh, sensitive and original as he could. The result was a beautifully crafted piece of work. But it was twenty-five pages long, and the producer and director were much dismayed. They saw it as a one-act play in its own right that would badly interrupt the progression of a film really intended as just a sequence of musical numbers. The playwright, a thorough professional, recognised this problem. But when invited to cut it down, he discovered he was not able to reduce it by more than three or four pages, and even those cuts were painful to him. He gladly agreed to let some other screenwriter tackle the job.

The second writer assigned was much more experienced in writing for film. One of the so-called rules of thumb at our studios in that period was that no scene in a film ought to be much longer than six or eight pages (four or five was what to aim for). This new writer was much impressed with the original scene (unlike most screenwriters, who always seem to discover flaws in the work of others) and worked hard on the cuts, even to the point of some drastic alterations of the original scene structure. But when she came back with a scene that was still a dozen pages in length, she had to confess she did not know how it could be further reduced without completely wrecking it. Producer and director felt they were in serious trouble. In some desperation, they remembered that the studio had on its payroll a young man who had been given his first job in the script department not because he was accomplished in writing dialogue, but because he compensated by using certain skills learned when he had been an illustrator and cartoonist. They handed the problem to me.

'How short do you want it?' I asked. 'Just cut it down as much as you can,' they said. I was impressed with the dialogue of both

1. The film Mackendrick is writing about here is *Dance Hall*, directed by Charles Crichton in 1950.

previous versions, well aware that it was better than I could ever do. Quite nervous, I spent a whole day in very careful analysis not of the lines of the dialogue but of the structure of the scene. I thought about the characters, I tried to define their feelings and impulses. I marked the beats of the scene, the identifiable moves, the shifts of intention and changes in mood. I also studied the placement of the scene within the story as a whole. Then, still highly insecure, I decided to go out and just forget about the problem. This, in fact, is for me a standard procedure. When a writing dilemma appears insoluble, it is not a bad tactic to push it deliberately out of your consciousness while you go off on other business, or indeed play. Find companions who will talk with you on other matters. Play a game of tennis. Go to a concert. Go for a long walk. Get drunk. Any preoccupation that, by preventing exercise of thought, pushes the problem down into your sub-, or at least semi-conscious mind. Then, just before going to sleep, briefly recapitulate the unsolved dilemma in your mind.

What happened to me was what happens to many of us who use this method. I was jogged into wakefulness in the very early hours by an idea that seemed rather preposterous. I got up at dawn and wrote a first draft. Then, after breakfast, I polished it a little and took it in to the studio. With some trepidation I gave it to the typists of the script department. These young ladies are very wise in the politics of the studio and I was not much reassured to hear them in fits of giggles just after I had closed the door on them. An hour later I was summoned to a meeting with the head of the script department. As I approached his room I heard more laughter. All too conscious that my contract was up for renewal, I entered to find that the producer, director and head of the script department were all there, all involved in the hilarity. Sobering up, the director told me that I had solved the problem and that he would shoot the scene precisely as I had written it.

I should describe my apparently brilliant solution and scintillating dialogue. The scene opens in the empty apartment of the would-be seducer. As he enters, he carries the shopping basket of the young wife that he rapidly discards, and moves toward a record player. By the time the young woman has appeared in the

DRAMATIC CONSTRUCTION

doorway, looking round the room that clearly holds some memories for her, music has begun to play, emphasising those recollections. The man moves over to her, saying nothing, and offers to help her with her overcoat. With only the slightest of hesitations, the young wife lets him take it, and he deposits it in a chair next to the side table on which he starts to mix a drink, again without needing to ask her what she wants. Accepting it, she obviously notes he has remembered her tastes. She smiles at him and goes on listening to the gramophone record. But when he joins her, carrying his own drink, he leans close to kiss her lightly on the nape of the neck. She turns quickly, with a small shake of her head.

> YOUNG WIFE
> (*negative inflection*)

Mm-mm.

> WOULD-BE SEDUCER
> (*makes face, questioning*)

Mm-mm?

She looks at him. He looks back at her, and his expression becomes more serious.

> YOUNG WIFE
> (*quietly, with tenderness*)

Mmm-mm.

The seducer accepts the rejection with good grace. He moves away, opens a closet, and after a moment returns to present her with the skates. He is amused but respectful.

> YOUNG WIFE
> (*giving the word several meanings*)

Thank you.

There were two results of this version that consigned to the waste-paper basket the costly efforts of writers with vastly greater talent than my own. The first was that, as played by two actors of considerable ability and naturally appealing personality, the scene worked much better than it may have deserved to, and since the other versions were never seen, nobody could ever tell if they would have played any better. The second was that my contract was renewed and I was privately noted by the Chief Executive of the Studio as a youngster who might eventually be better at directing than at writing. (Years later, I read that Raymond Chandler felt that one of the best dialogue scenes he had ever written in a Hollywood movie contained only one word: 'Uh-huh', spoken three times with different intonations. It is the same anecdote.)

It may be worth reminding students that such wordless scenes are, in some respects, just as challenging to the screenwriter as scenes of snappy and clear dialogue, since they depend on very careful examination of the mute behaviour of the characters, the use of props, and the staging of the action. Such scenes, of course, must also take into account those situations that have preceded it, as well as the entire dramatic structure underlying the film as a whole, an understanding of which must always precede the invention of dialogue. To a strong degree, in cutting these twenty-five pages of dialogue to three non-verbal noises and a single word, I had remained absolutely faithful to the playwright's original story.

The Solomon Exercise

In his book *The Empty Space*, the director Peter Brook writes about a scene in Shakespeare's *Romeo and Juliet*. Brook invites the reader to consider how, if the scene had been written as a screenplay, the dramatist might have replaced a large proportion of the lines with cinematographic images, drastically cutting the dialogue. In Brook's words:

1. *The Empty Space,* pp. 135–6.

[The actors] were asked to select only those words that they could play in a realistic situation, the words that they could use unselfconsciously in a film . . . Then [they] played this as a genuine scene from a modern play full of living pauses – speaking the selected words out loud, but repeating the missing words silently to themselves to find the uneven lengths of the silences. The fragment of scene that emerged would have made good cinema, for the moments of dialogue linked by a rhythm of silences of unequal duration in a film would be sustained by close shots and other silent, related images.[1]

As I see it, this exercise relates closely to what every film director must do when confronted with any text. In making the action playable, the director and his team of collaborators work backwards from the words, retracing the work that the writer has done before the lines of dialogue were even written. Though screenwriters are apt to declare 'In the Beginning is the Word', the truth is that the first step in all dramatic writing is visual. The film-writer's literal sense of imagining is actually the process of creating images in his head. It is the visualising of people, places and activities, out of which comes the impulse for dialogue.

Here is a primitive effort at how I have used ideas taught in the Dramatic Construction class to prepare a version of the biblical story of Solomon. You will recall the tale, found in I Kings, chapter 3, verses 16–28. Two prostitutes come to see Solomon,

King of Israel. The first woman explains how she had given birth to a baby, and that three days later the other woman had also given birth. One night, the first woman explains, the other woman had smothered her own child and replaced the body of the dead baby with the first woman's living child. The second prostitute denies this, saying the dead baby actually belongs to the first woman. To settle the dispute, Solomon calls for a sword with which he will cut the living baby in two, giving one half to each woman. While the first woman thinks this a good idea, the second woman is horrified, and Solomon immediately gives her the baby, knowing full well she must be the child's mother.

At first glance, the false mother is by far the most interesting character. How did she come to 'overlay' (smother) her child? Was she perhaps drunk? The loneliness of the harlots' lives also occurs to me with the line 'there was no stranger with us in the house, save we two in the house' (verse 18). But the line that sticks in the mind is, 'But the other said, Let it be neither mine nor thine, but divide it' (verse 26). Indeed, my first reaction is that no actress could find a way to play such a line without being wholly unbelievable as a character. But it is, of course, the task of the writer and director to find some way of making character-action believable, and as one learns from experience, it is this effort that provides unexpected insights into character. When you do finally discover how to believe in it, the line that at first glance seems unplayable may turn out to be the most important piece of dialogue of all.

So how could she possibly say such a thing? One way to approach this biblical story is to frame it as the practical reporting of a very real incident (one that happens to have become something of a myth). What I decide to do is explore the possible motivations of these characters found in the story's subtext. Through a process of what I call disciplined daydreaming, I let my mind wander on a number of possibilities, but I fix on none of them as I want as many options as possible. Though I am seeking to keep the characters as shifting, changing and nebulous figures, I try all sorts of faces, temperaments and behaviour as colouring for the as yet lifeless characters. I let my imagination explore the life of the two harlots. What is their relationship? It is said that prostitutes so deeply resent their degradation by men that they rely on friendship, companionship, and sometimes sexual intimacy with other women. Would this help explain the venomous attitude of the girl who would prefer to see a child dismembered than have it returned to its real mother?

I sense (at the emotional level, not the analytic) the ferocious malice of this woman who wants a child dismembered. Why? It can only be because she wants to inflict the most horrendous agony and injury on the other prostitute with whom she has shared a brothel. But why the jealousy? Because the other woman is younger, more successful as a whore? Possibly, but I reject this as dramatically undesirable (it's just too obvious). I suspect it might be better to work on the question of guilt at having killed her own baby through, perhaps, drunkenness. If it is the false mother who smothered her own infant, is she projecting her self-hatred onto the other innocent mother?

Again about that line ('Let it be neither mine nor thine, but divide it'). Certainly any woman saying this speech must recognise that it completely condemns her. It proves her guilt, and that is why my first reaction was that it was not a playable line. But now I see a possible solution: play the line as a savage admission of guilt. Play it as a ferocious and defiant reaction to the fact that not only Solomon, but all those present, have seen her for what she is. As I began to sense the dramatic impact of this, I got my first taste of the tone of how to construct the scene dramatically. It began to make me think about the character of the innocent mother, the real mother. How does she feel about her erstwhile companion? They surely know each other well and, even in this dreadful bitterness, the true mother must understand the false mother only too well.

At this point I begin to see that for an effective peripeteia, the scene has to be constructed so that, on the surface at least, the false mother seems the more piteous. The performance of the guilty woman, her show of distress and injury, has to be exceptional. To produce the required shock and peripeteia, we should load the situation so we are expecting and hoping that it is the guilty woman who is the true mother. What will be the shock and revelation in the scene? It is that she is ready to see the infant dismembered because this means revenge on the true mother. This works, and the image that springs to mind is the expression on the face of the guilty woman as she sees in Solomon's eyes, and then in the eyes of everybody else present, how the King has unmasked her. The shock (and it has to be as forceful as we can devise) has to cause a shift in our feelings about the two women. Here again I see the false mother as the more appealing. The more apparently vulnerable at the beginning, the more tragic after the unmasking.

My next thoughts concern Solomon. I have seen him as a stereotype, the all-knowing and all-powerful patriarch with a flowing white beard. Experience warns me that if he is the protagonist, then this characterisation is a mistake. But is he actually the protagonist? If the women are more dramatically interesting, why not tell the story from the point of view of one of them? I reject this because Solomon is so very obviously the principal activist at the climax: it is the trap he sets that provides the main crisis.

I see immediately why I had started on the character of the false mother: I was doing precisely what Solomon has to do – he has to unravel the mystery of these female characters. So I begin a process of thinking not of a character as a character-in-itself, but of character interactions. I start by asking: What Does A Think B Is Thinking About A? It sounds complicated (and it is), but this is the very essence of giving some density to a character, and in turn a scene. The simplest way to make Solomon more interesting is to ask, 'Why does he have to be so all-powerful and secure? What is at stake for him?' Preliminary reaction: not much. He's the King, he's secure, all he has to do is be wise. This is a little dull. I would like there to be something at stake from his point of view. Going back to the text, something occurs to me. I find it where it usually is, at the end: 'And all Israel heard of the judgement which the king had judged; and they feared the king: for they saw that the wisdom of God was in him, to do judgement' (verse 28).

This prompts me to follow through with another 'rule': when searching for fresh insight into a text, it can be useful to do background research. Don't limit yourself to the material within the scene – make a study of the larger context. I put down the Bible and pick up the encyclopaedia to find out more about King Solomon. It seems there was considerable controversy about his

DRAMATIC CONSTRUCTION

ascension to the throne of David, and that Solomon had not actually been regarded as the son most likely to succeed his father. This idea gives an entirely different feel to the final lines of Solomon's story and at once produces a switch in my vision of the King.

In the Bible story, the incident of the judgement of the two harlots is not placed at any particular moment of Solomon's long reign. As I said, I had originally seen him as a wise and all-powerful priest-King. Quite abruptly it occurs to me that it would be far more interesting if the scene took place when he was much younger, new to the throne and its responsibilities, surrounded by elders who are not until this moment convinced that he deserves his royal authority. I realise again the validity of looking to see what happens in the end for clues to what might be the possible theme of the story, and what might happen at the start. I get the idea for a further peripeteia after the unmasking of the false mother: a turnabout of the attitude of these older men as they sense not simply that the young man is shrewd, but that his insight is from God. This is actually the more significant peripeteia in the scene (providing that Solomon is the protagonist). It is something of an axiom in dramatic construction that the protagonist is the one whom we feel has most at stake and for whom the obligatory moment is a confrontation with the main dramatic tension holding up the scene.

I see Solomon being brought in to solve the problem that has, up until this point, been confronted by three separate judges. Why three? Because a trio seems to represent an abstract of a larger community, and also because it presents a group figure within which there can be represented two who are sceptical of young Solomon and one ready to have faith in him. There can therefore be a shift of balance as Solomon wins the admiration of the majority. All this is still an unstructured exercise of the imagination. I have not yet got down to the real work. And I should emphasis that I have been thinking about the end situation, ignoring the start. With this in mind, I begin to select the dramatis personae of the short scene. They are:

1. Solomon, as a young man, new to his responsibilities, not yet fully secure and aware of the scepticism of his critics and rivals.

2. Solomon's supporter, perhaps some kind of chamberlain or functionary, probably one of the judges.

3. Two other foils: the sceptics who have failed to deliver judgement on the case.

4. The False Mother. The prettier and younger of the two harlots, and a much better dissembler. Her very real tears are the result of self-disgust and guilt. Guilt because she not only inadvertently smothered her own baby, but also because she knows that she could never have been a fit mother for her child. She is smart and sees at once when and how Solomon has unmasked her.

5. The True Mother. A woman of real feeling for her child, probably with real understanding of the pain of the other woman and the motive for her action. Not necessarily a wholly sweet character. She might feel rage and anger against the judges, even against Solomon for his suggestion of cutting the child in two (Solomon's trick is, after all, very sadistic).

6. Some supernumerary characters, necessary to the action only as reacting observers: a Bailiff or Sergeant of the Court, a Nurse, into whose hands the infant has been given during the litigation, a Guard.

Had I decided we should make one of the mothers the central figure, we could probably have done without the two characters who represent the different sides of the case (the foils). But now that we have them, and now they are to take part in the real point of the scene (Solomon's success in persuading those who have doubted him), I realise the scene needs to focus on them. Their relationship to Solomon has to be established before the problem of the rival claims of the two mothers, or at least during it.

One more note. If we attempt anything realistic in terms of style, the result will be either embarrassing or farcical. Students in bedsheets trying to declaim phoney biblical language can be nothing but ridiculous. We have neither the time nor money, and perhaps not even the skills, to try for that kind of thing. Accordingly, I suggest an approach that is safer and, in some ways, more experimental: an abstract effect, in the sense that it deliberately abstracts from different and even contradictory or incompatible scenarios. On the one hand we have the biblical origins of the story, on the other hand an updating of the emotions of these characters as might be experienced by youngsters living in Southern California in 1976.[2]

SCENE ONE

*A hearing room of some kind, a set that could be acceptable as contemporary or a symbol for the early Hebrew reality. Large and gloomy, empty except for one figure, a young man wandering about in the shadows. He seems depressed, insecure. He approaches the raised platform and the long bench behind which are judicial-looking chairs. Before the central one, the most imposing, is a candelabra of vaguely religious character. Also some large books, sacred or legal in appearance. Staring at the big chair behind the bench, the youth (*SOLOMON*) finds a cigarette in the pocket of his jeans, lights it at the sacred candle and*

2. Mackendrick also produced a handout which contained storyboards of the script he had written, giving a shot-by-shot layout of a proposed three-camera set-up in the CalArts studio. Some details from these notes are included here.

Below: The 'Solomon' set.

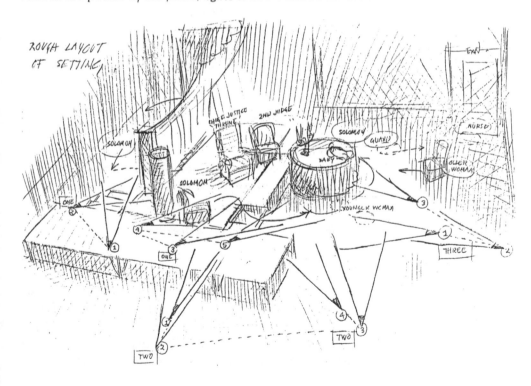

then, brooding, squats to sit on the edge of the platform, and lies flat on his back, eyes closed and smoking. Camera with wide angle lens mounted on dolly at low level. Lighting for low-key effect, as if main illumination is from the candles. Religious atmosphere, music both awesome and uneasy. On the sound-track, a whispering narrative voice with some echo. Cut from establishing shot to close-up of SOLOMON.

> VOICE
> (*very small, 'interior'*)
> Now when the days of David drew night that he should die, he charged Solomon, his son, saying, 'I go the way of all the earth: be thou strong therefore, and show thy-self a man . . .'

SOLOMON *opens his eyes a moment. He looks towards the big chair, the candles before it. Their flames flutter in a draught.* SOLOMON *closes his eyes again.*

> VOICE
> (*continuing*)
> In Gideon the Lord appeared to Solomon in a dream by night. And God said, 'Ask what I shall give thee.' And Solomon said . . .
> (*close up on Solomon's face, his lips move slightly,
>   as if speaking in a half-waking state*)
> 'Thou hast shewed unto thy servant, David my father, great mercy, according as he walked before thee in truth. Thou hast made thy servant king instead of David my father, and I am but a little child. I do not know how to go out or come in.'

The candles flutter again before a dissolve to

SCENE TWO

An area behind the hearing room with corridors, stairs. Music fades out. SOLOMON *comes through a doorway, pushing past various characters who are loitering in the precincts of the Hearing Room, petitioners, counsellors and such (close-up of* SOLOMON). *They make way for the young man but show no particular respect for his arrival. He makes it clear he is late. At the top of some steps is a door that opens onto the platform where the judges seem to be already in session. About to enter,* SOLOMON *hesitates, unsure of how to make his appearance. Just inside the door is a* BAILIFF *who notices* SOLOMON, *hesitates, and then starts to move to the bench to call the court to attention. But* SOLOMON *quickly and unobtrusively discourages him from this interruption of the proceedings that have started without him. During this we have heard some of the preliminary interrogation. (Important to have shot of room that establishes as much as possible the geography of the set and of the characters in place.)*

CHIEF JUSTICE

And the child? Where is it now?

COURT OFFICER

It's here, sir. The nurse has it here.

CHIEF JUSTICE

I see. But there are no witnesses, no others to give evidence. Just the two women in the dispute.

The CHIEF JUSTICE *occupies the central chair behind the judge's bench, clearly the position of authority. The* SECOND JUDGE *sits beyond him. Of the other chairs, the one nearest the door is unoccupied. Below the steps down from the judge's dais is a small table with the large book. Here those who give testimony stand as they address the judges. Behind the* COURT OFFICER, *a kind of constable or official, stand two women, the plaintiffs. Between them is a* GUARD *who is armed with a short sword. In the background is the* NURSE *who has been referred to, carrying the swaddled bundle, the* CHILD. *The* SECOND JUDGE *has noticed the arrival of* SOLOMON *and indicates his presence by getting from his chair. This prompts the* CHIEF JUSTICE *to turn, recognise* SOLOMON *(reaction shot) and, after a barely noticeable hesitation, also get up, thus vacating his position of seniority. But* SOLOMON *is already moving to sit at the chair at the near end of the bench. (Shot that shows* CHIEF JUSTICE, SECOND JUDGE *and* SOLOMON *sitting on judge's bench together.)*

CHIEF JUSTICE
(*hesitant*)
We had begun, sir. We were not certain that you . . .

SOLOMON
You were right to do so. Sit, please.

The CHIEF JUSTICE *indicates the central chair, but* SOLOMON *is already in the empty chair, looking at documents before him and glancing at the figures in the Hearing Room. (Shots of documents, geography of Hearing Room from* SOLOMON's *point of view.) Uncomfortable at the lack of ceremony, the* CHIEF JUSTICE *exchanges a look with the* SECOND JUDGE *as he resumes his seat (reaction shots). Still unsure of whether he should continue or start over, he glances at the young man who does not look up from the papers. The* CHIEF JUSTICE *resumes. (During this speech, cut to shots of* YOUNGER WOMAN *and* OLDER WOMAN *standing together. Reaction shots from* SOLOMON.)*

CHIEF JUSTICE
You've been warned, both of you, of punishment for those who, coming here for judgement, take in vain the name of the Lord. You know of the statutes and the commandments against the bearer of false witness?

The YOUNGER WOMAN, *who has been watching* SOLOMON, *nods dutifully to the* CHIEF JUSTICE. *The* OLDER WOMAN *has her hands behind her back and is silent, expressionless. As the* CHIEF JUSTICE *inclines his head, the* OFFICER *prods the* YOUNGER WOMAN *to advance and begin her testimony. (Shots of* CHIEF JUSTICE *and* SECOND JUDGE *without* SOLOMON.)*

YOUNGER WOMAN
(*emotional but with great sincerity*)
I – I and this woman live in the same house. I had a – I was delivered of a child – while she was there in the house. Then – afterwards – three days after – she had a child.

While the YOUNGER WOMAN *is trying to control her emotions, the* SECOND JUDGE *intervenes. (Move in on shot of* YOUNGER WOMAN *and* OLDER WOMAN.)*

SECOND JUDGE

Was there anyone else there? The fathers?

Both woman make no reply. The YOUNGER WOMAN, *distressed, shakes her head. It is left to the* OFFICER *to answer.*

OFFICER

No sir. Just the two women. They –
(*he hesitates*)

CHIEF JUSTICE

They are harlots, I take it.

OFFICER

Yessir.

A beat. The YOUNGER WOMAN *continues pathetically.*

YOUNGER WOMAN

There was no one else, only this – this woman and myself.
(*a beat*)
And the child died.

SOLOMON
(*gently*)

How did it die?

The YOUNGER WOMAN, *tearful, looks at the other woman who shows nothing but stoic bitterness. She is aware that* SOLOMON *is looking at her. The* YOUNGER WOMAN, *weeping, shakes her head.*

YOUNGER WOMAN

I – I don't know. It died – it died in the night. I don't know how, perhaps she – lay on it. She had been drinking and –

The OLDER WOMAN *shifts on her feet and we become aware that her hands seem to be tied behind her back.*

SOLOMON

Why is she bound?

OFFICER

She was violent. She would not come with us here. She was very violent so we –

I don't know how it died. But when we were both in
bed, she – she got up – she got up in the night, and took
my own from me – while I slept. She took my baby from
me – took it to her bed and laid her dead child in my
bed – at my breast . . .
(*weeping*)
I woke – I woke in the morning to feed my baby – and –
and it was dead. But it wasn't my baby! It wasn't mine! It
wasn't my child, my son, my baby – the baby that I . . .

At this moment the OLDER WOMAN *sharply turns, looking off
towards the* NURSE, *and we hear a very small whimper from the*
CHILD *(the* OLDER WOMAN *has heard it first). The* YOUNGER
WOMAN, *glancing at the* OLDER WOMAN, *reacts a moment later
and moves towards the* NURSE, *but the* OFFICER *blocks her, indicating that she remain before the judges. The* CHIEF JUSTICE
looks across at SOLOMON *who is watching the women. The*
NURSE *has tucked the swaddled* CHILD *under her shawl so as to
feed it unobtrusively. The* CHIEF JUSTICE, *after conferring with
the* SECOND JUDGE, *again turns to* SOLOMON.

CHIEF JUSTICE
Sir, if you wish to question these women, or if you have
an opinion?

SOLOMON
Bring it closer, the baby.

SOLOMON *gets up, descends the steps into the court. At the sign
from the* OFFICER, *the* NURSE *comes forward. She is nervous, but
at a gesture from* SOLOMON *lays the* CHILD *on the small table.*
SOLOMON *stoops to examine it. The judges watch, the* CHIEF
JUSTICE *with some impatience (reaction shots).*

SOLOMON
(*smiling as he watches the infant*)
It is asleep.

With a fairly abrupt change of manner, SOLOMON *turns to
address his colleagues on the bench. In the course of a short
speech (reaction shots throughout), he builds from a casual and*

cool disinterest to a kind of ruthless and logical cruelty.

SOLOMON

One of them is lying, that's clear. And, as you say, that is
serious, intolerable. It demands punishment, the most
severe penalty. Excuse me –
(*turns to the* GUARD *and indicates that he wishes
to be given the sword*)
One women is lying. But which? Without other evidence
we must treat each of them equally and impartially.
Justice must be equal, and so we will divide. We shall
give half to one, and half to the other.

SOLOMON, *without warning, spins around and raises the knife.
After a moment of stunned silence there is a scuffle and a cry of
pain that comes from the* GUARD *who has tried to seize the*
OLDER WOMAN *in order to prevent her from throwing herself at*
SOLOMON. *She has bitten him. In spite of her tied hands, in spite
of the* GUARD'S *intervention, she is already on her knees, blocking the possibility of* SOLOMON's *murderous act. Gasping, she
cries out with savagery.*

OLDER WOMAN

No! No! Let it – let her have it! It's – it's hers. I was the
one that lied before. It's her child. Let it live.

For some moments there is confusion. Then, as SOLOMON *lowers
the upraised knife, they begin to realise he is unconcerned with
the woman at his feet. He is looking at the* YOUNGER WOMAN. *As
the significance dawns, and as the* YOUNGER WOMAN *recognises
how she has been trapped, she begins to tremble (close-ups of*
YOUNGER WOMAN, SOLOMON *and* OLDER WOMAN). *The*
YOUNGER WOMAN *drops the mask of the pathetic victim.*

YOUNGER WOMAN
(*shaking her head, then savagely*)
Kill it! Kill it!
(*choking an admission*)
It's better dead! Like . . . like . . .

She turns to run. The GUARD *goes after her, pinions her. But*
SOLOMON, *with authority, gives him an order.*

SOLOMON
(*sharply*)
Let her go! Leave her alone!
(*turning back to the older woman*)
And let the mother take her child. She should not have
been bound.

As the GUARD *releases the* YOUNGER WOMAN, *she collapses to
the floor, sobbing.* SOLOMON *gives the sword back to the* GUARD
who uses it to cut the cords binding the hands of the OLDER
WOMAN, *freeing her to pick up the crying* CHILD. SOLOMON
takes a step to the YOUNGER WOMAN *and helps her to her feet.*

SOLOMON
Get up. No one will punish you. You have been pun-
ished enough.

*During the above business, we have been following other reac-
tions. The* JUDGES, *at first appalled, progressively begin to
recognise the cunning of their younger colleague (reaction
shots). All are still shocked, but also impressed. The most sober
is the* CHIEF JUSTICE. *First he sits down in his chair, then he rises
again, goes slowly to meet* SOLOMON *who has already been
joined by the* SECOND JUDGE. *Dissolve to*

SCENE THREE

A night scene. SOLOMON *is alone, but now he is seated in the
central chair and is reading from a book, smoking again,
thoughtfully watching the fluttering candle flame as he considers
some problem. The soft whispering voice fades in.*

VOICE
And all Israel heard of the judgement and feared the
King. And God said, because thou has asked for thyself
an understanding heart to judge thy people and hast not
asked for thyself the life of thine enemies, behold I have
done according to thy words. And I have also given thee
that which thou has not asked, both riches and honour,
so that there shall not be any among the kings like unto
thee all thy days.

DRAMATIC CONSTRUCTION

The Director and the Actor

Finally, before we launch into Film Grammar, some thoughts on the working relationship between the director and his most important collaborator: the actor.

How much does the film actor need to know about the work of the film director? This is a controversial issue. There are some actors who prefer to bother as little as possible with the cumbersome technology of film production and its problems, while a few directors declare that the less the actor knows the better. An extreme case is Antonioni, who has been all too candid on the subject, arguing that that actor 'does not need to *understand*, he needs to *be*'. I have some problems with Antonioni's view. But while I sympathise with actors who find his pronouncements insulting to their profession and who suspect (not without some reason, perhaps) that Antonioni is defensive because he has had certain difficulties with actors (and especially actresses) who have challenged him for explanations, he might not be entirely wrong.

As a general rule, the director is an interpretive artist and is often called upon (by the actor, no less) to be critical and self-consciously analytical in his approach, full of verbal explanations rooted in deep thought. The actor of talent, however, works from intuition, instinct and impulse rather than critical and intellectual comprehension (though of course a good director will, to a certain extent, also work from his imagination and impulse). Jean Renoir put it both more tactfully and probably more wisely: 'Some actors are very intelligent, but it is not necessarily with their intelligence that they act.' In this context impulse would seem to be the opposite of thought, because thought is the result of premeditated and conscious awareness. For the actor, then, knowing is a gut thing. He learns about his character through intense imagining (imagination being the faculty of creating images in the mind, recapitulations of sensory and emotional experiences).

It has been said that an overly conscious understanding of the techniques of the film director on the part of the actor may, in some cases, hamper his ability to give a good performance. Thinking too much, the argument goes, might inhibit this magical process. While the director needs to be very much aware of the range of potential possibilities confronting him on set and in the editing room, some believe that if an actor is fully conscious of the film-making process, his performance might be too premeditated and not spontaneous enough. But acting is a strange and magical craft that involves a kind of split consciousness. The actor is at once totally absorbed in a fantasy, yet at another level retains a sense of the other dimension, the reality that lies outside the arena of the make-believe. An actor's control is, at its best, automatic. Like the trained athlete, he needs reflexes that have been developed through rigorous and highly conscious discipline. These are skills he must know so thoroughly that he can use them without any deliberate premeditation at all. They need to be inbuilt and, if not unconscious, then at least unselfconscious.

Because the actor's imagining needs to be controlled at all times, I believe there are certain basic things actors (particularly those trained in the theatre) should be aware of before they step in front of a camera. Very generally, they include the unselfconscious and automatic ability to adjust to the position of the camera, a sense of its place (including a theoretical grasp of the principle of the axis, eye-lines and eye contact), and an understanding of continuity. Some actors even have a good knowledge of specific camera lenses, which means they know how they will be framed within the shot. In this context, allow me to reiterate in more detail some technical ideas about which I have spoken many times in class, but this time direct them specifically at the actor.

Theatre is predominantly an art of the spoken word, and in an effective stage performance a skilful actor can, through shifts of intonation, phrasing and subtle timing in the delivery, reveal the subtext of his lines. If there is a difference in cinema, it is that what is unsaid is made dramatically explicit via film grammar (for example camera moves, long shots, atmospheric lighting).

In other words, the director and editor have as important (if not more important) a role to play in creating effective performances on screen. In a situation where there is a subtle exchange of looks between two characters involved in an emotional interaction, the intercutting of close-ups can frequently be quite complicated, involving a sequence of swiftly alternating responses. In such a scene, words might become a mere after-effect of emotion, as director and editor seek to uncover those motives and thoughts in the footage that prompt the action (using the word not just in its physical sense, but in its dramatic significance too).

Consequently, the timing of an actor's looks can have considerable effect on the editing pattern and, in this sense, may have more impact on performance than many actors realise. For example, when a character 'takes a look' and flicks a swift glance to a person or object on a certain word, the editor will frequently make the cut to the point-of-view angle precisely on the frame (or maybe two or three frames immediately after) when eye contact (or otherwise) is made. This is the instance at which we, the audience, feel the need to see the cutaway point of view, a shot that need not be longer in duration than a few seconds, during which time the audience can read its meaning. And as soon as it has been read, the editor might return to the reaction of the person making the look, for often the real action in a scene is actually the reaction, the impact of what has been observed or said as seen through subtle facial responses. It is precisely those looks that the editor wants to find when he explores the footage of the interplay of two characters.

Experienced screen actors seem to have quite remarkable expertise in the timing and precision of their looks, something that can be just as important as the intonation, phrasing and timing of a line of dialogue. And while the stage actor who has mastered the technique of listening will be admired by other actors and by the stage director, the film actor who knows how to use close-ups of his performance that have subtlety and intensity in reaction is likely to discover more footage of himself on the screen when the film has been edited.

Related to this is the fact that some of the most basic elements of film grammar are, to a certain extent, relative rather than absolute in nature. Consider a speech by an actor. How does he give meaning to certain words rather than others? A famous stage actor of the nineteenth century gave his name to a trick of delivery still known as a 'McCready Pause': that fractional hesitation before a word or phrase in which the actor seems to be groping for the word. It is a vocal equivalent of the kind of trick a graphic designer might use.[1] Putting air around or in front of a word makes it jump out of the surrounding context (although like everything else, it can be a profoundly irritating vocal mannerism if overused, or if it is so clearly deliberate that the effect becomes self-conscious). All actors punctuate points of importance in a speech in some way (for example by varying the tempo and melodic pitch of certain words and phrases), inevitably de-emphasising some passages, while stressing certain others, giving them more meaning. In fact, actors are liable to sound monotonous when they don't do this. The ability to throw away part of a line, while still keeping it crisply audible, is part of the craft of the actor who knows how to sting the words that have more bite.

The best screen actors are those who not only give attention to the words, but also provide the audience with a clear understanding of those reactions and emotions that lie within the subtext of the scene at hand, the space between the lines, the feelings and thoughts that serve as preparation for the dialogue (or lack thereof). As specifically applied to the actor's craft, subtext reflects the psychological realities of a character, clarified and articulated (to the audience) when he speaks his lines. For the actor, comprehension of subtext means he is better able to understand the material he is working with and so define that material from the point of view of his character's inner life.

How is this done, practically speaking? The actor must decide what the character is saying to himself at all times, as if he were writing a continuous inner soliloquy that expresses his character's thoughts, responses and attitudes. An actor who has mastered a role is able to speak this soliloquy out loud. He is, at all times, able to answer the question 'What is this character really trying to say with his line?' (even if his character is not). In this way, subtext can develop during rehearsal, quite unconsciously, as a way of controlling the inflections of words, the timing of gestures, and the length of silences. Try these examples. In each case mumble the framing lines but speak the middle line aloud. Notice how this emphasises the spoken word and reduces the sense of conscious control.

Unspoken: How disgusting!
Aloud: No thanks – nothing to drink for me
Unspoken: You stupid fool!

Unspoken: He's handsome!
Aloud: No thanks – nothing to drink for me
Unspoken: And how thoughtful!

Unspoken: Now what?
Aloud: No thanks – nothing to drink for me
Unspoken: Aha! Trying to get me drunk!

If screen actors are to apply this idea specifically to their craft, they must be aware of the fact that the camera is able to photograph thought. Movement and expressions that work on the stage are liable to appear as gross exaggeration (as weak acting) on screen.

Something else the theatrically trained performer working in film should understand is related to Stanislavsky's recommendation that actors 'play to the eyes of acting partners'. It is good advice, but when applied to film needs some qualification. In actual everyday behaviour, a continuously sustained look into someone else's eyes is very rare indeed. It is, in fact, apt to look quite unnatural. As a demonstration, try this experiment. Sit opposite someone and start by looking down at the floor. Then raise your eyes to look accurately into the eyeballs of your partner. While you are speaking, maintain this fixed look. If you carefully examine your feelings and thoughts, you are apt to find the image of your partner is interesting and meaningful for only a few seconds. Within a moment or so the meaning of the image is likely to vanish and become insignificant. You have momentarily slipped out of the intense concentration of make-believe and have allowed a degree of self-consciousness to create a false moment. Your look has become phoney.

To emphasise this issue, consider something that has been

discovered by those investigators of the psychology of visual perception as it applies to the use of film grammar. The fact is that rather than being stationary, the human eye is actually highly mobile in two different ways. First, there is a completely unconscious and constant oscillation of the pupil that seems to be designed to prevent the retinal image from ever becoming fixed, keeping it in a state of constant instability and agitation. This means that the signal from the retina to the visual cortex is constantly recurring and renewed, permanently unstable. Second, the eye muscles keep the focus of the eyes constantly flicking across the field of vision, searching the object at which we are looking like a scanner. If these muscles are treated by a drug that freezes the position of the pupil, keeping the optical image on the retina absolutely steady, the mental awareness of what is seen virtually disappears. We are, in short, unable to see a static image because the eye is perpetually scanning what we look at, which means there is always fresh information being delivered to the brain. Visual information is, in this sense, never static. A look is brief – it is the spark of recognition, the instant of registering meaning in what we see. And it rapidly loses its impact, for the meaning will evaporate if we continue to look at something that provides no fresh visual information.

Conversely, if you avoid eye contact by looking only during those brief instants when you have a real need to see something, then your mind is constantly at work. Thus to scrutinise an object with extreme concentration, you must keep the focus of your attention in constant motion. Try the fixed look at your partner again but now keep the look moving from the mouth to the eyes, the left eye to the right, the eyebrows to the chin. This will, on film at least, appear as a fixed concentration of your attention. (Add to this the fact that when two people know each other extremely well, they seldom need to observe each other's faces, until or unless they are expecting some reaction.) On film, the tiniest of shadow movements of facial expression can punctuate private and unspoken impulses. An important and sustained look from the actor is thus apt to lose the spark of its intensity, the snap of a sharply indicated betrayal of interior feeling or thought. In dramatic terms, a screen actor's performance is likely to be much more useful to the director and the editor if

DRAMATIC CONSTRUCTION

his looks are not sustained but are rather a series of sharply defined flicks of the eye to check for information. These almost imperceptible shifts of eye focus can, in close-ups, be enormously expressive and significant, as the audience reads them as the outward evidence of internal thought and feeling. This means the director should ensure that his actors save these glances for the swift instants where they have real meaning.

The final technical point about which the screen actor should have some knowledge is called 'business', the incidental unspoken activity of the performer that helps conveys subtle details of characterisation. The experienced actor will make a habit of furnishing himself with possessions, clothes and objects that provide him with easy, unaffected and natural physical behaviour (obvious examples are lighting a cigarette, cutting the pages of a book, or even the way Alec Guinness uses his scarf in *The Ladykillers*). The value of such material objects to the film director is that they are a way of making an actor's behaviour visible and practical, physical and material, inevitably forcing dialogue into a position subordinate to on-screen action. Good film actors understand how cinema functions at the most basic level (through action, not dialogue), and by manipulating the audience's attention through the movement of certain on-screen objects they are able to assist the director in his own job.

Once such actions have been devised (either by the writer months before, sitting at his typewriter, or by the director and actor exploring the filming location), it is far easier to isolate those lines of dialogue that are essential to the comprehension of the story. These are the ones that, in a silent film, would be title cards. In a sound-film version they become the lines more likely to be shot full-face and close-up so they have full emphasis. Note that the director's task is already half done if he is working from a screenplay written by a dramatist who has been thinking behaviourally rather than verbally. Such a writer will have provided his characters with a range of props within their on-screen environments to work with. Objects can be brought into play during a later stage of the film-making process, through the input of, for example, the costume designer, the production designer, and, naturally, the actor himself. But in such cases, the effective staging of actors in a scene will often depend on a director's ingenuity in devising business with these props, or stimulating the actors to do the same.

Though the actor need not realise precisely what he is doing, it is actually through the strategic placing of props on set that the director can control an actor's staging within the frame. To be candid, when dealing with the amateur performer who is agonisingly self-conscious, or the over-confident actor who is enjoying his role with too much theatrical relish, a director might find no better way of discouraging the actor from his artificiality than inventing for him the kind of activity that – while it occupies the mind in a mechanical and unthinking fashion – releases much more natural and unselfconscious expression of feeling.

For the actor, the handling of such objects might involve essentially meaningless actions that have hardly any significance at all and are performed in an absent manner. In fact, it is one of the inherent values of such incidental activity that it can be made to be relatively undramatic. But, if a few moments later, there is an offstage gunshot, then the reaction of the actor might qualify as a significant piece of dramatic action. It is the interruption of these seemingly unimportant activities that makes visible the impact of more significant thought: the cessation of some relatively insignificant action is a way to accentuate certain reactions. This is less complicated than it sounds – comedians do it all the time. To mark with some precision the instant of a strong reaction, a comedian will arrange to be caught halfway through some bit of incidental and perhaps unconscious business. He will be in mid-gesture, for example, about to take a drink, when hit by the impact of something unexpected.

There are several devices a director can use when he wants to stimulate the actor into this kind of active performance, all of which have the indirect added effect of isolating things that need underlining, and of developing characterisation through nonverbal behaviour (the very essence of good cinematic storytelling). The phrase used by directors to describe this is the 'sweeping the floor' routine. It supposedly comes from an occasion when a scene was repeatedly ruined by a self-conscious line delivered by a bad actor, a bit player. The unfortunate man had only one line to say but several takes were ruined because, under pressure from the impatient director, he tried to deliver the line without making it sound embarrassingly and unnecessarily significant. No amount of rehearsal helped the actor play his dialogue in a throwaway fashion. The solution was finally found when the director handed the man a floor mop, spilled some water on the floor, and instructed him to mop up every drop of water while the scene was shot. Concentrating on this bit of business produced the desired effect: the actor was so absorbed in the irrelevant activity that he hardly reacted at all to the protagonist, delivering the line in a completely natural, casual and convincing manner.

For a more ingenious example of the same device look at one of the love scenes between Marlon Brando and Eva Marie Saint in *On the Waterfront*. It is reasonably well written, but might have seemed over-saturated if the actors had played it while looking at each other directly. Instead, Brando uses a couple of props, one of which is a child's swing in the playground of the park where the scene takes place. Incongruously he sits in the swing, giving a slightly self-deprecating tone to his performance. The other prop is a glove the girl has dropped. Brando picks it up and does not return it, absent-mindedly trying it on his own much larger hand. This purely incidental activity means that for much of the dialogue he avoids eye contact with her. Because of this the scene is less sentimental and creates an impression of unpretentious and natural screen presence (though it is, needless to say, just as contrived and premeditated as any other piece of acting).

A brief aside. Few interesting situations are drawn in black and white. Few well-drawn characters seem absolutely confident of right and wrong. In too many scripts this is transformed into phrases like 'He's angry, but a bit pitying', or 'She's a bit resentful, but at the same time intrigued'. This is not much use to the actor, as such compromise is likely to produce a drab and confused result. The character who is 'almost angry but a bit pitying' will achieve this effect with more vitality if he shows an impulse to anger, quickly checked by a contradictory moment of pity, then by another flash of annoyance. If the girl who is resentful but intrigued alternates between moments of resentment and moments of interest, it is much clearer for the audience. And clarity, of course, is perhaps the key to efficient storytelling. An analogy

3. After several years of careful preparation, and with the assistance of the Deans of the film/video school and the theatre school, an interdisciplinary directing programme was created at CalArts in 1985 called Directing for Theatre, Video and Cinema. Students on the programme, even those who wanted to become film-makers, not theatre practitioners, were required to take a certain number of acting classes. One of the entry requirements to the programme was for each student to produce a video tape of themselves telling a story. Actors, wrote Mackendrick, 'teach more to directors than directors ever teach to actors. The emphasis in the directors' programme is actually theatre, because students whose only passion is film tend to be dull.'

from impressionist painting may be relevant here. The impressionists were fascinated by the nature and energy of light, so they did not mix colours on the palette. Using pure pigments in small fragmented brushwork meant the fusion took place in the eye and mind of the observer. So with performance.

A few notes here about the practical problems the director faces and about how he should approach his job.

There are many practical steps a director can take to ensure a smoothly running set and a good working relationship with his actors. Perhaps the most important is to appreciate that the actor is the director's most valuable collaborator, to the point where I believe the director should go out of his way to ensure he has a rudimentary understanding of the craft of acting. It is not necessary for him to be as good a performer as the actors he is working with, only that he has basic comprehension of the problems the actor faces when standing on the other side of the camera. It does seem clear that a director who has an intuitive understanding of the way an actor feels is likely to be much more successful than the one who hopes to communicate at an intellectual level – through words.[3] My advice to students is liable to lean very strongly on negative admonitions, things the director should never do when dealing with actors. (Or, to be more honest, should never appear to be doing.)

Never ignore the actors. Humility is the main thing to learn, though this is not easy because sympathetic understanding of your crew and, especially, the actors will come very slowly and only through experience (for which there is no substitute). Humility is, needless to say, not a gift but a technique that can be learned through training. Admiration for actors is the prerequisite for working well with and controlling them (without them knowing it). One of your first exercises as a director, therefore, is to develop your ability to become infatuated with an actor whom, in other circumstances, you would feel free to dislike.

A note here about the value of listening and watching with real attention and concentration. These are not passive activities for either the actor or the director. Nor are they things that are done well without considerable effort and a good deal of experience. In a workshop that he gives to beginning directors, a cer-

DRAMATIC CONSTRUCTION

tain CalArts teacher invites two or three actors to play a scene in front of the directors in the class. He then questions the directors to find out what they saw, for example: 'The actor was sitting here on the sofa. Did he have his legs crossed or uncrossed? If he uncrossed them, on exactly what line in the dialogue did he uncross them?' Through such an exercise, one is apt to find that many directors are scarcely aware of the actor's body language, something that can be an extraordinarily revealing clue to his often quite unconscious feelings.

Never appear to be overly distant from the actors. A fine performance is always tuned to the feedback of those who watch it. This is why a stage performance in a huge auditorium is quite different from one in a small and intimate space, why a performance to a cold audience will be different to one before an audience that is supportive and enthusiastic. The audience itself is, in a sense, an instrument upon which the actor plays. The performance both controls the audience and is controlled by it. Though there is no such large-scale feedback on the film set, to say nothing of the fact that the processes of cinematography and post-production often rob actors of their own control of audience response, the response of the future audience (whether a mass of people or a solitary viewer) needs to be felt by the actor. This is perhaps the primary function of the director: to provide his actors with the same kind of support and stimulus the stage actor gets during a live performance.

Never be afraid to do anything it takes to protect the actor. Anything that intrudes on the actor's sense of security or distracts from his concentration is a menace to his or her performance. And since it is the performance about which the director must feel passionately, he must be a fierce ally of the actor against all sources of irritation or distraction. The director has to be enormously accessible. The archetypal director is a bully, a screaming megalomaniac (though in professional practice one encounters very few directors who let their real aggression show, at least not in front of the actors). But the fury of a director is likely to be the obverse of his tremendous patience with things that really matter, like the work of the actor. Of course the director's other functions, such as instructing the camera crew, deciding on camera set-ups and camera coverage, and working with technicians, are all important. But the director who lets these tasks distract him from his responsibilities to the actors is incompetent.

How does the director get an actor to do what he wants? This was a question I was asked many years ago when I first began my work as a teacher, and the way it was phrased took me off guard as I had never asked myself the question in these terms. The student who challenged me grew impatient at my confused attempts to answer and he repeated the question with more vigour. Surprising myself I said, 'You don't. What you do is try to get the actor to want what you need.' It was the first moment when, instinctively, I stumbled on a point that I believe in with great passion: the film director must have respect for his actors. This is the reason why, in the vast majority of cases, the director who demonstrates to the actor by acting the role himself, by reading the line of dialogue for the actor to mimic or by performing the gesture so that the actor can copy it, has already failed.

There are two reasons why this can be disastrous. First, if you happen to have less talent than the actors you are working with, he or she will instantly recognise this and, if intelligent, ignore you. Second, if you happen to be more talented than the actor you are directing, the actor may try to imitate you. Since there is no one who can imitate you better than you can imitate yourself, you have already abandoned your real responsibility: to help the actor discover within himself a sense of truth, his own understanding of the character, how he feels and behaves within his role. There is, in addition, an even greater failing. While you are intent on imagining how you would say the line or make the gesture, you have been unable to really listen to and watch your actors. Blinded by preconceptions, you may well have closed your mind to what he or she is able to contribute.

Just as the most careful tracing of any drawing will always seem inexpressive compared with the original, so an actor's copy of somebody else's performance is liable to be unconvincing and false. Explanations to an actor that are some kind of critical analysis of the meaning of a line, which you as director are trying to convey, are apt to be just as unhelpful. They make you feel intelligent and wise. They may even impress the actor and anybody else who happens to be listening. But it is rare that they assist in stimulating a more effective performance. For the intelligent actor and equally intelligent and analytical director there may be considerable satisfaction in sitting down to discuss their interpretation of a script's theme or of the relationships between characters. Talk of this kind might be stimulating, particularly if it brings to mind examples illustrative of their ideas. But there is no guarantee that a director who is able to explain such things to his actors will be of real help to them. (He is certainly not likely to be much use if he is more a critic who is unable to give tangible guidance and ask useful questions of his actors.) Such an approach can help, however, if it contributes in some very practical way to the act of imagining the action.

Anything that helps the process of bringing the characters and situations to life will stimulate the actor's imagination. This is why, in my opinion, it is quite legitimate for a director to tell any story about some incident or person if it is evocative of the feelings that the actor and the director are trying to recreate. Not infrequently, one of the most helpful things the director can do is invite the actor to improvise scenes that do not appear in the script but that in narrative terms have taken place just before the scene that is being presently explored. And remember that questions are often more helpful to the actor than any answers the director might be able to offer (a good example being something like, 'What happened to your character after the last scene and before this one?').

A director contributes not by instructing the actor but by inspiring him. A performance is wholly the creation of the actor's imagination, of the control he has over his expressive instruments (voice, body), and even more significantly of his emotions, sensory feelings, intuitions and mental attitudes. (This is why they say once a role has been properly cast, the director has done ninety per cent of his work.) So listen. Listen hard. Observe the actor minutely. Watch closely for his body language, those subtle qualities of personality that belong utterly to this particular individual. Imagine how these might be absorbed into the role. Where there are qualities that do not seem right to you, be patient. Remember these may, in fact, be due to your own inability to see beyond your preconceptions. Remember that, in any event, to call attention to what is wrong may inhibit the actor. Where he or she has mannerisms you are anxious to eliminate, other tactics may be necessary.

Never proceed until you are absolutely ready. Remember: the meaning and structure of a particular scene can be truly understood only in the context of the whole. So read the script through, preferably in a single sitting, then put it aside and forget about it for a while. The point of this is to let it all soak in, to prevent you from jumping too quickly to conclusions. Once you have read a script once, perhaps twice, and have then spent some time away from it, try to recap the story in your mind. This helps the subconscious to absorb and internalise things, to feel the behaviour of the characters in ways that lead you to think of their impulses more than their words. Often, when I have done this before going to sleep, I find quite vivid impressions of it in my mind the next morning. In a sense, I am well on the way to visualising (reconceiving) the story non-verbally.

What I do then is carefully go through the whole story again, remembering 'who does what with which to whom and why?' This involves a lot of work – not just time but also energy, imaginative effort and real concentration. Not just random freewheeling and daydreaming (though this is an absolutely essential aspect of the effort) but a really disciplined study. This is a point worth emphasising. It seems that many students do not look at precisely what has been put down on the page with enough care. To be candid, I have to admit I have a certain amount of sympathy with the superficiality that is all too apt to accompany one's initial reading. I have been guilty of it myself. But on almost every occasion when I worked from a script by another writer, one of the first steps of my own method of script study was to copy out, in laborious longhand, every single word. The physical effort involved in this labour of calligraphy was such that it forced me to use my imagination in a way that internalised what I believed to be the writer's intentions, to repeat all the thoughts and emotions experienced by the writer. As a matter of rigid self-discipline, I made sure every single phrase and sentence was gone over very carefully before I started thinking about translating them into cinematic language. Only at the point when all the sequential connections in the story were

DRAMATIC CONSTRUCTION

known to me inside and out was I ready to proceed. On those occasions when I did not do this, I lived to regret it.

Having absorbed the whole story so that the characters have come alive in your imagination, start your study of particular scenes. Look especially for the connections that one scene might have with what has come directly before and what is going to happen next. An important principle of dramatic structure comes into play here, because every step within each scene should be a progression along the line that leads to the story's climax (this is the principle of dramatic momentum). Every entrance is an exit from a previous situation and every exit is an entrance to somewhere else. Indeed, if this is not the case you should ask yourself whether or not the scene is necessary. At the end of this period you should know your story so completely that there is no question any actor can ask you about a character (including aspects of off-screen life and back-story) for which you cannot instantly improvise a convincing answer. (Good actors will test you this way, and you will lose their respect if you don't know more about the characters than they do.)

For me, and I believe many directors, the next important stage is again a solitary one: a quiet and uninterrupted period of walking through the places where the scenes will be shot. During this time you become each character in turn. You should concentrate on body language. This will obviously come out of your capacity to see and hear the performance in your head, but the lines of dialogue are much less important than the physical behaviour of the characters (what gestures he or she might make, whether he slouches about, whether she picks her teeth). Take care, of course, never to become too enamoured of your own interpretations, because odds are that once on location an inventive actor will provide you with his or her own much more effective activities. Your private and secret rehearsal of the role is not because you intend to show the actor what to do and how to do it, where to stand or when to move. This is for the actor to discover himself. But you will be better able to appreciate his performance if you have already been there on your own.

General practice is to work out the details of the actors' staging before camera set-ups have been fixed. But actually it is likely to be more complex than that. From your first reconnaissance of the location, and then during your secret rehearsal, you will inevitably have devised specific shots in your head. Don't bother to explain this to actors except in a most general way ('The camera will be over there'). In reality you are leading the actor on a very short rein, gently coaxing him into a performance that he must believe is entirely his. If, by any chance, he happens to do exactly what you thought you might tell him to do, congratulate him for his inspiration. If he has an idea that for some dramatic reason is quite impossible for you, show slightly less enthusiasm, look a little worried and explain that it might cause you some technical problems (upon which you do not have to elaborate). Then wait till he comes up with another idea that you can use. In this respect, your job is to gradually jockey the actor into thinking up what you've already thought up.

Infinite patience is necessary. This will be very difficult for you because privately you are under horrendous pressure. Never let it show. During all this the cinematographer, camera operator and script clerk should be observers. They should not participate in any way, for it is not their job to make helpful suggestions, even when these are blindingly obvious to everyone present except the actors. The suggestions should come either from the actors or the director, and when coming from the director should always seem to be unplanned and spontaneous, even when, in fact, you have prepared a detailed shot list and set of storyboards.

DRAMATIC CONSTRUCTION

PART TWO

Film Grammar

The Invisible Imaginary Ubiquitous Winged Witness

When on set or location, a film director is apt to have an absent manner, as if his mind were in another place. In a way this is true, for he is not really there. In spirit he has removed himself into the future and is already sitting in the movie-house, watching the screen as if it were a window into an imaginary world. Already a member of the audience for his as yet unmade film, the director is feeling what the future spectators of his work might feel and reacting as they might react.

As someone who seeks to know what will 'work' for the audience, the director becomes this audience whilst making his film. He looks at the crowd of people surrounding him in the studio in a strange way, blind and dead to much that is going on. Why? Because his mind is fragmented. He is screening out everything not relevant to the as yet not-present world of the story being told. Concentrating only on what he can see, he is busy arranging in his head the short, narrow segments, those disorientated pieces of this soon-to-be-assembled reality that will be seen and heard through that open window of the cinema screen. He is, in his mind's eye and ear, involved in make-believe just as complex as that of the actors before him. He is living not only in the future but also in the past, when, during the writing stage, he was gradually constructing a fully focused concept of the film: its atmosphere, its visual qualities, its characters' appearance and behaviour, their emotions and interactions.

Though nothing is fixed and finalised in his mind, standing on location as the individual personification of his future audience, he is able to run the film though in his mind's eyes and ears. As he looks through the viewfinder and puts the jigsaw together, he is using his memory as a guide to the hundreds of decisions he has to make. His dream film is becoming progressively more concrete and specific: the actors have been chosen, the sets have been designed and constructed, the locations found, the dialogue revised and polished. Even though when shooting starts the director will be working just as much from his memorised fantasy as from anything that might appear in the typed-up shooting script, every single decision related to camera position, image size and editing pattern is determined by the question 'What do I need to see now?' – with the 'I' being that which exists only in the future: the potential audience.

I have tried to illustrate these ideas by creating a character who represents the director at this stage: the Invisible Imaginary Ubiquitous Winged Witness, a creature designed to personify the mind's eye and ear of the director leaping about in the time and space of an imaginary world constructed in front of the camera lens. This movement, this shifting point of view, is what the director needs when planning camera set-ups and staging performances.

The camera may be a mechanical instrument that records images, either static or in motion. But the Witness is an utterly different kind of creature with a magical and mythic presence that has very human qualities and characteristics. Far from being passive, it is an active participant in the imaginary events being portrayed. It is the embodiment of the audience's curiosity, a creature whose attitude to persons and events is coloured by feeling: sympathetic on occasion, alienated at other times. It can watch as an imaginary observer or it can feel as a participant. It has, in other words, a point of view, seeing at all times from one precise point in space, but able to shift that viewpoint in an instant. To answer a complex question very simply: where does the director place the camera? Answer: at the precise spot from where at any given instant the Witness can see all that needs to be seen and only what needs to be seen. Whether it is a long shot, a medium shot or a close-up, the Witness is able to observe it all. This is no simple matter since, as every cameraman and director will tell you, the real world in which the filming is done may be intractable in providing, within the limits of the viewfinder, all that the Witness desires to see.

Every cut in action is always something of a disorientating shock for the audience. This is sometimes forgotten by the film-maker who thinks that all cuts in action must be smooth. The way to make a cut *seem* smooth is to make the jump of the mind's eye one that the audience wants to make. Simply, the cut to an image is accepted when it supplies to the viewer the satisfaction of some curiosity stimulated by the previous image, or when the shock of the cut is a surprise presentation of something that is interesting and stimulating, even if unexpected. To answer a second complex question simply: when should the director make a cut in the action? Answer: when the Witness wants to see something it cannot yet see. As such, the motivation for every cut should always be built into the preceding angle. There should automatically be within every shot something that creates in the audience a desire to move at the right moment, along with the Witness, to the next angle. This is what the film editor looks for: a motive for a move within space and time.

In this respect, the Witness is a strange disembodied and mythic creature. It has magical faculties, living in an entirely fictitious and imaginary world, oblivious to real space and time. It is a being able to leap about with total freedom, taking up impossible positions in space, as for instance when it hovers outside a top-floor window of a skyscraper looking in to see the action. The Witness is able to look not only through solid walls, it can even take up a position inside a brick wall. It can fly in close to enough to study the facial expressions (those secret and private reactions) of a character who is sitting alone. Or it might fly out to allow the audience an appreciation of the geography of a crowded room. From this it will be clear where the characters lie in relation to each other and where the objects that surround them are standing.

The Witness can make leaps in time too. Intensely inquisitive as well as somewhat impatient, and because it is in touch with the desire of the audience, it tends to anticipate. Seeing what may happen next, it jumps to the next interesting action, thus telescoping time. Seeing an intention, it might even leap to the conclusion, while on other occasions it will explore the realm of memory by retracing time into the past.

How to be Meaningless

Framing and editing determine the eye-path of the viewer. It might not be too much to say that what a film director really directs is his audience's attention.

In this sense it is secondary that he tell the actors where and how to stand and move, and how quickly, slowly, loud or soft to play the scene. Equally secondary are his suggestions to the cinematographer about where he wants the camera to be placed, whether it should move or not, what needs to be included and (just as importantly) excluded in shot. All such directions are ultimately means to another end: manipulating the perceptions of the film viewer. Direction is a matter of emphasis. In telling a story, the task of the director is to emphasise what is significant by under-emphasising what is less so. The actors' performances, the camera's coverage of the performances, and the film editor's reconstruction of these during post-production: all are designed to make certain things more significant than others to the audience.

Long before I got the chance to work in film, I had a job in the art department of a large advertising agency. Though I was very junior and inexperienced, within a short time I became the assistant to an experienced art director from whom I learned a great deal about the craft of the layout in designing advertisements. The layout man is given the words of the advertisement (the headlines, captions, slogan and logotypes) and either asked to design illustrations, drawings or photographs, or given already completed texts and illustrations with the instruction to arrange them within a given space. The space may be a full page in a newspaper or glossy magazine, or it may be a one- or two-column space in another publication.

It was a good many years afterwards when I belatedly recognised that in this very early and crassly commercial task, thanks to what I learned from my boss about the layout man's trade, I had been given some first-class training in my future career as a director of feature films. The important thing was to decide which things needed to be made more emphatic over others and which had to strike the reader/viewer's eye immediately. By placing the varied elements on the page (both words and images), the layout man intuitively learns which should catch the audience's attention immediately and which should be legible only as a consequence of this initial impact. In short, he leads the eye and ear of the audience by designing the visual track of the reader's eye through his arrangement of words and images, all according to their sequential significance. (In the cinema, of course, this is partly the role of the cinematographer. As a cameraman friend of mine once noted, when playing with lightness and darkness, 'It's not about where you put the shadows, it's about where you *don't* put them.')

Making something eye-catching is not always a matter of making it bigger. Rather, it is about it being that little bit different from everything else. It is the overall design – hence the relative nature – of spatial patterns that can make one thing more emphatic than another. As you contrive to make the eye fall upon one element, you ensure that it passes over and thus dismisses others. A standard problem for the typographical designer is that he is often required to include in the available space a number of relatively uninteresting elements. One way is to make them less legible. For example, text will seem monotonous and meaningless if you manipulate the space of the lettering so there is not quite enough space between the words. A typographer might use this design for the kind of copy that has to be included but that should not call attention to itself, while type that is important can be made more noticeable when placed in a box. Also to consider are contrast of colour or tone, the spatial surround, and the amount of air around the words. A director of film images and sounds is faced with a similar task – the leading of his audience's eyes and ears – though at a much more complex level. Where graphic design has only two-dimensional patterns to work with, the film director works in several dimensions. The manipulation of time and space all play a role, though the key is still the same: emphasis has to be created by contrast. To stress one thing is to underplay and dismiss something else.

When it comes to the relative rather than the absolute nature of film grammar – how dramatic effects are achieved by comparison and contrast – the scale of sound amplification is also of great importance. The most important thing to remember, a principle on which a whole philosophy of sound design can be based, is that the absence of sound does not necessarily read as silence. For example, in order to create the dramatic illusion of quiet in an empty room, the sound designer might add in unnaturally loud sound effects of things that the ear would not normally pick up, like a dripping tap or ticking clock. Perhaps these sounds might even be contrasted with the faraway barking of a dog or distant traffic noise. (Experienced sound mixers will tell you of directors who, hoping for powerful sound effects, keep urging the mixer to turn up the controls. The effect is quite unimpressive.)

Sound influences what you see. Images alter how you hear things. The mind's ear, like the mind's eye, can select what it chooses to hear and be deaf to what it considers irrelevant. The brain is able to edit what the ear supplies to it, just as it interprets what information comes from the eye. At a dinner table where there are many simultaneous conversations, for instance, it is possible to focus your hearing attention on two people talking across the table while at the same time tuning out the voice of somebody beside you, even though that voice might be much louder. It has also been noted that emotion can influence auditory perception: for example, the mother of a young child can be quite oblivious to loud noises while at the same time acutely sensitive to the slightest whimper from her child in another room. The microphone and audio tape, however, have no such capacity, and this is why it may be necessary to think of sound in film very differently.

Consider the story of a problem confronted by BBC radio producers who wanted to open a programme with a soundtrack of street noises heard on a busy night. They sent a crew to record those sounds for real but found that the track was unusable, a mush of incomprehensible and indistinguishable noises. They realised that to create the desired effect it was necessary to record each single sound effect quite separately (sounds of car horns, squeaks of brakes, noise of gear changes and car engines, chatter of passers-by, cries of newspaper boys, clang of bus bells, the conductor's shouts to a boarding passenger). When these were all very carefully orchestrated on various tracks and mixed in a clearly and carefully balanced design, the effect of what the engineers had heard at the location was recreated. In this way, the effect of a totally natural sound environment may need to be contrived with a great deal of skill and artifice.

Mental Geography

Our perception of what lies around us is a mysterious thing. Is it something absolute or a purely personal subjective construction? For the film director (and, if he is doing his job properly, his audience), it is to a certain extent both, sometimes synthetic and fictional existing in the imagination, sometimes absolutely real and tangible.

In 1920, at the age of twenty-one, the Russian Lev Kuleshov started the world's first film school. His pupils included Vsevolod Pudovkin, later to become one of the most important directors of early Soviet cinema. Kuleshov is famous in the history of film theory for two or three experiments designed to demonstrate basic principles of the art of the cinema and the way in which the medium differs from that of literature and theatre. The Russian pioneers were great admirers of the contemporary American directors, in particular of D. W. Griffith, whose films they studied with passionate interest. As the Americans in Hollywood were a good deal more practical in their approach to film-making and not much given to theorising, it was left to the earnest Russians to study the work done quite instinctively by the pragmatic directors who had recently arrived in California and who were developing new approaches to the medium of film.

Kuleshov believed that montage, the juxtaposition of shots, was the very essence of cinema. Going much further than the Americans, Eisenstein held that each shot in itself was without much meaning until it had been organised into a pattern of editing. Thus the whole is not just greater than the sum of the parts but something different (an idea supported by much Marxist dialectical argument: the clash of opposites, the contradictions that produce a new reality). Today, much of this theorising from the Russians seems to be little more than an elaboration of basic film-making practices: it is hard to recapture the excitement the theories provoked at the time. But they are nevertheless worth studying, for example one of the experiments made by Kuleshov called 'artificial landscapes', a development of a problem he had encountered earlier when shooting a film of his own.

Nowadays the principle that Kuleshov was demonstrating (the idea of continuity of action and consistency through editing) is such universally accepted practice that it is taken for granted. But it does make a very important point about editing and the structuring of dramatic material. When shooting his 1918 film *Engineer Prite's Project*, wrote Kuleshov:

[W]e encountered certain difficulties. It was necessary for our leading characters, a father and his daughter, to walk across a meadow and look at a pole from which electric cables were strung. Due to technical circumstances, we were not able to shoot all this at the same location. We had to shoot the pole in one location and separately shoot the father and daughter in another place. We shot them looking upward, talking about the pole and moving on. We intercut the shot of the pole, taken elsewhere, into the walk across the meadow.

This was the most ordinary, the most childlike thing – something which is done now at every step.

It became apparent that through montage it was possible to create a new earthly terrain that did not exist anywhere, for these people did not walk there in reality, and in reality there was no pole there. But from the film it appeared that these people walked across a meadow and the pole appeared before their very eyes.

A few years later I made a more complex experiment: we shot a complete scene. Khokhlova and Obolensky acted in it. We filmed them in the following way: Khokhlova is walking along Petrov Street near the 'Mostorg' store. Obolensky is walking along the embankment of the Moscow River – at a distance of about two miles away. They see each other, smile, and begin to walk towards one another. Their meeting is filmed at the Boulevard Prechistensk. This boulevard is in an entirely different section of the city. They clasp hands, with Gogol's monument in the background and look – at the White House! – for at this point, we cut in a segment from an American film,

1. From *Kuleshov on Film* (University of California Press, 1974), pp. 51–3. In his book *Film Technique*, Pudovkin writes of this experiment, noting that 'Though the shooting had been done in varied locations, the spectator perceived the scene as a whole. The parts of real space picked out by the camera appeared concentrated, as it were, upon the screen. There resulted what Kuleshov termed "creative geography". By the process of junction of pieces of celluloid appeared a new, filmic space without existence in reality. Buildings separated by a distance of thousands of miles were concentrated to a space that could be covered by a few paces of the actors' (pp. 60–1). In today's parlance, read 'cheating' for 'creative geography'.

The White House in Washington. In the next shot they are again on the Boulevard Prechistensk. Deciding to go farther, they leave and climb up the enormous staircase of the Cathedral of Christ the Savior. We film them, edit the film, and the result is that they are seen walking up the steps of the White House. For this we used no trick, no double exposure: the effect was achieved solely by the organisation of the material through its cinematic treatment. This particular scene demonstrated the incredible potency of montage, which actually appeared so powerful that it was able to alter the very essence of the material. From this scene, we came to understand that the basic strength of cinema lies in montage, because with montage it becomes possible to both break down and to reconstruct, and ultimately to remake the material.[1]

As Kuleshov sought to demonstrate, physical space and real time can be made subordinate to montage. The sense we sometimes have of geography (our perception of a consistent spatial relationship between people and objects and furniture, interior architecture or exterior landscape) may, in film or video, be quite fictitious. It is something the imagination pieces together as the mind's eye and ear synthesise the images and sound presented to them into a logical and believable, if non-existent, environment. Note that eye-lines (the degree to which an off-screen look is wide or narrow to the lens) play a vital role here. In the editing room, if confronted by shots of different locations filmed at different times, it becomes clear that if one character is looking off-screen at the same eye-line angle of a different character in a different shot, these shots when intercut will produce the effect of eye contact, even if the two characters were never meant to be together in the same location, let alone looking at each other.

What is important for students to understand is that the geography of a scene must be immediately apparent to an audience. The editing in a film such as D. W. Griffith's *Intolerance*, for example, is at times extraordinarily fast. There are shots that are only three or four frames long, almost too short for the eye to see. In such scenes, the pace of intercutting is possible only because the performance areas have already been very clearly established, with the result that the layout of characters and objects is extremely clear in the mind of the audience.

Once the geography has been clearly defined, the director and editor are able, essentially, to do anything they want without confusing the audience, including, for example, playing with eye-lines and the juxtaposition of shots.[2]

Critics have said that Aristotle's principles, including that of 'unity of place' (the idea that the action of a story takes place only in one location) no longer apply. It is also true that few stage plays nowadays seem to stick closely to the 'unity of time' (requiring that the action not extend beyond sunrise and sunset of one day). But it has been said that a sense of what has been called the 'closed world' is a considerable asset in certain types of comedy or drama. We thought *The Ladykillers* was a comedy of this kind. At an early stage of production on the film, when the story was in outline and before the screenplay had been written, it was apparent to the screenwriter, myself and the associate producer that the bulk of the scenes should take place inside Mrs Wilberforce's house. In fact we realised there could be some problems in comic tone whenever we moved outside because the film had to perch on the edge of fantasy. All the main characters are exaggerated cartoon-like figures and when set against natural backgrounds, interacting with real persons, they were in danger of losing conviction.

So with the exception of the prologue and epilogue at the police station, there is only one scene (the robbery) that does not take place in Mrs Wilberforce's house. But if every scene was to be played in an interior, we were afraid the effect would be of a photographed play or a television show. Accordingly, while the screenwriter started to work on the scenes, the art director and I began to prepare plans for the sets and the location. When a screenplay and pre-production proceed together in this way, the result is that the story is more likely to be conceived in cinematic terms from the outset. This particular screenwriter was able to construct scenes and dialogue within the context of a narrative that was already taking shape in images and in action, all too seldom the professional procedure.

The logistics in the case of *The Ladykillers* were complex. Parts of scenes were filmed in three different places at widely separate points on the shooting schedule, and this high-speed comic action had to match seamlessly. There were three sets

2. See the example of *Le jour se lève* in 'The Axis' below.

built inside the studio: one was an elaborate composite of two downstairs rooms, a hallway and a double-clad section of the front entrance to the house. A second was of the two upstairs rooms of Mrs Wilberforce's house, with part of the landing and staircase. The third set was the police office. All were essential elements for the 'mental geography' of the story. Note too that the sequence when the sinister figure of Professor Marcus follows Mrs Wilberforce home – one that gives us that high-angle establishing long-shot of the cul-de-sac street, the dilapidated but elegant little home at the end of it, the vista of railway yards seen beyond, as well as the house itself – was also crucial for the audience's appreciation of exactly where the story was taking place.

Condensing Screen Time

Pacing is occasionally a problem for the inexperienced director. Let me give an example. Assume that a screenwriter delivers you a page of dialogue, a scene in which a young woman calls on her fiancé in order to take him to the airport where they are both to catch a plane to take them to the formal wedding of the young man's aunt. The girl is eager that the young man should not be late, and is exasperated to find that he has slept in and that they might miss their plane. I have chosen a banal situation because we are interested only in certain technicalities of how the scene can be shot. The content is essentially unimportant. As a director, you have been furnished with the following lines of dialogue:

> GIRL
> What's the matter? Aren't you ready?

> BOY
> When is the plane? I thought it was this afternoon.

> GIRL
> No. I told you I changed it. It's at ten-fifteen. We've got twenty minutes.

> BOY
> Why can't we take the afternoon flight?

> GIRL
> (*on telephone*)
> May I have the Bell Captain, please.
> (*to* BOY)
> Because it won't get there in time.

(*on telephone*)
This is Room 304. Can you send a boy up for the bags.
And order a taxi please.

BOY

Why not? The wedding's not till tomorrow.

GIRL

You've got to be there this afternoon.

BOY:

Why?

GIRL

There's a rehearsal.

BOY

A what?

GIRL

A rehearsal, at your mother's place. You promised her
you'd be there.

BOY

No I didn't. Not for the rehearsal. What does she need a
rehearsal for? She's been married twice already.

GIRL

I promised her we'd be there. You know how she feels
about these things.

BOY

And she knows how I feel.

At the end of this not-too-inspiring dialogue, the screenwriter,
who has assumed that the scene will start with your young man
asleep in bed, has invented for you some piece of business
involving tipping the hotel bellboy. The actions involved are:

1. the BOY gets out of bed, puts on a dressing gown, goes across
to the door and opens it

2. the GIRL enters, reacts and begins the dialogue

3. the BOY gets his trousers from the chair, takes off his pyjama

pants (under the dressing gown) and puts on the trousers

4. he takes off his dressing gown and pyjama jacket, finds a shirt and climbs into it

5. he fastens his shirt buttons

6. he finds his socks and his shoes

7. he sits on the bed, puts on one sock, then the other, one shoe, then the other

8. he finds a tie, puts it round his neck, knots it

9. he puts on his jacket, checks his wallet and plane tickets

Your problem is that when you time this dialogue, you find that these actions have to be played at great speed. In fact, the dialogue will be finished by the time his trouser fly is zipped. This is even before you confront the next problem: who does the packing? Or has he already packed? (It hardly seems in character.) Somebody has to get the suitcase, open it, start to empty the contents of drawers into it, go to the bathroom for shaving things. And how does the bellboy arrive? Your screenwriter hasn't thought it through.

The answer to this problem is pure film mechanics: planning the action so it breaks down into shots that progressively jump the continuity, thus drastically telescoping the action. The scenes detailed below are present on-screen so that we don't actually see stages 1 to 9. Instead we see the start of every action, then cut away and almost immediately reintroduce the action at a more advanced stage. It will appear to the audience as though it is all one uninterrupted process. Something like this, for example.

1. MEDIUM SHOT – BOY

Overscene, the sound of knocking. The heap of bedclothes stir. The BOY's *head appears, bleary-eyed. Knocking resumes. Reluctantly, he decides he has to get up and gropes for a dressing gown that lies at the foot of the bed, mumbling complaints.*

2. MEDIUM LONG SHOT – DOOR

The door handle is rattled. More knocking. After a moment, the BOY *appears in shot wearing his dressing gown.*

(This has already cut considerable business: climbing out of bed, putting one arm into a dressing-gown sleeve, then the other. More importantly, because of the editing, the tempo of the scene is established very quickly. The BOY can move quite slowly, but the GIRL moves fast, and the editing makes the scene move at the brisk pace of her impatience.)

As the BOY *unlocks the door, the* GIRL *enters at once. She looks at him and at the room.*

> GIRL
> What's the matter? Aren't you ready?

She walks through the shot. The BOY *consults his bare wrist where his watch ought to be but isn't.*

> BOY
> When is the plane?

FILM GRAMMAR

3. MEDIUM SHOT – GIRL

The GIRL, *taking initiative at once, is already snatching up his trousers that are on a chair, picking up his watch from the table beside the bed.*

BOY'S VOICE
(*overscene, continuing*)
I thought it was this afternoon.

Camera pans back with the GIRL *as she thrusts the trousers into the* BOY's *hands and gives him his watch.*

GIRL
No. I told you I changed it. It's at ten-fifteen. We've got twenty minutes.

The BOY *has turned to camera. Still groggy, he complains.*

BOY
Why can't we take the afternoon flight?

Overscene, under this dialogue, there is the noise of a telephone being dialled. The BOY *has started to take off his pyjama trousers under the dressing gown.*

4. MEDIUM SHOT – GIRL

The GIRL *is already connected with the hotel desk (in films, hotel telephone service is always miraculously rapid).*

GIRL
(*to phone*)
May I have the Bell Captain, please.
(*to the* BOY)
Because it won't get there in time.
(*to the phone again*)
This is Room 304. Can you send a boy up for the bags.
And order a taxi please.

5. MEDIUM SHOT – BOY

The BOY, *having now pulled on his trousers, takes off the dressing gown and the pyjama top together.*

> BOY
> Why not? The wedding's not till tomorrow.

The GIRL *appears in shot carrying the* BOY's *suitcase. She takes from him his dressing gown and pyjama top, picks up the pyjama trousers he has thrown on the bed, and thrusts his shirt at him.*

> GIRL
> You've got to be there this afternoon.

> BOY

Why?

CAMERA *is panning with the* GIRL *to exclude the* BOY *again as she sets the suitcase down on a chest of drawers, and starts to open it.*

> GIRL
> There's a rehearsal.

6. MEDIUM SHOT – BOY

Having already got an arm in the shirt and feeling for the other, he reacts.

> BOY

A what?

7. MEDIUM SHOT – GIRL

The GIRL is filling the case with clothes from the chest of drawers.

GIRL

A rehearsal, at your mother's place.
(*closing the case*)
You promised her you'd be there.

Slamming the case shut, she carries it off towards the door, CAMERA pans with her to include the BOY. He has the shirt on and has buttoned all but the collar. As the GIRL walks through shot, he sits down on the bed, looking around the floor.

BOY

No I didn't.

8. INSERT SHOTS

Beside the BOY's feet are his shoes. One sock is also on the floor. The BOY's hands pick them up. Camera tilts up as he speaks.

BOY
(*continuing*)
Not for a rehearsal.

While he is putting on one sock, he is looking around for the other.

9. CLOSE-SHOT – GIRL

Having set down the case by the door, she stoops to pick up the other sock and throws it at him.

10. MEDIUM SHOT – BOY

The sock hits him. He has the other shoe and sock on, and now begins to put on the second sock.

BOY
What does she need a rehearsal for? She's been married twice already.

Overscene, sound of the door buzzer. The BOY *glances at the door.*

11. LONG SHOT – DOOR

The GIRL *is already on her way to open the door.*

GIRL
(*as she goes*)
I promised her we'd be there.

A BELLBOY *appears in the doorway as she opens it. Indicating the suitcase, the* GIRL *walks out of shot towards the* BOY, *while the* BELLBOY *goes for the case.*

GIRL
(*continuing*)
You know how she feels about these things.

12. MEDIUM SHOT – BOY AND GIRL

The BOY, *now standing, has his shoes and socks on and his tie in his hand, He puts the tie round his neck as the* GIRL *lifts up his jacket to help him put it on.*

BOY
And she knows how I feel.

FILM GRAMMAR

13. MEDIUM LONG SHOT – BELLBOY

The GIRL *re-enters shot and indicates to the* BELLBOY *that he is to carry out the suitcase, then turns impatiently, as the* BOY *comes into frame, finishing the knot in his tie. She then explores his pocket to produce his wallet and check the plane ticket.*

Drawing Lesson

When you are planning camera coverage, what notation do you use to indicate the set-ups? This is presuming you find it useful to design your camera coverage on paper before you arrive on the studio floor. Do you make a ground plan of the setting, then draw V-shaped camera angles? Or do you make primitive thumbnail sketches that represent the film frame and the size of the figures in the shot? You can, of course, do both. Or neither.

As a system, storyboards suit the temperament of some directors and not others. Personally, I believe they can be useful in certain circumstances. A scene that involves very complicated and expensive logistics, crowds, special effects and elaborate production design can very profitably be planned in very precise detail beforehand. But if you are working on a scene with a lot of dialogue and the possibility of complex movements of actors during a sustained scene, it can be a mistake to plan the camera set-ups in advance in any rigid way. The argument for this often takes the form of a case on behalf of the instinctive contribution that good actors can make, as they are often able to assist the director enormously in exploring how the scene might be staged. It can certainly be a mistake to plan camera coverage in a way that locks you in so you are unable to seize unexpected opportunities that arise while rehearsing or shooting.

There is actually no real contradiction between preparation and improvisation. The director is constantly doing both and, paradoxically, a well worked-out plan for the staging and camera coverage ought to give you *more* freedom to improvise, not less. Planning how a scene should be directed is, in my opinion, a great deal like planning a battle. All your moves should be worked out as carefully as possible, given the fact that you cannot be sure of what your opponent has in store for you. Or, to use another metaphor, it is like preparing to hunt big game. You build your hidden vantage point as near as possible to the waterhole, you keep your ammunition and gun at hand, but your preparations are utterly dependent on the unpredictable: the behaviour of the wild animal for whom you are lying in wait (in our case, the actor).

I have for some time urged all students, both writers and directors, to develop some competence in drawing. Having graphic skills, even of a very humble kind, will enable the director to produce basic diagrams at high speed in the margins of a script. This is an invaluable aid at the stage of planning the coverage of a scene and the creation of a shooting script, and is essential as a means of swift and clear communication with the actor, camera operator, and film editor. Being able to prepare a basic ground plan on paper that shows the scale of your location, possible positions of actors, and placement of furniture and props, can also be useful. (It may even be a mistake to illustrate things in any greater detail since this will slow you down. The precise photographic imagery is something you should be able to leave to the cinematographer and art director.) With such competence in visualisation you may find it easier to be free of the actualities and potential problems of the given geography of your location, and very much clearer in your use of film grammar. Being able to prepare elementary storyboards can force you to think much more precisely, from the outset, in the medium of cinema. It requires you to see and think in the visual structures you need to master.

'Of course, you know I can't draw,' says the film student, without any trace of self-criticism, as if the ability to draw was something for which one had no personal responsibility, like having been born with brown or blue eyes, a genetic trait. Well, I admit to a prejudice. It seems a little odd to me that a student pays exorbitant tuition fees to attend one of the professional schools that deal with the visual image, without having bothered to acquire any skill in draughtsmanship whatsoever. A real command of figurative drawing may indeed be a gift, an inherited and instinctive ability. But it is hardly more than the knack of reasonably legible handwriting (which, admittedly, is occasionally also absent in a good many of students these days), and anyone who can, with reasonable effort, write legibly or draw the lettering for a sign, has the requisite skill. As all of us are, surely, meant to be studying skills of 'communication', there is far less excuse for us to be wholly inept in these matters.

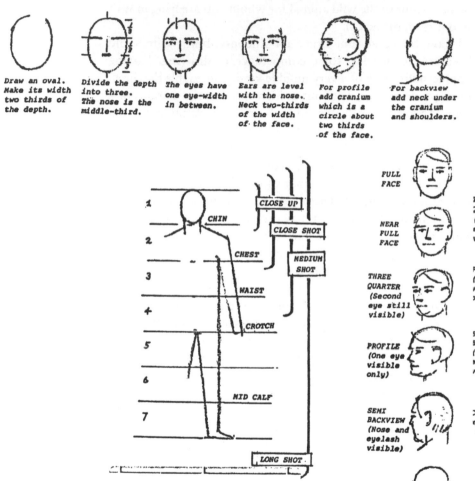

Draw an oval. Make its width two thirds of the depth.

Divide the depth into three. The nose is the middle-third.

The eyes have one eye-width in between.

Ears are level with the nose. Neck two-thirds of the width of the face.

For profile add cranium which is a circle about two thirds of the face.

For backview add neck under the cranium and shoulders.

Some tips about drawing the human form. The face is very roughly oval, about two thirds the width of its depth. If you divide it vertically in three, the eyebrows are on the line of the upper third, the nose is the middle third. Between the eyes, there

220   FILM GRAMMAR

is the width of one eye. Ears are about the depth of the nose, the neck is about two thirds of the width of the head. To complete the head, add the cranium behind and slightly above the face, a circle of about two thirds of the face. To indicate a back view, show the neck under the cranium and ears.

The same formula for drawing the face and head can be used to diagram, in very primitive fashion, the eye-line in close-ups. Some sense of the expression of the face is still present in semi-back-view if we can see the curve of the cheek and eyelashes of the eye. Back view leaves the expression to be imagined.

The head is very roughly one seventh of the height of the whole body. Two sevenths cuts at the chest, i.e. at close-shot size; three sevenths is waist-length, i.e. medium shot. Six-sevenths, cutting below the knee, is a medium-long-shot, and anything that shows the full length counts as a long-shot.

Point of View

1. See Hall's *The Hidden Dimension: an anthropologist examines man's use of space in public and private* (Anchor, 1969) and *The Silent Language: an anthropologist reveals how we communicate by our manners and behaviour* (Anchor, 1973).

At each particular moment of any given scene, the position of the camera is a point in time and space from where the Invisible Imaginary Ubiquitous Winged Witness, the observer to the action, implies a specific point of view. It is from this spot where the audience views the story, from where the Witness prompts the audience to feel sympathy for one character over another. One of the most elementary decisions the director must make in this respect is about the size of shot. At each precise moment of a scene, how close is the subject to the lens? How much is included in the frame? How much is left off-screen?

A popular psychologist, Edward T. Hall, has written a couple of books about what he calls *proxemics*, a theory that purports to be a study of how people's behaviour and attitudes are affected by the physical distances between them.[1] Hall suggests that these can be divided into certain categories: intimate, personal, social, public and remote. According to Hall we all have a sense of 'psychological territory'. He gives the example of how, in eras past, a king would not allow his subjects to come too close, also insisting that subordinates were not permitted to sit in chairs higher than his own. Watch strangers who are crowded together in an elevator or a bus and you may notice the curiously frozen facial expression they assume, a kind of mask protecting them from the indignity of uncomfortable proximity to strangers.

As a science I think proxemics theory is probably not to be taken too seriously. But it is quite useful when thinking about film grammar: when and how to use long-shots, close-ups and such. The film industry has given names to the various shot sizes you will see in many films.

Important to understand is that the most basic elements of film grammar have the potential for dramatic irony. The camera

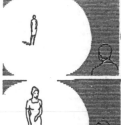

REMOTE DISTANCE
The individual person is not identified as a particular person. Figure is recognised only by costume or because of the situation or context.

PUBLIC DISTANCE
This distance will be maintained by people who have to establish a 'public status', who are 'unapproachable' as individuals.

SOCIAL DISTANCES
At fifteen feet to ten feet, deportment and dress are on display. In a social environment manners are likely to be self-conscious.

Speech and gesture are apt to be fairly deliberate, formal and still a little 'projected' if in the presence of a group of people.

PERSONAL DISTANCES
Reserved for close acquaintances or friends. A stranger who invades this 'private space' may be regarded as an intruder.

Closer still implies that the relationship is 'one-on-one'. The presence of others is ignored. Speech will be impromptu and the communication more 'non-verbal'.

INTIMATE DISTANCE
Physical involvement. Acceptable in public if participants are 'family'. It does imply exclusion of others, normally demands some degree of privacy.

PROXEMICS THEORY

A popular psychologist, Edward T Hall, has written a couple of books, 'The Hidden Dimension' and 'The Silent Language' on what he calls a theory of proxemics'. It purports to be a study of how peoples behaviour and attitudes are affected by the physical distances between them.

Hall suggests that these can be divided into four categories: INTIMATE DISTANCE, PERSONAL DISTANCE, SOCIAL DISTANCE and IMPERSONAL DISTANCE.

According to him we all have a sense of 'psychogical territory'. He gives the example of the way in which in other days kings would not allow their subjects to come too close, also insisting that subordinates were not permitted to sit in chairs higher than the king's.

always takes what could be construed as a psychological attitude to what it is filming, an attitude that directly affects the story being told. By using different shot sizes and placement of camera, a director is able to make a clear statement about his thoughts and feelings concerning the story's characters, and the situations they find themselves in. One of the most obvious examples might be when the camera angle is high and shooting down, something that seems to encourage the audience to feel superior to those characters on the screen, while an angle that is below eye-level, shooting slightly upward, seems to indicate a point of view that is more sympathetic and deferential.

If the physical position of the Winged Witness always implies some degree of psychological participation, it is possible

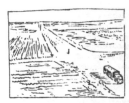

EXTREME LONGSHOT
Example: the opening shot in the scene of the attack by the crop-dusting plane in Hitchcock's 'North by Northwest.

It's an image of 'the environment'--little emphasis on the figures in it. It's generally considered that if a figure is less than one fifth of the height of the screen, you can use doubles for the actors. They are recognized only by the clothes they wear.

LONGSHOT
Example: the second shot in the same scene. It's full length figure or more.

As an image, it reads as 'The Landscape-with-Figure'. The figure in relation to the surroundings.

Here the framing deliberately emphasises the emptiness, the surrounding 'nothing.'

CLOSE SHOT
Example: this shot, coming at the moment when Cary Grant realizes that the plane is directly attacking him.

The shots cuts off at the chest leve, now excluding much of the 'body language' of torso and arms to put more emphasis of facial reactions. It's 'personal distance.'

CLOSE UP
Example: The shot where Grant stands waiting in the middle of the road in order to force the oil truck to stop.

It's head and shoulders only. Strong emphasis on the feeling and thought of the character. 'Personal' or even 'intimate' distance. Better and more typical uses are elsewhere in the film; the close-up is standard screensize for moments where the feeling and thought, the 'subtext' to verbally expressed ideas is at least as strong as the literate meaning of the words.

BIG CLOSE UP
Example: the end frame of the above shot after a track-in on Grant's terror stricken face.

MEDIUM SHOT
Example: Third shot in the 'North by Northwest'.

It cuts the figure off at the hips. At this distance, we read fully the 'body language' of the actor's stance, his way of holding himself--his 'overt' attitudes and the extraverted behavior. The voice would be projected as off talking to someone across a room or a couple of yards away in a public place. Performance scales is projected to 'social distance'.

MEDIUM CLOSESHOT
Example: a few cuts later in the sequence. Slightly closer waist length.

We get a slightly stronger impact of facial impression, seeing enough to appreciate feeling and thought in the face. It's a 'social distance' with a little more personal feeling.

MEDIUM TWO-SHOT
Example: a three quarter length shot of the two figures seen in profile. The shot is distant enough to be more or less 'impersonal' and it is 'neutral' in emphases. It shows the spatial distance between the characters.

OVERSHOULDER CLOSE-SHOT
Example: the cut following which is a little closer, more full face on Grant, showing more of his thought and feeling and 'favoring' him at the expense of the girl who is backview.

'COMPLEMENTARY' TWO SHOT
Example: intercut with the above. Same screen size so that it can be used as the 'complement', having an equal but opposite degree of emphasis on the girl.

POINT OF VIEW CUTAWAY
Example: by including the shoulder of Grant at the edge of screen in foreground, it emphasizes the 'subjective' viewpoint, 'as seen through the eyes of' the girl.

FILM GRAMMAR

to detect rather obvious 'attitudes'. First, an attitude of disinterested, objective and neutral interest. Second, an attitude of balanced sympathy alternating between two or more characters in the scene. Third, a strong sense of empathy with one of the characters whose point of view is seen subjectively, with the other point of view seen merely in cutaway. There are, needless to say, many variations on this. Within any given scene there can be several shifts of sympathy and attitude. There are also at least three interrelated factors that seem to determine the audience's degree of identification with one character over another.

First, the relative screen sizes and placement of camera. If one character is seen in close-up and the other in medium shot, our feelings of sympathy and/or identification are with the figure seen at the closer distance. Increase in shot sizes generally creates a rise in tension, while a decrease relaxes our feelings of participation. Camera movement not only directs the attention of audiences but indicates how we should be feeling. If the camera follows a particular character, this encourages identification with that person, while a tracking shot from a character's point of view underlines its subjective quality.

Second, the eye-line, the degree to which an off-screen gaze is given either narrowly or wide to the lens. The narrower the eye-line, the more we seem to feel identification, because when confronting the face directly, we feel much more of the impact of the subject's personality. The feeling is one of greater involvement and there is more sense of identification.

Third, the timing of the interactions. If one character is on-screen for longer than another, and especially if the edits are timed to capture the thoughts of that character, then the scene will often appear to be from his or her point of view.

Objective and Neutral

Three angles and one master-shot (overleaf) of the two characters composed for equal pictorial emphasis, plus two singles in semi-profile, not particularly close, and with very carefully matched screen sizes and eye-lines.

Medium Shot of Girl.   Master Shot.   Matching Shot of Man.

In this pattern there is equal sense of identification with two people, and no clear point of view (except that of an uninvolved third party).

Balanced Sympathy

Five angles, one master-shot of equal emphasis, two matched over shoulder close-shots, plus two close-ups with fairly narrow eye-lines.

Overshoulder onto Girl.   Master Shot.   Oversholder onto Man

Girls Closeup   Man's Closeup

With this pattern, there is more sense of involvement with the two characters, though the point of view is alternating, which means there is no special identification with either person.

Strong Emphasis on the Point of View of One Character

Emphasising a particular character can be done in a number of ways (overleaf).

1 By framing one character in positions where he appears larger on screen than the other character.
2 Through camera movement that can carefully centre his figure when the camera is in movement and following his moves, while the other character is left in relatively static positions and is treated as part of the environment.
3 Use of an over-shoulder shot where the character to be emphasised (a man) is seen large in the foreground with the other character (a girl) in a longer distance.
4 A fairly big close-up of the man, with his eye-line very narrow to the lens.
5 A medium- (or medium-long) shot of the girl, in which her eye-line is somewhat wide of camera.

These angles should be edited so that much of the footage is either on the big close-up of the man or the master-shot. Both the medium shot of the girl and the over-shoulder shot should be used quite briefly, held for no longer than is necessary as a cut-away point of view angle or as a brief linking shot to remind us of their spatial relationship. When editing, much of the girl's characterisation would be played off-screen, or on the master-shot where concentration is on the man.

The placing of the subject matter within the film frame is a matter of personal aesthetics. As any painter or illustrator will tell you, it depends on many factors (the balance of shapes, colours, light and shade), while the film-maker also has to consider the images (and emotions) that precede and follow in the sequence of events. For sequences designed with great attention to image composition, look at films such as Carl Dreyer's *La passion de Joanne D'Arc* and the work of Eisenstein (who was a graphic designer before he became a director). Montage sequences

Mastershot. When Camera pans, it always keeps the Man in center frame, following him not her.

Overshoulder onto the Girl, the Man framed large in foreground.

His point of view of the Girl. A cutaway

A Big Closeup of the Man, Matched to the size of him in the Overshoulder.

The timing of the shots in editing should be to underline the impact of unspoken responses seen in the Man's Big Closeup, with the other angles used as coverage of the dialogue to which he is reacting. Cutaways never long enough to interrupt the Man's performance.

in Soviet cinema of this period paid great attention to the framing of shots and the patterning of sequences. John Ford's films are also worth your examination for classic image composition. They illustrate the value of traditionally balanced and restful long-shot images that can be effectively used in what stage directors would call tableau effects, the kind of picture-postcard staging that can be used to mark the end of an act in a play.

Framing can be defined as the composition of the pattern of visual elements within the rectangle of the cinema screen. Though it is a matter of concern to several people on the film set (including the lighting cameraman and camera operator), most directors insist on the right to design their own camera style. This is because the smallest details of the camera set-up, movement and framing all have an immediate effect on the narrative/dramatic meaning of the shot and hence the film as a whole. Though audiences may not (indeed should not) be aware of it, the exact framing of a shot has such an influence on the drama being played out that relatively small matters of visual composition may completely alter the storytelling significance of the shot.

When thinking about framing it can be useful to discuss what we call off-screen space. The thing to remember here is that whatever is left off-screen or hidden behind things that are within the frame might be just as important as what is visible. By masking things from our view and controlling the precise point at which we see them, the director manipulates the timing of visual information and, in turn, our attention and sympathies. The most obvious example of traditional off-screen space is a setting that has entrances and exits used in the way they might be in a theatrical play, where characters appear and disappear into the wings (classic slapstick often exploits this stage tradition). Several European films have also used off-screen space in very interesting ways, as they literally guide the viewer through complex tracking shots, taking us from one incident and character to another.

Here is a scene from *The Man in the White Suit* as an example, staged in one static master-shot. (For some reason, slapstick tends to work best when it is played in long-shot as continuous action, and without the use of closer angles.) When everybody vanishes from the shot and the camera remains on the empty corridor (with noises off), the staging makes use of the oldest of comic formulas beloved of the oldest music-hall clowns.

OFFSCREEN SPACE

The most obvious example of the use of 'offscreen space' is a setting which has entrances and exits which are used in the way they might be in a theatrical play. Characters appear and disappear 'into the wings'.

Classic movie slapstick often exploits this stage tradition. For some reason, slapstick tends to work best when it is played out in longshot

as continuous action and without the use of closer angles.

Here is a scene from 'The Man in the White Suit' as illustration. It is staged in one static mastershot. When everybody vanishes from the shot and the camera remains on the empty corridor - with noises off - the staging is using the oldest of comic formulas beloved of the oldest music hall clowns.

Pursuing SIDNEY, BERTHA trips over a bicycle left at the bottom of the stairs...

But SIDNEY is similarly held up, trying to unlock the back door. BERTHA tackles-

-hurling him through the door of the scullery. Both of them disappear inside.

As terrible sounds emerge from the scullery, the LODGER comes out of his room-

just as SIDNEY appears with BERTHA in pursuit. The LODGER is caught between them.

SIDNEY, defending himself with a wooden lid from a boiler, grabs a balustrade-

but it breaks ollapsing into the LODGER's room as BERTHA locks the door.

Protesting, the LODGER tries to escape to the back door. BERTHA pushes him through-

the scullery door and locks that as well. Both of them are her prisoners.

Cameramen use the slang word 'dingle' to describe an object that can be used as a foreground piece at the edge of the frame. It is sometimes used to make the pictorial composition more interesting. For example, a blank area of blue sky may be felt to be more picturesque if a tree branch is tipped in at the top of the frame to lend depth and perspective.

But foreground pieces can also be used for reasons of exposition. It is always desirable to keep reminding the audience of the geographical relationships between characters and objects, and in some cases this is essential to the clarity of the scene. Below are several examples. In the *North by Northwest* images, it is the tyre wheel and the man's arm in the foreground that make the shots dramatic. The image with the corn stalks in foreground show just how far the camera is from the road and the dangerous space across which Cary Grant must run. And in the drawings from *The Man in the White Suit*, it is the helplessness of Alec Guinness that requires that camera to emphasise the window bars, while the pressure that Marlon Brando's character is under in *On the Waterfront* is indicated by the framing of the bodies in the foreground as they confront him.

<u>Framing - Foreground Pieces.</u>

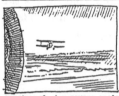

A point of view camera angle in 'North by Northwest'. Cary Grant has been nearly run over by the huge gasoline truck. He now looks off to see the crop-duster plane diving to attack him again. The wheel of the big truck is used as a 'dingle' in the foreground to emphasise that it is Cary's point of view.

Moments later, in the same scene. The plane smashes into the truck and they both explode. The arm of one of the bystanders is framed in the foreground, emphasis on the danger to them. This reads as a 'point of view' but, interestingly, it is not cut with any reverse angle closeshot of Cary or the other bystanders.

On the right, Cary Grant's point of view of the oil tanker coming down the road. The stalks of corn are used as 'dingles' to frame the scene - to establish the distance that Grant must cross to reach the road.

'DINGLES' AND FOREGROUND PIECES

Cameramen use the slang word 'dingle' to describe an object that is carried about and can be used as a 'foreground piece' at the edge of the frame.

It is sometimes used simply to make the pictorial composition more interesting. For example a blank area of blue sky may be felt to be 'more picturesque' if a tree branch is 'tipped in' at the top of the frame to lend depth and perspective.

But foreground pieces can be used for important reasons of exposition. It is always desirable to keep reminding the audience of the geographical relationships and in some cases essential to the clarity of the scene. On this page are several examples. On the left, the tire wheel and the arm of the man in foreground are what makes the shots dramatic. At the top it's essential to show how far the camera is from the road and the dangerous space across which Cary Grant must run. Below the helplessness of the imprisoned Alec Guiness requires that the camera emphasises the window bars. On the right, the pressure on Marlon Brando is indicated by the framing of the bodies in the foreground as they confront him.

In 'On the Waterfront', a shot across the shoulder of Karl Malden onto Brando. The framing stresses the pressure that the priest is putting on Brando, urging him to fight back against the mobsters by testifying against them in court.

Later, in court, Brando is in the witness chair. Again the masking by the arm of the interrogating lawyer helps the dramatic tension.

On the left, complementary angles shooting through the bars of a window (from 'The Man in the White Suit). In this case the window bars are used as foreground pieces in both shots. It is more usual to put them in only one of the angles.

A useful class exercise is to take any scene of dialogue between two performers, shoot it, and then edit it in a number of different ways to accentuate different points of view. As an example, I will use a scene from one of the first features I worked on, *Saraband for Dead Lovers*. The plot concerned an adulterous affair between an unhappily married German princess and the military commander of her husband's army. The scene I have in mind was simple and wordless. The hero K has returned from a campaign and, after an interview with the Prince, is on his way through one of the antechambers of the palace when he sees the Princess with whom he is still in love. He is unable to talk to her, nor she with him. They are at the opposite end of a room filled with other people. They see and acknowledge each other according to the formal etiquette of court behaviour. That is all that happens.

In an example like this, it is often the editing that makes the scene work. The director covered the action in six shots. Here, as I remember, is how the editor assembled the scene:

1 Medium shot of K accompanied by his companions. He enters the room and stops as he sees the Princess.
2 Reverse angle. K in foreground, the Princess with her womenfolk at the other end of the room. She notices him.
3 Close-up of K reacting.
4 Medium shot. Princess with her friends. She has seen K first, and now the other womenfolk are looking at him.
5 Resume close-up on K. Sensing others are watching, he makes a small formal bow.
6 Long-shot, reverse angle. The Princess framed in foreground. K and his companions beyond.
7 Resume medium shot of Princess as she formally acknowledges him. She turns to her womenfolk.
8 Resume long-shot. Princess in foreground with K and his companions beyond. K looks at her for a moment before he turns and goes on his way, his companions following.
9 Close-up of Princess. Listening to chatter of womenfolk, she glances after K. We see the effort with which she controls herself.

It is the sequence of changing image sizes that determines the point of view from which the action is seen, the identification of the audience with, in this case, K, until the last shot of the scene. A literary version of the scene might read as follows:

K came through the doorway followed by his companions and was halfway across the antechamber before he saw her. She was at the other end of the big room, surrounded by some of her womenfolk. He had not expected to meet her, and it was a moment before he could recover his composure. She wore the same dress that he had seen her in the day that he left. Conscious of the others that watched, he managed the formal inclination required by court etiquette. She acknowledged him and turned back to her friends. K hesitated and started again towards the other exit from the antechamber, along with his companions, but as he disappeared, the girl glanced after him. Listening to the meaningless gossip of her friends, she managed to conceal her emotion.

Each sentence in the above (very corny) passage represents a shot. Now compare this with another version. Another editor, using exactly the same footage, might have put together a sequence that covered the same action but where the emphasis was sufficiently different for the content to be the story of the Princess, not K.

1 Close-up of Princess. Listening to off-screen chatter of womenfolk. She happens to glance across the room.
2 Long-shot. Princess framed in foreground. Beyond at the other end of the antechamber, K comes into the room followed by his companions.
3 Resume close-up of Princess. She reacts.
4 Medium shot of K and his companions. He sees her, stops in his tracks. His companions follow suit.
5 Reverse. Medium shot of Princess and her womenfolk. Seeing her, they look towards K.
6 Close-up of K. Sensing their scrutiny, he makes a bow to the Princess.
7 Resume medium shot of Princess and womenfolk. They sense tension, watching her now.
8 Close-up of Princess. No trace of emotion.
9 Resume long-shot. Princess framed in foreground with K and other beyond. He hesitates, starts on again with his companions.
10 Medium shot. Panning with K and his group to the door. As he leaves, he looks back towards the Princess.

11 Resume close-up of Princess. Overscene, the chatter of womenfolk. She is not listening. We are close enough to see the struggle not to show her private misery.

The literary version might be:

She knew he was in court and was torn between the hunger to see him again and the fear that her feelings would betray her. She was in the anteroom with her women when he appeared. She struggled to hold back tears. He looked thinner, under strain, as he saw her and stopped. Her womenfolk, seeing him enter, had sensed the tension.

K was as careful as she, as formal in his manner. Aware that her women were watching, she drew strength from him as she matched him in discretion, equally formal. She was perfectly under control, dismissing him as she turned to the women again. Then he was gone. And it was then that she had to fight hardest for self-control, unable to concentrate on the gossiping of her women friends.

The Axis

As audiences we are, it seems, remarkably perceptive in observing very small shifts in the direction and focus of people's eyes. These barely visible movements of the face are important clues to a person's feelings and thoughts, and like us, the camera is able to read them with astonishing speed and accuracy. Thus in a scene involving two characters who are involved in some interaction, we seem to feel there is an imaginary line that represents an axis of their relationship. It can be thought of as the line connecting their looks, the eye-line. There is an invisible line connecting the eyes of two characters even when they are not looking at each other. When the camera moves from a master-shot of two people, cutting to closer angles of each of them separately, this line becomes significant. It seems to be disorientating if the closer angles 'jump' this axis, moving to camera positions on the opposite side. As will be explained, this is much simpler than it sounds.

The standard shooting pattern is that camera set-ups should be kept to the same side of the axis. To do otherwise is called 'crossing the axis', something that can create disorientation in the audience if the geography of the scene – the layout of the environment and the orientation between characters – has not been adequately revealed. Overleaf is the most elementary pattern of camera coverage involving the eye-line axis. The master-shot shows the two figures in their geographical relationship to each other. We see the distance between them from a third-person point of view with some degree of objectivity. The move to the close-up from camera B excludes the man, concentrating on the woman, and gives us a shot angled so we get much more of a sense of what she is feeling and thinking. The shot from camera C does the same for the man. Because the two close-ups are matched in both screen size and eye-line, the balance of our interest is equal (assuming they are given equal time in editing). Note that the eye-lines meet in this series of shots. In effect, this is because shots B and C are equidistant from the (x–y) axis, as well as from the line that bisects it (e–f). The angles are complementary because she looks off-screen right to him, and he looks off-screen left to her at the same angle.

ESTABLISHING SHOT
Figures in profile.
The Woman looks <u>Right</u>
at the Man. The Man
looks left at her.

CLOSE SHOT OF WOMAN
She looks towards the
man. Her eyeline is
camera <u>Right</u>.

CLOSE SHOT OF MAN
He looks towards the
woman. His eyeline is
camera <u>Left</u>.

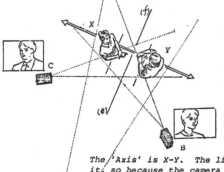

'GEOMETRY' OF
EYELINES AND
SCREENSIZES

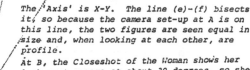

The 'Axis' is X-Y. The line (e)-(f) bisects it, so because the camera set-up at A is on this line, the two figures are seen equal in size and, when looking at each other, are profile.

At B, the Closeshot of the Woman shows her look past camera at about 30 degrees, so she is semi-profile. The eyeline angle is B-X-Y.

At C, the Closeshot of the man is about as far on the other side of (e)-(f), so the two Closeshots are equal in screensize.

And since the eyeline -(C-Y-X)of the Man is equal to that of the Woman (B-X-Y) so their looks are exactly matched.

FILM GRAMMAR

Note what happens when the shots cross the axis. Because both characters are looking off-screen in the same direction, both seem to be looking at the same thing, and if the two close shots need to be inter-cut, their eyes will not meet.

A) M.S. MAN AND WOMAN
Establishing two-shot.
The Man looks LEFT At
the Woman. The Woman
looks RIGHT at the Man.

B) C.S. MAN
He looks offscreen
LEFT towards the
Woman, the same
direction as in the
establishing shot.

C) C.S. WOMAN
She looks offscreen
LEFT, the same
direction. The
eyelines do not
connect.

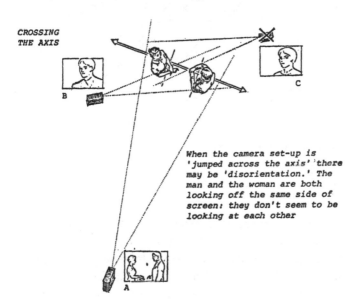

CROSSING
THE AXIS

When the camera set-up is
'jumped across the axis' 'there
may be 'disorientation.' The
man and the woman are both
looking off the same side of
screen; they don't seem to be
looking at each other

A) ESTABLISHING SHOT
Angled to shoot more
along the axis showing
the Young Man a bit
more frontally (both
eyes) but the Young
Woman profile

B) OVERSHOULDER SHOT
Another two-shot but
closer. The Young Man
is framed in fore-:′·.′
ground on screen Left.
The Young Woman is in
Medium Shot beyond,
looking narrowly Left

C) C.S. YOUNG MAN
A 'single' of the
Young Man. Eyeline
matching B) as he
looks offscreen to
the Right towards
the Young Woman.

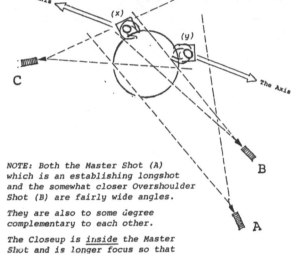

NOTE: Both the Master Shot (A)
which is an establishing longshot
and the somewhat closer Overshoulder
Shot (B) are fairly wide angles.

They are also to some degree
complementary to each other.

The Closeup is inside the Master
Shot and is longer focus so that
the Young Man is seen more frontally.

In the example above, the master-shot is angled to favour the man with the woman in profile. Another two-shot, somewhat closer, is angled towards the woman, while the man is framed in the foreground. The effect of this is a very different sense of the points of view. B and C are quite accurately matched as regards eye-lines, and there is a strong sense of eye-contact at moments when they look at each other. But there is a contrast in the size of the shots. The single close-up on the man is much bigger than its reverse angle of the woman, and it invites us to identify with him rather than her.

FILM GRAMMAR

FRONT VIEW. Eyeline narrow to the lens. In a close shot this is commonly the image that a director uses for the full impact of personality. Our sense of empathy with the character is strong.

THREE QUARTER VIEW. Eyeline is wider. The impression of empathy is not quite so strong. But we still see the thoughts and feelings and, depending on the context, will 'identify' with her.

SIDE VIEW. Eyeline is now very wide and we can see only a little of the eye that is furthest from camera. We now seem to be looking at the character. It's a more 'objective' shot.

COMPLETE PROFILE. As soon as we can see only one eye the shot becomes much more impersonal. Camera feels like an onlooker. We may or may not feel empathy, but we are likely to feel a degree of objectivity, a distance.

SEMI-BACKVIEW. If we can see enough of the curve of the cheek and eye to recognize what expression there might be on the face that is turned away, we may still get some sense of personality. But it is likely to feel like a point of view angle.

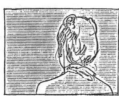

FULL BACKVIEW. Nothing of the face can be seen. Because all expression is left to our imaginations, paradoxically, a backview can sometimes be used--in certain contexts--to produce a very strong sense of empathy.

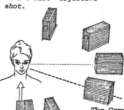

THE 'COMPASS POINTS'

OF THE EYELINES

The Camera is a 'presence'. It is a kind of 'stand-in' for the audience. Though in fiction film it is usually (not always) the convention that the actor avoids looking directly at the lens, and thus suggesting a conscious awareness of the audience, nevertheless there seems to be another level of awareness at which the character played by the actor is involved in something that might be a 'psychological interaction' with that oddly magical creature the 'Imaginary Observer'.

Note that the eye-line is a measure of our feeling of empathy with a character. The more frontal the camera angle, the greater our sense of subjective involvement. Interactions shot in semi-profile are relatively objective. We, the audience, remain outside and relatively neutral observers. With the three-quarter eye-line, there is some greater involvement. When the eye-line is very close to camera, tension is at its maximum. It is common practice, as a scene builds in dramatic tension, to use eye-lines closer to the camera.

Important to remember is that in these diagrams, for the sake of simplicity, the eye-line has been drawn as if the look of the eyes is always in the same direction to which the face is turned. Obviously this need not be so. Overleaf are sidelong off-screen looks where the face is turned in one direction, but the eye-line is a look in another direction. What is important is the eyes, not the face. Note that when the eye-line is not in the same direction

Eyeline is narrowly to Left though the face is turned to the Right of camera.

Eyeline is NARROW LEFT though the face is turned slightly to the Right of camera.

Eyeline is NARROWLY RIGHT though face is turned towards the Left of camera.

Eyeline is WIDE RIGHT though the face is turned narrowly to the Left of camera.

When the eyeline is well above the level of the lens, the offscreen look will sometimes - in some situations - imply a feeling of awe or admiration, literally of 'looking up to' the offscreen person or situation.

Conversely, when the eyeline is underneath the lens, a closeup may have a sense of more 'interior' and private thought or feeling. It is we (the camera) who are looking for what is 'behind the eyes'.

© 1988 A.Mackendrick

EYELINES AND THE CAMERA

In many of these diagrams, for the sake of simplicity, the eyeline been drawn as if the look is always in the same direction as the face is turned. But obviously this need not be so. Above are 'sidelong' offscreen looks: the face is turned in one direction, but the eyeline is a look in another direction.

In <u>matching</u> what is important is the eyes, not the face.

Notice that when the eyeline is not in the same direction as the face, there is apt to be a suggestion of slyness in the expression.

An eyeline just below the level of the lens may - in some contexts have a slightly more 'introspective' feeling than one over the camera. Needless to say, however, these are things about which it is dangerous to theorise. A good actor will have an instinct - a 'sense of camera' which the director will learn to respect and encourage.

as the face, there is apt to be a suggestion of slyness in the expression, and that an eye-line just below the level of the lens may, in some contexts, have a slightly more introspective feeling than one over the camera.

Following on from our look at Kuleshov and his discovery of 'mental geography', note that these principles relating to the eye-line can be played with. Through the matching of eye-lines and the editing, the director can convince us that characters who have never even met other are engaged in quite intimate interactions.

A) *ESTABLISHING TWO SHOT*
The Woman is turned
away from the Man,
busy with some files.
Ignoring him, she is
looking off Left.

B) *MEDIUM SHOT. MAN*
Impatient, he glances
at his watch. He is
turned away from her,
looking downward Right.

C) *MEDIUM SHOT. WOMAN*
She is in backview.
The angle is from the
Man's point of view
- if he did look at
the woman.

'NON-EXISTANT EYELINES' THAT ARE IMPLIED

We start by demonstrating so-called
'principles' of the axis and eyelines by
using only the simplest of situations -
two characters who face each other and
look directly into each others faces.

Once you've grasped the principles,
however, you should note that this is a
situation that occurs rarely in normal
behaviour, and looks distinctly strange
if it is maintained for very long. Two
people do not ordinarily hold eye-contact
for longer than the very brief glance that
is necessary to check for a reaction. The
moment is fleeting - even if it is also
a significant moment.

This 'axis' is, of course imaginary - but so
indeed is all 'cinematic space': it exists only in
the mind's eye of the audience.

A common problem for the student who is not
yet experienced in film or video is to become so
involved in the actual geography of the location
or the set that they do not realise that it is
quite possible to create an illusion of spatial
relationships - by intercutting shots that might
be taken anywhere but that seem to 'connect' by
matched eyelines.

There are countless illustrations of this.
One can cite examples of 'intimate' scenes of very
strong emotional relationships between two actors
who, in actual fact, were never together in the
same setting at the same time.

Indeed, one of the best arguments for the
study of how to match eyelines and so produce the
illusion of 'eye-contact' is that it can help you
put together scenes out of shots where it wasn't
possible to stage the scene as it might have
occured 'in reality'

Here is conventionally
matched camera coverage
of 'eyelines' - at a
point where characters
are not, in fact, looking
at each other at all.
Oddly, the principles
still seem to apply.

Two shots taken in wholly
different locations - and
on different occasions -
without the characters ever
actually having met each
other will appear to make
eye-contact if the eyelines
are 'correct' and the edits
make good sense.

While the so-called 'rule' against crossing the axis is one that
you should understand, it is important to recognise that it
should not be regarded as some kind of law never to be broken.
A common problem for the student who is not yet experienced
in film is to become so involved in the actual geography of a
location that he does not realise that by intercutting shots that
might be taken anywhere but that seem to be connected by
matching eyelines, it is possible to create an illusion of spatial
relationships. Like most things discussed in these classes, examine the standard usage of certain techniques so you can determine just how to break them most effectively to create the effect
you want.

1) M.S. MAN AND WOMAN
Over her shoulder onto
the Man. He looks Left
at her. She looks Right.

2) C.S. WOMAN
She looks offscreen
Right towards the Man.

3) C.S. MAN
He looks Left at her.
Then he turns to look
Wider Left towards –

4) CUTAWAY OF CLOCK
From the Man's Point
of View. Detail of
the Clock on the shelf.

5) C.S. MAN
(New angle). He looks
offscreen Left. Then
he turns to look Right

6) M.S. MAN AND WOMAN
Over his shoulder onto
the Woman. He looks
Right, she looks Left.

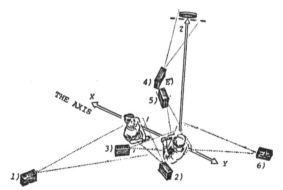

One way a director can add variety to a scene is by crossing the axis in a way that does not produce disorientation through use of a cutaway. Illustrated here is an example. The man, while in conversation with the woman, glances off-screen at the clock on the mantelpiece. Following his close-up is the point-of-view insert of the clock. As we resume his close-up, the camera set-up is shifted so that he is seen a little more full face. As he looks to the woman again, his eye-line is screen right, not left as it was before. In effect, during the cut to the clock, we have moved our position so that we are looking at the two characters from positions that are on the opposite side of the imaginary line between them. The cutaway has been motivated by the look at the clock.

Here are images of a couple of scenes from Marcel Carné's *Le jour se lève* that are examples of how the axis can be changed. Here we see a point-of-view cutaway that establishes the geography of the scene. The off-screen look by Jules Berry provides good reason to resume the scene of the two men at the café table from a new angle.

1) C.S. JULES BERRY
He looks Right across the cafe table at Jean Gabin seen backview on the edge of screen in foreground. He glances more narrowly Right over Gabin's shoulder.

2) L.S. INT/EXT CAFE
Berry's point of view. Outside the window of the cafe, a street musician is playing. (Beyond, on the other side of the street, we see the Girl as she walks past.)

3) REVERSE ANGLE
Gabin, with his back to the window, is now on screen Left and is looking Right at Berry (Camera has now crossed the axis) Berry is backview on screen Right.

4) C.S. JULES BERRY
Complementary angle towards Berry now on screen Right, facing Gabin who is on the Left of screen in foreground back to camera.

1) M.S. GABIN AND ARLETTY
Gabin on Left of screen and Arletty on the Right. They have their backs to the bar - until Gabin starts to turn away -

2) M.S. ARLETTY AND GABIN
- to face in the opposite direction. Over the cut the movement is overlapped. And they have now switched sides, Gabin Right and Arletty on the Left. But because we want to see their faces, the jump across the axis is quite acceptable - 'smooth'.

CROSSING THE AXIS

While the so-called 'rule' against 'crossing the axis' is one that you should understand, it's important to recognise that it shouldn't be regarded as some kind of 'law' that must never be broken.

Here are a couple of cases from 'Le Jour se Leve'. On the left is an example of how the axis can be changed after a point-of-view cutaway. The offscreen look by Jules Berry provides good reason to resume the scene of the two men at the cafe table from a new angle.

Above is another scene from the same film where the 'direct reverse' is unavoidable. But because it shows us what we want to see it is quite natural

Let's now look at what is called staging in depth, where both foreground and background are in shot as much as possible. The diagram overleaf is an illustration of a point one would think is almost too obvious to mention: that by placing the camera so that it shoots from positions closer to the axis, by lining up characters so that you shoot in depth, the screen sizes are increased.

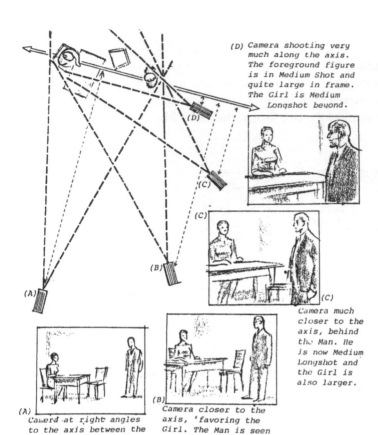

(D) *Camera shooting very much along the axis. The foreground figure is in Medium Shot and quite large in frame. The Girl is Medium Longshot beyond.*

(C) *Camera much closer to the axis, behind the Man. He is now Medium Longshot and the Girl is also larger.*

(B) *Camera closer to the axis, 'favoring the Girl. The Man is seen fulllength, but both figures are larger in the frame.*

(A) *Camera at right angles to the axis between the two characters. Both are seen in longshot*

Images that are composed in depth have certain advantages. The frame can include a figure seen relatively close in the foreground, as well as others seen full-length beyond. This may make not only for a more interesting composition but also, through the variation of sizes of characters, indicate point of view in the scene, thus increasing our dramatic involvement.

Further, it means that the upstage character, if he or she is looking at the nearer figure, is seen more frontally, showing more facial expression. Though the nearer figure may be seen in either an over-shoulder angle or in a semi-profile, it is often easy to devise some incidental business that gives him the excuse to turn around and face more towards the camera so that you present a close shot of one of the figures and a longer angle of the other at the same time.

Now study this example. The scene calls for a woman to enter a room, cross it to sit at a sofa, and begin a conversation with a man sitting at a desk. The location or the set has all the necessary furniture, the door, desk and sofa. Question: where do you put the camera?

FILM GRAMMAR

Here is the set we are working with. It is typical of the inexperienced director to accept the position of the sofa and the desk, placing the camera in the centre of the room and facing the corner of the room, with the result that the figures are seen in medium shot size and against a background of the wall a few feet away. It makes a pretty dull image. A more practised director is likely to take a very different approach. Arriving on the set or location, he looks first for the longest axis he can find, no matter if this means rearranging things. In this case it is retreating to a point that faces the windows and the door.

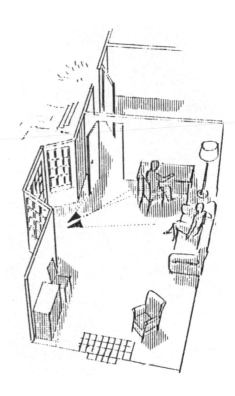

Placement of the camera along this axis means that the shot will be staged in depth. It often means that with limited camera moves, the director is able to hold figures both in the far background, in the middle distance, and in close shots near to the lens. The result is not only that the frame is kept full of visual information, it also means there may well be a condensation of the action because, while present action is shown in the foreground, we might also be able to see what is about to happen next. While one thing is happening, the audience can be prepared for the next piece of action. It also means the story being told is more likely to be about the transactions between characters, rather than merely

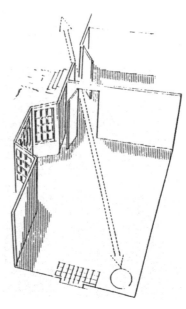

THE AXIS

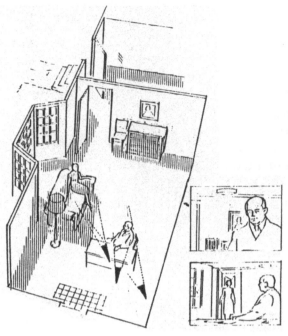

individual actions. Thus the dramatic action is richer, increasing the density of the scene. In this case it means the man can be framed facing the camera in the foreground, while the girl is seen full-length at the door, moving along the axis into close-shot as the man turns around to face her.

Now look at this as an alternative. Virtually the identical screen images could be achieved in a single camera set-up by contriving a series of moves by the actors that move them to and from the camera lens. If you develop some skill in the staging of actors, and give some thought to providing motivations for their behaviour through the layout of furniture and the positioning of props (so the moves are not so self-conscious), the scene can work just as well.

(1) *Medium Shot. The Man is seated in a swivel chair behind the desk in the window. He is facing Left. At the sound of a door opening, he swivels the chair to look offscreen to the Right -*

(2) *- and camera follows the move by Pulling Back and Tracking to include the Woman who is seen full length in the doorway in the background. As she starts to come forward into the room-*

(3) *- camera continues the Track to the Right, holding her as she comes round the desk and Panning with her as she crosses and is framed backview on the Left of the screen in foreground -*

(4) *- Camera Tracking further to the Right and moving in as the Woman moves to the window behind the desk, turning back to look at the Man seen who is now framed profile in forgground -*

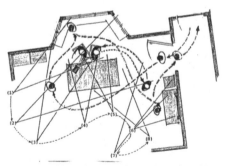

But consider this as an alternative. Virtually the identical screen images could be achieved in a single camera set-up - by contriving a series of moves by the actors which move them to and from the lens of a camera that is following them in a continuous 'long take'. If you develop some skill in the 'blocking' of actors moves and are ingenious in providing motivations for their behaviour, through the layout of furniture and the positioning of 'props', so that the moves are not self-conscious, the scene can work just as well.

FILM GRAMMAR

(5) *The Woman crosses behind him, exiting frame Right. The Man turns round into a Closeup. He rises from the desk and camera Pulls Back with him* –

(6) – *moving to include the Woman at the mirror. Camera shoots over her shoulder at a matching Close-up of her with the Man seen beyond her in background. She turns* –

'7) – *and camera Pans to shoot over her Right shoulder on to the Man again. After a moment, the Woman starts towards the door, moving past him*–

(8) – *and camera Pulls Back to a longer angle as the Man turns away to look off at the Woman. She pauses in the doorway, looks back before she exits. Camera Pans with the Man as he returns to his desk.*

The problem with the so-called 'rule' that forbids crossing the axis is that in many cases the axis actually shifts as the actors move about. To keep eye-lines consistent, the director will sometimes design camera movements where the camera tracks across the axis in order to reverse the eye-lines. In such a case, a director will prefer to shoot master-shots and long-shots first, then move in for closer coverage. In this way he can plot the moments when closer angles are needed, those shots that punctuate the master-shot. In (C1) below, the man is seen on the right of screen. When he walks off to the left, the camera tracks with him, moving past the woman. When the man rejoins her, moving left to right, the camera does not track, it pans, and the axis has been crossed.

A) *C.S. WOMAN*
She looks offscreen to camera *Right.*

B) *C.S. MAN*
Complementary angle. He looks off *Left.*

C1) *M.S. MAN & WOMAN*
Overshoulder shot. She looks *Right* at him. He looks *Left* at her. But now he moves Left, crossing behind her. Camera *TRACKS LEFT* to –

C2) *M.S. MAN*
– the Man picks up some object, looks back *Right* to her. As he moves back to rejoin her, camera *PANS* with him –

C3) *M.S. MAN & WOMAN*
–over her shoulder. She now looks Left at the Man, He looks Right at her. Their looks are now in the reverse direction.

D) *C.S. WOMAN*
Now she is looking offscreen *Left*

E) *C.S. MAN*
He looks off Right. (Directions Reversed)

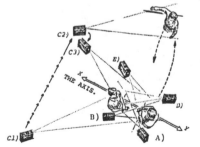

In a scene involving three characters, there are likely to be three axes. In the diagram below, (A) to (B) is the axis of exchanges between mother and son. The axis between mother and father is (A) to (C), while (C) to (B) is the axis of father to son. During the scene, the eye-lines will change according to these axes.

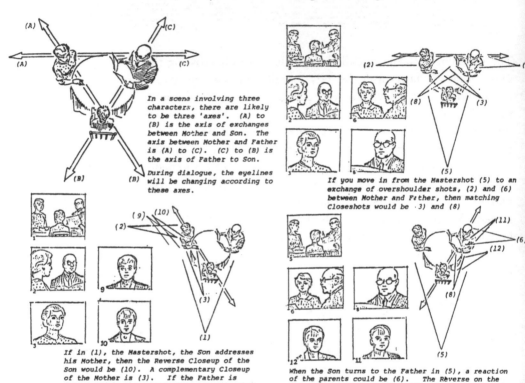

In a scene involving three characters, there are likely to be three 'axes'. (A) to (B) is the axis of exchanges between Mother and Son. The axis between Mother and Father is (A) to (C). (C) to (B) is the axis of Father to Son.

During dialogue, the eyelines will be changing according to these axes.

If you move in from the Mastershot (5) to an exchange of overshoulder shots, (2) and (6) between Mother and Father, then matching Closeshots would be (3) and (8).

If in (1), the Mastershot, the Son addresses his Mother, then the Reverse Closeup of the Son would be (10). A complementary Closeup of the Mother is (3). If the Father is introduced in the overshouldershot (2), then the Reverse angle of the Son should be (9) in order that his eyeline is wider to the lens.

When the Son turns to the Father in (5), a reaction of the parents could be (6). The Reverse on the Son could be (12), eyeline wide of camera. But if the Closeup of the Father is (8), then the matching Closeup of the Son (11) should look closer to the lens.

1 MASTER SHOT
The MOTHER, SON and FATHER
The SON is in Backview. He looks Left to the MOTHER.

2 TWO SHOT
The MOTHER, in profile, the FATHER in backgound beyond. They look offscreen Right.

3 C.S. MOTHER
The MOTHER looks offscreen to the Right. (Either to the Son or to the Father.

4 C.S. MOTHER
The MOTHER looks offscreen to the Left. (Either to the Son or the Father)

5 MASTER SHOT
The MOTHER, SON and FATHER.
The SON is in Backview. He
looks Right to the FATHER.

6 TWO SHOT
The FATHER in profile, the
MOTHER in background beyond.
They look offscreen Left.

7 C.S. FATHER
The FATHER looks offscreen
to the Right. (Either to
the Son or the Mother)

8 C.S. FATHER
The FATHER looks offscreen
to the Left. (Either to
the Son or the MOther)

9 C.S. SON
He looks offscreen to the
Left - wide of camera.

10 C.S. SON
He looks offscreen to the
Left - narrow to camera.

11 C.S. SON.
He looks offscreen to the
Right - narrow to camera.

12 C.S. SON.
He looks offscreen to the
Right - wide of camera.

When cutting from a long-shot to a closer angle, it is generally a good idea to change the angle. You might think that to move the camera forward toward the subject on the same line (called an in-line cut) would be a most natural jump in space, one that involves no disorientation and results in a smooth cut. But it can, paradoxically, make us more aware of the edit (though this, of course, may be the desired effect).

When the edit is the equivalent of a visual enlargement of the preceding picture, the problem is likely to be that we do not really see anything we haven't already seen. We may, of course, get more concentration on one of the characters to the exclusion of another, but this doesn't seem to be enough. Think about it: there is not enough reason for the dislocation that will inevitably take place due to the jump of the mind's eye. (A possible exception is a cut from an extremely distant view in which the detail was too distant to be observed, to a close shot where it is visible for the first time.) Note that this applies less in a cut that takes us further away from the scene, since the change of angle means new visual data has been added to the shot.

Note also that when cutting from a long-shot of very fast action to a closer angle of the same, it does not look right if you do it honestly. The action of the closer shot has to be taken a little slower before the cut can be made smoothly. There are valid

A) _M.S. MAN AND WOMAN_
Establishing two shot
Both of them are seen
in profile.

B) _C.S. WOMAN_
Closer angle. Because
camera has moved but
is on the same line
it is still profile.

C) _C.S. MAN_
A matching shot. Also
a profile since the
camera is on the
same line.

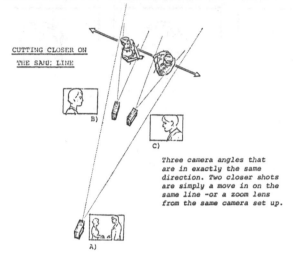

CUTTING CLOSER ON
THE SAME LINE

B)

C)

Three camera angles that
are in exactly the same
direction. Two closer shots
are simply a move in on the
same line -or a zoom lens
from the same camera set up.

A)

theories of perceptual psychology that will explain this phenomenon. The mind's eye will accept the slight shock of disorientation involved in a big jump of mental geography, but does so more readily when there is some compromise. Very fast movement that is seen in an extreme long-shot (a big frame) is, in actual fact, a relatively small and slow movement. When the frame is dramatically smaller, the relative movement is unexpectedly swift.

Shot-to-Shot Relationships

The phrase 'a smooth cut' is an obvious contradiction in terms. All cuts are, to a greater or lesser degree, a potential disorientation for the audience. But if the cut is timed to precisely the moment when the viewer (and the Invisible Imaginary Ubiquitous Winged Witness) has the impulse to see from a new vantage point, then it will seem smooth. In such cases, there is meaning given to the cut.

When the director plans the shifts of set-ups intelligently, each incoming image will have contained within it the impetus for a jump to the next angle. It should coincide with some cue found in the outgoing shot. Moreover, each angle should be significantly different in a way that adds or subtracts to the pictorial narrative, and in turn advances the story. The move from one shot to another might answer a question that is posed by the previous angle. It might satisfy some curiosity on the point of the viewer by showing more clearly what is already visible, perhaps cutting out information that is now irrelevant, or shifting the angle to include new information that an action in the previous shot has led us to want to see.

The key is that every cut should have a purpose, that it follows the momentum of the viewer's interest, that each shift of angle is motivated by the audience's desire to see something that has been promised to them. Of course the editor can manipulate the perceptions of the audience, but there is a sense in which the cutting is determined quite precisely by the mental and emotional responses of the viewer, as anticipated by the film-maker.

(a) Two shot
A young woman hands to the seated man something she wants him to read. The shot, since it holds two people, is an objective

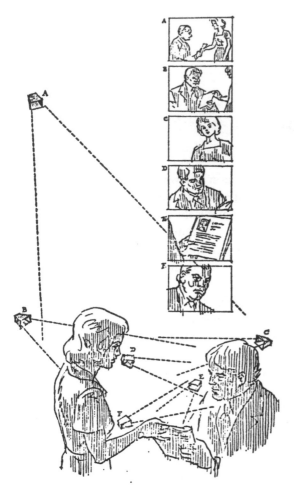

view of the situation, the relationship, and the action. At some particular instant (and a good editor will find the precise frame on which to cut) we will want to see a . . .

(b) Medium Shot

. . . of the man. The imaginary observer is prompted to jump closer, to see better. The new shot is not just closer, but angled to see more frontally the man's face. It is as close as necessary, meaning close enough to include all that is relevant: the man, the thing that has been handed him, and perhaps enough of the girl's body to keep us reminded of her presence. Again, the image contains within it the reason for the desire to cut to a . . .

(c) Close Shot

. . . of the girl. Upward at her, because she is looking down at what we have just shown in (b). Also a little closer than (b) because it is an image of her reaction. And, of course, it creates the desire to see the . . .

(d) Close-up

. . . of the man. This is now downward. It is from the point of view of the girl standing over him. It is what she is looking at. But the man is looking at . . .

(e) Insert

. . . the object in his hand, over his shoulder, and from his point of view. It has to be held for only as long as the time necessary for the audience to grasp its significance. This prompts a cut to the . . .

(f) Big Close-up

. . . of the man. His reaction. This is closer than (d) because we want more emphasis on what his feelings or thoughts are. Where (d) was downward, this shot may be upward if we want to underline the axis between the man and what he is looking at. If, for example, it was just as close as (d) but downward, then the impression would be that we are looking at him from the point of view of the girl. Such a shot would de-emphasise our view of his responses.

1. Focal Press (first published 1953, second edition, 1995), pp. 237–41.

A shock cut is one that makes deliberate use (sometimes a carefully designed misuse) of the craft of film editing. In Karel Reisz's *The Technique of Film Editing* (the best book on the subject, and one of the few works that successfully combines theory and craft), there is analysis of a well-known example from David Lean's version of Dickens's *Great Expectations* that I urge you to look at.[1] On paper it may not sound impressive, but on the several occasions that I have seen the film projected under good conditions to an audience of any size, this particular moment produces a real shriek of terror from susceptible viewers that quite disrupts the flow of the film for a minute or so. And the effect is achieved entirely by the grammar of set-ups, sound effects and skilfully planned editing.

The example Reisz uses (Pip encountering Magwitch in the cemetery for the first time), is an instance where the intention was to take the audience by surprise, and is one you would do well to study carefully. To achieve this, it is not enough to let the surprise appear unexpectedly. Rather, it needs to be planned from some way back. In the scene from Lean's film, an atmosphere of mystery is conveyed, a danger is established. This is done through the creative use of sound effects and ominous lighting. Then, just as a rather frightening image (a distorted, almost human tree) has been shown, Pip starts to run away, and it is at this point of slackening tension and audience relief when the really frightening image appears. Lean and his editor deliberately contrive to make the spectator believe that the danger is over, and then catch him on the rebound.

If Lean's intention had been to give suspense to the sequence, he would have edited it differently. He might, for example, have shown us a shot of Magwitch watching Pip in the cemetery. The audience's emotional reaction would have been the suspense of waiting for the moment they know is about to happen. What is worth noting here is that, whether the effect comes after the spectator has been pre-warned, or whether it comes as a shock, it must be planned some way back. If suspense is aimed for, the spectator must first be shown what to wait for. If a shock is intended, the pre-warning must be, so to speak, negative: the spectator must be deliberately led away from the significant event before it can come to him as a surprise.

The choice between anticipating a climax and it being a surprise arises on a routine level every time a particularly startling event is just about to occur. Take, for example, a character who is just about to drink poison. Should there be a cut to a close-up at the crucial moment, or just before? If the cut occurs some time before the actor swallows the poison, then the very fact of a close-up makes the audience anticipate a climax and feel suspense for it to happen. But if the cut to the close-up coincides with the moment the lips touch the glass, it will come as a surprise. In the example we have just quoted from *Great Expectations*, after giving the spectator a shock, the editor chose to hold back the really frightening image for a further fourteen frames, thereby adding a momentary uncertainty and suspense before the final revelation.

Editing is, in a sense, a performing art. Watch a good editor seated at the moviola and you will see that as he studies the footage on the screen, he is acting in sympathy with the performers, sensing the rhythm of the actor's delivery and responses. It has been my impression that one of the most common weaknesses among students, as they begin to edit their own material, is that their timing is never quite sharp enough. This is hard to explain, easier to demonstrate. At a primitive level of cartoon action, consider this custard-pie slapstick sequence.

1a. Ollie has the pie	1b. Stan, oblivious
2a. Ollie gets the ideas	2b. Stan, unprepared.
3a. Ollie decides	3b. Stan, defenceless
4a. He 'winds up'	4b. Stan . . .?
5a. He throws it . . .	5b. Stan gets it in the face
6a. . . . out of shot	6b. Stan just takes it

If these were two synchronous shots, which frames would you choose to cut from the pie-thrower to the victim? Typically, most students pick 5a and 5b. As Olllie's arm swings the pie past camera, the cut is made on the gesture, with the pie entering frame in 5b. This makes for something like a smooth cut, and in the flow of movement from Ollie to Stan, we are hardly aware of the edit.

But is this really what you want? In the smoothness, something of the impact is lost. If you want to feel the force of the pie in Stan's face, then a few frames of 4b are needed in advance of the impact of the pie. Indeed, there are a number of other ways to get even more impact. You might, for example, start on 1b, Stan's stupid look, and then cut to 1a and 2a, as Ollie makes his decision. Then resume 3b very briefly and only then go to 4a and 5a, before cutting on the action to 5b and 6b.

When editing, don't try to preserve every aspect of both performances. If you are filming a tennis match, for example, and you wait for A to complete his serve before cutting, you'll never see B returning his serve. Once the audience understands what is about to happen, when the impulse to act is clear, it's time to make your cut, so the audience is able to see the consequences of that action.

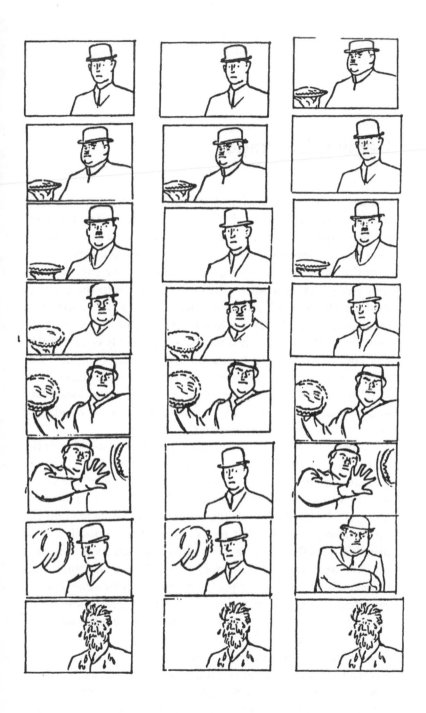

Camera Coverage

Camera coverage, like almost all aspects of film-making, is a matter of style and personal taste. The choices open to a director are like those made by the writer, who may have a preference for long or short sentences, polysyllabic or monosyllabic words.

In the early stages of student experience, my suggestion is that you experiment with various styles, even to the point of deliberately mimicking the grammar of some classic directing mannerisms (Hitchcock vs. Renoir, Antonioni vs. Lean). Your own personal and individual idioms will probably emerge not as any conscious decision but rather as instinctive impulse and habit. At its best, style is a matter of personal feeling, usually as unselfconscious as one's manner of speaking, one's vocabulary and phrasing. The thing is to be flexible. With this in mind, here are some thoughts on coverage when shooting.

On professional production crews, an essential member of the unit is the script supervisor, who is assigned the job of helping the director keep a close watch on continuity. Student crews frequently cannot afford this. Or, when they can, they do not have anyone who really knows the job and its problems, and the director often decides that he has to do it for himself. This is usually a mistake, for it requires great concentration and takes up time and energy that should be used on more important things. There is also the problem that a script supervisor is pointless if there is no script to supervise, and unless it is a screenplay and/or shooting script that is professionally conceived and written.

Simply, the role of the professional script supervisor is to ensure that the material obtained on location can be edited weeks – sometimes months – later. His primary job is to take detailed written notes about each and every shot, and observe what differences – however small – might exist between takes. A simple example might be that when working on a scene of Lonesome Bill walking into a saloon and ordering a drink, the script supervisor will remind his director that just after he pushed the doors open, Bill stopped and scratched his head, that the sky behind him was cloudy, and that the barman poured the whisky using his left hand. In short, the script supervisor is there to make sure that the footage will cut together without any glaring problems of continuity. He acts as liaison between the director working on the floor and the editor in the cutting room. In student films this is very often the same person at two stages of the process. But this should not lead you to forget that, in a very real sense, it is still two quite different people. This you will discover when, sitting at the cutting bench, you find yourself exasperated at that other character whom you were when you were shooting this material.

Many directors develop an extraordinary capacity for memorising the material they have shot, even the difference between specific takes of a certain set-up. To a greater or lesser degree, they remember which were the best parts of the best shots. Or so they believe. In fact, it can be hard to convince student directors that it really is necessary to write down all this information. Why does it have to be on paper if you have it all in your head? Many students have found the answer to this question, to their cost, in the cutting room. As such, I recommend that before you start editing, you prepare a detailed record of all the material that you have to work with. These are continuity sheets on which is a list of every camera angle, and what was seen and heard in the shot. Those takes not used are marked with the reason for their rejection. Variations between takes from the same set-up are also noted. You might also want to note down accurate timings of what little gestures or looks from the actor you find. What you are doing here is making a precisely detailed record of your options, the possibilities within the material that may be of value. This will save you a great deal of time once you start editing, as well as allowing you to prepare paper edits before you even start work in the editing room.

Between the period of the shooting and the editing stage some fascinating changes are likely to occur. Once principal photography has been completed, your role, as director, changes quite abruptly. It can be an odd switch in your way of thinking. You become almost another person, now standing outside the material you directed, exploring from an entirely new point of view. What you may have remembered may now present itself to you as having not only many problems, difficulties and short-comings, but also new and unexpected values. You should be able to see opportunities you did not previously appreciate, something that is a great deal easier if you have recorded on paper everything you have to work with.

It makes good sense to begin by shooting the master-shot of a scene, even if it is not the first shot in continuity. There are two obvious reasons for starting off with the largest angle that shows all of the important action, then moving close to medium shots and close-ups. One is that with a master-shot, you are better able to establish the tempo of the scene and the flow of character interaction. Another is that in earlier stages of filming, perform-ances are apt to be less subtle, and you will get into real continu-ity trouble if a performance is drastically different from one shot to the next. (When shooting a scene, always ask yourself, 'If I was allowed only one close-up, where would it be and which charac-ter would it feature?' Being able to answer this question means you probably know why that particular scene is necessary.)

If you are shooting scenes where there are longer and closer angles of the same action, do everything you can to overlap movements of the performers. As director you may chose to shoot in master-shot the angle where, for example, two charac-ters enter the frame, sit down at a table, and begin a conversa-tion. With this shot completed, you might then move to closer set-ups covering the ensuing dialogue. But because it is this dia-logue that concerns you, you might set up the closer angles with the characters already in position, already framed in the shot. This is a mistake. As a matter of routine, the experienced direc-tor will line up the closer angle with the actors in position and then instruct them to step out of the frame and move into posi-tion only after the camera is rolling.

Why? Because in your future role as editor, you are likely to discover that the most effective point on which to make the cut from one shot to another is on this matched action of the characters sitting down. Or perhaps because you find you can cut away from the proceeding long-shot earlier and, by beginning the closer angle before the entry of the actor, effectively speed up the action, eliminating dead footage in the long shot (always something to strive for). You may, of course, do neither, but the thing to note here is that by automatically overlapping the action, you will have left yourself the option.

Never say 'Action' or 'Cut' too soon. One of the most important reasons why you should pay attention to problems of coverage is to save footage and money. There is, however, one case in which this does not apply. In narrative films many shots are usually intended to cover the action of a scene at either the start or finish. Typical case: a woman enters a room to begin a confrontation with a man. For the inexperienced director, it may seem that the scene begins only after the woman has appeared, or that it is over as soon as the door is closed on her exit. Thus the inexperienced director might tell the cinematographer to cut the camera as soon as the woman is out of the scene. But do not take this for granted. As you set up any scene, consider: isn't it just possible that you could make good use of a couple of feet of the reaction after the exit? Or that there is value in a few moments of the man alone before the woman enters?

It is almost always a mistake to go back to a location for re-shoots before you have made an initial assembly of your footage. You may feel that since it is obvious that certain shots are unsatisfactory, it is best to redo them at once. Not so. Half the time you will find that there is another way to solve the problem in editing. And if you wait until you know precisely what is required because you have seen the problem in a rough cut, then you will be able to take unforeseen advantage of your mistakes and improve on the original concept. So before you decide on a re-shoot, keep in mind that no scene is ever exactly the way the inexperienced (or, much of the time, the experienced) director has foreseen it. As a beginner you may be so fixed in your pre-conception that you do not recognise any other way of seeing it.

And as far as acting is concerned, if you continue and try to impose your conception on the scene, you may do nothing but inhibit the actor who will get progressively worse, instead of better. Consider: was the entire shot unsatisfactory? Do you have coverage and cutaways? If much of the shot was, in your opinion, perfectly usable, you may still decide to go again in the hope of improvement. But be aware of what you are doing. Don't forget you can use parts of two takes as long as you have the necessary coverage. Consider, for instance, a short pick-up shot that will act as a kind of patch on the narrative.

As has been stated previously, cinema is not so much a medium for action as it is for reaction. It is with the timing of a reaction that the editor punctuates the significance of the action. Until students have had considerable experience in editing, they may be slow to appreciate this at a gut level. The thing to remember in any scene is that it is often the listener (the observer, with his or her introverted feelings or thoughts) who is more important than the speaker or the event being observed. It is the screenwriter new to the medium of film who imagines that his dialogue always represents the dramatic content of a scene. In this context, an important advantage of obtaining coverage of reactions is that it can provide you with the means to speed up a performance that lacks pace by shortening unnecessarily wordy dialogue.

As such, it is important to plan cutaway material. Like all the rest of my suggestions, this one involves an issue of style (which is why you should feel free to ignore it after you have tried it out). Indeed, the whole question of coverage assumes that you may be shooting your film in a way that means you will leave yourself some freedom at the editing stage. Several directors choose, quite deliberately, to shoot without coverage by using elaborately designed long takes. You are recommended to try this if only to discover how good you are at it, and how much it suits your particular talent and temperament (as well as the kind of stories you want to tell).

There is a phrase sometimes heard among film cutters: 'the cutaway to the seagull'. It seems to come from an apocryphal story about a film editor who found himself in trouble editing a dialogue scene on a beach. Unable to use the two-shots and close-ups because of bad matches and insufficient coverage, he found he could salvage the scene by adding a soundtrack of seagulls and using an occasional brief shot of a bird in flight with which to patch the unsatisfactory cuts in the scene. Plainly, this was a desperate attempt to rescue a scene that had, for whatever reasons, gone disastrously wrong (though some might insist that the better alternative would have been to leave the 'bad' or 'jump' cuts). But though cutaway footage can provide the editor/director with more freedom to shape a scene during the editing process, it should never be thought of as safety material, even though it may often turn out that way. If imaginatively conceived, it will have a relationship to the rest of the shots that can dramatically enrich the scene.

Plan for simultaneous action. Within ten years of the beginnings of cinema, the first film-makers had discovered the value of cross-cutting and inter-cutting simultaneous action. Common practice in most narrative films these days is to devise action that provides maximum opportunity for the editor to cross-cut. A primitive example: a scene of a maid who brings breakfast on a tray to her mistress, delivering a letter that has arrived by morning post. You could shoot this inside the bedroom, playing it either in one continuous shot, or in a master-shot with conventional closer coverage. But consider what happens if you also cover the maid arriving outside the bedroom door, knocking, waiting for the mistress to invite her to enter, and then finish with the maid coming out of the room, closing the door. For example:

1 Inside, the mistress asleep.
2 Outside, the maid arrives with the tray. She knocks (she might also glance at the letter).
3 Inside the bedroom, the mistress wakes.
4 Outside, the maid hears her mistress call to her to come in, starts to open the door.
5 Inside, the mistress sits up as the maid enters. The tray is placed on the bed beside the mistress
6 Outside, the maid emerges, closes the door.
7 Inside, the mistress reading the letter.

Is this way of telling the story, using seven cuts made out of two shots, any better? Not necessarily. But it does supply the editor many more opportunities of establishing a pace, even a dramatic drive, to the scene (and, naturally, has contained within it primitive elements of dramatic irony). Given this possible structure of cutaways and intercuts, the scene could be edited so as to give punctuation to specific points of view and performances.

Note that physical movement and shifts in the setting of a scene will not in themselves make a film more cinematic, though they may help in providing some visual variety – a kind of dialectic vitality.

In terms of dramatic construction (especially in dialogue scenes), this kind of simultaneous action can be even more advantageous to the director. I am thinking here of a lesson I was taught by another writer early on in my career. We were working on a very long expository scene with a lot of talk. The action: a messenger arrives at a palace and reports to the Servant. The Servant then takes the message to the Duke who is at that moment in bed with his mistress, a Countess. Four characters: the Messenger, the Servant, the Countess, the Duke. The information that has to be communicated is elaborate, almost a page of monologue if one single character had to deliver the entire message. The other obvious problem: redundancy. How do you avoid having parts of the speech repeated at each stage of the communication? The answer is intercutting. The speech is simply cut up and rearranged, and played in fragments.

1 *Exterior.* The Messenger arrives. The Servant emerges, hears part of the message, goes inside, telling the Messenger to wait. Servant knocks on the bedroom door.

2 *Bedroom.* Responding to the knocking, the Countess gets out of bed where the Duke still sleeps. She goes into an Anteroom with the Servant.

3 *Anteroom.* The Servant tells the Countess part of what he has heard from the Messenger. She tells the Servant to question the Messenger further while she wakens the Duke.

4 *Exterior.* The Servant emerges, starts to question the Messenger as they enter the palace together.

5 *Bedroom.* While the Duke dresses, the Countess tells him what she has heard from the Servant.

6 *Anteroom.* Messenger is talking to the Servant. The Countess emerges from the bedroom on an important line, reacting to it.

7 *Anteroom.* The Duke, now dressed, opens the door to overhear the next revelation.

8 *Anteroom.* The Countess, cross-questioning the Messenger and Servant, is told one more important fact as the Duke,

now joining them, appears for the final piece of the story to be related to him by the Countess.

A simple example, but note that at every stage there could conceivably be segments of dialogue that the characters hear, but which we as the audience do not. As such, there could be infinite variations of the above continuity. With the three locations and business to be played in each, this short sequence is not only full of activity and interaction of characters, it has a lively progression, interesting use of locations, and a build of reactions. All this without any of the speeches containing more than one single piece of exposition.

Always get alternatives of the same set-up. A standard complaint from the experienced film editor working with an inexperienced director is that the director shoots alternative takes, but gets insufficient coverage. The editor has different takes to choose from, but because of the problem of matching shots, if he uses one no part of the other is useable. The director with expertise (and we are talking about experience here, not necessarily talent) who has learned how to make maximum use of film stock and filming time will shoot alternative versions of the same shot that the editor will be able to intercut. This is not easy to explain except by example.

Take a scene that starts on a close-up of one character, one of a group. At a certain moment, the camera pulls back to include the entire group. In the first take there are moments when the performance of the principal actor leaves something to be desired, but everybody else in the shot gives good performances. In making a second take of exactly the same action, the director can tell the cameraman to stay in close-up, with no pull back. If this shot is satisfactory and the performance of the individual actor good enough, the close-up coverage can be intercut with the shot that includes the full group. A carefully thought-out variation between two alternative takes of the same set-up provides the editor with all that is needed for an effective assembly (even if the director may have wanted his shot, from close-up to master-shot, in one continuous move).

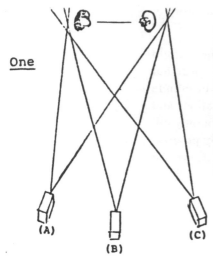

One

Illustrated here are examples of three-camera coverage. The first, an all-too-common pattern of inexperienced students, is one that should be avoided. Here we have three cameras in a row, all in much the same direction, all with the same lens width and at almost the identical angle and length from the subject. The result is not useful for the editor who wants to cut a new angle, because cutting from one camera to the other will present the audience with no substantially new information.

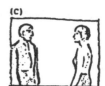

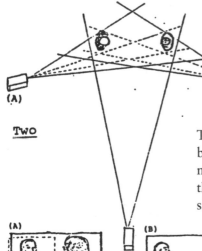

Two

The second is more useful and is standard practice both in film and television because it provides an infinite number of options for the editor, and dramatises the point of view of either character. The closer over-shoulder shots that have a character in back-view provide for effective cuts to the reverse angles. They both exclude certain pieces of visual information and can help motivate the edits. The master-shot (B) in set-up below is the same as in the first set-up, but (A) and (C) are now both shooting along the axis.

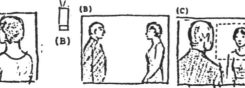

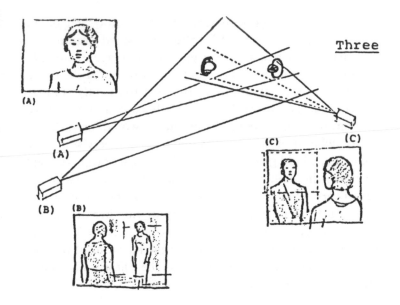

Three

The third is also a standard formula, one that offers an even richer variety of screen sizes. Designed to shoot in depth along the longest axis, the shot from (B) is likely to be more visually effective and dramatic. (C) is in the reverse direction with complementary matching eye-lines, and the zoom also provides a single shot.

A more complex version of a dialogue exchange between two characters might need at least five angles:
a) the master-shot
b) and c), two complementary over-shoulder shots (that favour each of the characters)
d) and e), two matching singles

The now classic taxicab scene between Rod Steiger and Marlon Brando in *On the Waterfront* is a good example of a scene that uses a five-angle set-up. Full coverage of this kind gives the maximum number of options available at the editing stage. Coverage as elaborate as this was frequently standard practice in the days when the major Hollywood studios were run on a conveyor-belt system. The producers would insist that the director, who in those days was under close supervision of the head office, would give such a complete range of camera angles that when the dailies were supplied to the editor (who also worked very much under the supervision of the producer), the scene could be cut in an almost infinite number of ways. In effect, the direction of a scene can be completely redone in the cutting room. As far as the subtext of the reactions of the characters is concerned, with full coverage, the editor is able almost to rewrite the scene on the editing bench.

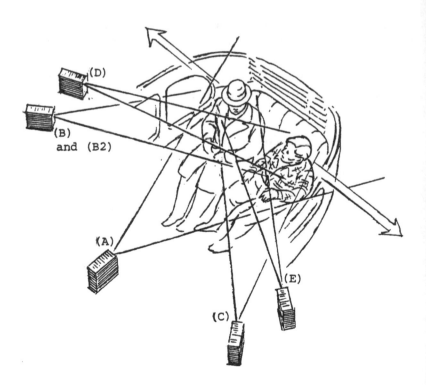

C.S. FAVORING STEIGER
Camera shoots over the
shoulder of Brando on
to Steiger.

C.S. FAVORING BRANDO
A matching angle over
Steigers shoulder and
favoring Brando.-

- which holds Steiger
in foreground as he
turns front. Emphasis
on Steiger, Brando is
seen beyond.

MEDIUM SHOT OF BOTH
Longer angle. We see
both men in profile.
A 'master shot' with
neutral emphasis.

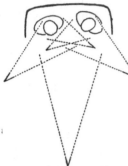

The scene was probably
covered throughout in
all five angles: one
mastershot, two over-
shoulder angles. two
single closeups. This
is the 'full coverage'
which provides for the
maximum number of
options in the editing.

FULL COVERAGE

The now classic scene between
Marlon Brando and Rod Steiger in
'On the Waterfront' is a scene
which has been shot to the formula
of 'full coverage'. There are five
angles; one master, two matching
'complementary' over-shoulder shots,
two matching closeups.

With coverage like this, there
is enormous freedom in editing. As
far as the 'subtext' of the scene
is concerned, the producer, the
editor and the director can almost
'rewrite' the scene at the editing
bench.

Study the scene carefully on an
flatbed and you will see what I
mean. After the first establishing
mastershot, most of it is played in
alternating two-shots, favoring now
one character now the other, timed
not to dialogue but to the inward
thoughts and feeling.

CLOSE SHOT STEIGER
A single showing
Steiger from Brando's
point of view.

CLOSE SHOT BRANDO
Matched eyeline, a
single of Brando -
Steiger's P.O.V.

After the initial establishing shot of the scene, most of the dialogue is played in alternating over-shoulder shots, favouring one
of the characters and then the other, timing the cuts to the interaction of thought and feeling as much as to the exchange of
speeches. Close-ups are delayed until the later moments where
feelings are more intense and thoughts more interior. Music also
marks mood shifts. The remarkable thing is that this formula for
shooting, considered by many young directors to be so traditional that it is a cliché, nevertheless turns out to be the simplest
and most effective method to cover a scene where performance
is very much more important than fancy camerawork.

There is no harm in experimenting as you plan camera coverage. In fact, you are encouraged to experiment, to copy any

CAMERA COVERAGE

interesting moves and shots you have seen in films, to play with the 'rules'. Remember that there is, in any scene, an almost infinite combination of possibilities. Allow me to finish with these (not so experimental) examples that will, I hope, give you an indication of just what is possible in the editing room if you have been adventurous in your camera coverage and moves. After all, there can never be a single correct way to edit a scene.

The standard pattern of full coverage may not need three setups. By devising some piece of business that prompts one of the characters to turn toward the camera, for example, it is often possible to achieve the same coverage. Another variation might be a move by an actor who is given a reason to walk away from the camera. In fact, when working with an experienced camera operator and actors, the variations of camera choreography are infinite.

1) Medium Two-shot across the Girl in foreground at the typewriter. She is in profile. The Man is seen -over her shoulder beyond.

1a) But, instead of cutting to the reverse angle closeup of the Girl, she uses business with the typewriter to turn her towards the lens. Camera makes a small move in excluding the Man in the background.

2) But a matching closer shot of the Man is also covered to use for intercutting with the closeup of the Girl.

The standard pattern of 'mastershot' with two complementary close shots may not need three setups. By devising some piece of business which prompts one of the characters to turn towards the camera, with an unobtrusive move by the camera, it's often possible to achieve the same coverage.

3) For further coverage that can be intercut with these shots, it's useful to make an extra take of 1) without the camera move, a medium two-shot.

1) The same Medium Two-Shot of the Girl at the typewriter. She is in a profile, he is seen full face over her shoulder.

1a) But, instead of turning towards camera, she gets up and moves away from it and the camera zooms or tracks to follow her, excluding the Man. Having 'upstaged' him, she turns to look back at him.

2) A reverse angle of the Man may be needed for intercutting as he turns 'upstage' to look at the Girl.

Another variation is a move by an actor who is given a reason to 'upstage' the other by a walk away from the camera. Moves of this kind usually need the 'motivation' of some piece of incidental action that involves a 'prop' - I.E. the typewriter or the filing cabinet.

3) Again, it's useful to make an extra take of the first set-up - without the camera move, holding both of them in an overshoulder shot with the Man backview.

As you plan camera coverage there is no harm in thinking of it in terms of a number of separate setups which provide the traditional screen sizes, 'mastershot', 'overshoulder shot', closeup', etc. But you should be prepared to change the plan as you begin to work with actors on the set or location.

You are very likely to find that the rehearsals with the actors, particularly if you're able to rehearse with furniture and props (always remember the value of props), that the actors can find ways of making moves that combine the setups or suggest camera moves instead of cuts.

1) An overshoulder shot with the Man backview and the Girl seen beyond. She gets up and moves towards the camera, exiting frame on the Right-

1a) -so that the Man is turned to the lens as he looks offscreen after her. As he moves after her camera pulls back with him to include the Girl again -

1b) -while she is at a card-file and is seen facing the camera. The Man crosses behind her and is seen over her shoulder on the Right -

1c) -until she turns backview, facing him in another overshoulder 'shot', while he moves to the Left again and is seen over her other shoulder.

When you can work with a camera operator and actors who have a little experience, the variations of the 'choreography' of camera an performers are infinite. The kind of 'waltz-step' by which you can achieve alternating over-shoulder shots is a common formula.

FILM GRAMMAR

One final note about camera coverage. It should be clear, by now, that with careful choreographing and blocking of an actor in relation to the camera and his surroundings (to say nothing of the other actors), the director can tell the story just as effectively – if not more so – than with dialogue. When talking to students during the planning stages of their film projects, it has become increasingly clear to me that many are anxious to use several cameras in order to obtain a great deal of coverage of the scene in question. Such an approach will, most probably, give the director and editor, when sitting at the cutting bench, a great many opportunities to explore their footage, even to change its narrative thrust quite radically. It is, of course, important that the film-maker understands such a thing is possible. The careful ordering of material obtained on the set or on location weeks, sometimes months later, is in many ways the key to effective storytelling in the cinematic medium.

But beware of giving yourself *too* many chances to chop and change your film, and in turn the story you are telling. I cannot help but feel that wanting countless set-ups to ensure coverage from every conceivable angle betrays a fundamental lack of understanding of how the scene being shot needs to fit into the overall story being told. Though on the morning before a shoot the director might not know precisely what angles he needs or exactly how he wants the actors to move through the set, he should be very aware of the purpose of the scene when it is placed within the context of the story as a whole. He must know what story beats need to be established and what kind of emotional tone is to be created. To put it another way, if you know the precise meaning of a scene (in narrative terms), you will probably have more than a rough idea as to where to put the camera, how to move the actors on the set, and how to cut the footage. How often have we seen films or television programs where there is no real meaning to *any* scene because there is no meaning inherent in any shot, camera move or cut? This issue is all the more acute in the days of cheap videotape which tempts many students into shooting what I consider to be an excessive amount of footage, and only afterwards deciding what the story they want to tell actually is.

Camera Movement

When it comes to the study of camera movement, the descriptions and explanations I can give here are generally going to be harder to understand than to recognise in practice. Moreover, perhaps more than any other element of the film-making craft, students need to get practical experience of handling cameras and lenses, as well as looking carefully at films themselves. Writing about it just seems redundant. But though this could probably be said about almost everything we have discussed in class, allow me to give you some general points to think about when considering camera movement.

For most directors and cameraman, the details of camera movement are a question of style and personal preference. One director may like the effect of a fluid camera constantly moving, another may prefer the severity and discipline of static set-ups. But when you think of certain shots within the context of film grammar and dramatic construction, there are other considerations. Be sure to watch for interesting tracking and panning moves that reveal certain pieces of information at specific times. Watch how a figure moves in relation to the world around him. Notice if he is isolated from his environment or made a part of it through his interactions with on-screen physical elements. Look for subtle moves that contain within them elements of dramatic irony, for example a move that reveals something to us, the audience, of which the on-screen character is unaware. In this context, always consider what has been left out of the frame, why and when the director has chosen to show us certain things and to avoid others. Think about how a camera move can radically and rapidly shift point of view from one character to another and about how a scene with long, sprawling takes might look (and, more importantly, feel in relation to the story) when played out in a series of carefully edited shorter shots.

All movement is relative. For the film-maker this means that the camera and the eye will observe an object in movement only when it is seen in relation to something else. A simple idea, but one often forgotten by beginners. Example: footage shot by a student who has been asked to photograph a dancer performing in a setting containing a large mobile sculpture. For some reason the student decides to use a hand-held camera, and the result is confusion. The movement of the sculpture might have been interesting but we cannot see it properly and have no sense of its movement. As the eye reads the situation, the movement could have come from either the camera or the sculpture itself. The situation is unclear to the audience because it is not anchored by the image of any stable environment, meaning there is no chance to distinguish between gestures of the dancer and those of the camera operator. Because everything is in floating movement there is, paradoxically, no comprehension of any movement at all. This is not to deny that such confusion can frequently be effective. Ambiguity in perception is one of the most interesting tricks the film-maker can employ. But what is sometimes infuriating is student incoherence that comes from ignorance of the principle of visual perception.

There are three basic things to consider when dealing with how a camera might move:
  a) the (stable) environment
  b) moving figure(s)
  c) the camera's point of view (moving or not)

There are four types of camera movement from a stationary set-up:
  a) Panning (a swivel movement left or right)
  b) Tilting (a similar movement up or down)
  c) Canting (a tilt from the vertical to left or right)
  d) Zoom (an apparent movement, where the image is optically enlarged or reduced)

These should be distinguished from the following where the entire camera set-up itself (camera plus dolly) is in movement:
  a) Tracking (forward and backwards)
  b) Tracking (left or right)
  c) Craning (up or down)

There are infinite combinations of the above, as well as free (unsteady) hand-held camera operations and shots obtained from Steadicams, mechanisms upon which the camera balances and that give a flowing movement to the shot.

At this juncture, let me say that much of the prejudice against hand-held camera movement is probably based on the extent to which it has been used by amateurs and students who are apparently uninterested in the pictorial aspects of the film frame. The amateur is, quite understandably, so entranced by the exciting experience of actually shooting the film, panning and tilting and zooming as he or she responds to the activity seen through the lens, that everything else is forgotten. It is the more experienced cinematographer or director who, even while film runs through the gate, is concerned with how the film will actually appear to audiences.

The decision to let the actor move within the design of a static frame, as against the camera moving with the figure in the environment, may be a matter of taste, but it can also contribute greatly to the dramatic narrative, giving certain psychological/perceptual clues about the characters. It is, after all, through the precise framing of a shot that the meaning of an image is communicated to the audience. A mistake in exposure or a poorly lit scene can be damaging to the atmosphere a director is trying to create. But a camera move that is mistimed or a poorly planned and executed set-up can, in only a second, destroy the dramatic sense of the scene and wholly confuse the audience.

A simple example: a scene of a woman entering a room, moving to look out of the window, then crossing to the fireplace, all seen in a long-shot. The director, in consultation with the lighting cameraman and the camera operator, has to decide: will the camera follow her about, panning so the audience sees her roughly in the centre of the frame at all times? Or will the frame be rigid, with the figure moving about within the picture? Some third alternative perhaps? (One useful rule of thumb is that camera moves ought to be as economical as possible: the minimum movement needed to provide the maximum of new visual information within the frame.) When the moving camera holds the woman in a relatively fixed central position in the frame, with the background environment somewhat out of focus, we are generally liable to focus our own attention on her. A static set-up with the woman moving within the pictorial composition, on the other hand, allows the audience to study her in relation to her environment. Both shots have different dramatic meaning to them, with the static set-up probably proving less revealing of character, less involving and sympathetic when we observe the woman within the scene.

Consider slight variations on this. The woman enters the room, pauses, and looks towards the window. Before she moves to it, the camera makes a slight movement that pans to include the window, then stays framed on this shot while she crosses to look out of the window. As she turns away and moves back to the fireplace, the camera does not follow her but stays on the window, leaving the woman framed at the edge of the screen near the fireplace. Here, the barely noticeable camera movement seems to place more emphasis on the atmosphere of the room itself and perhaps the view from the window than on the woman herself. Of course her move to the window, and our ability to see both her and what she is looking at, also helps to underline her mood, albeit indirectly (also revealed by, for example, the lighting, music, set design, business with props).

These are examples of what we call motivated and unmotivated camera moves. An example of a motivated camera move is when the camera follows Cary Grant in a scene from *North by Northwest*. Here, the audience is not strongly aware of the camera. Such moves can be motivated either by an actor's walk, or by an off-screen look that prompts a pan in the direction of the look, both of which make the action seem very natural.

EXT. U.N. LOUNGE
Cary Grant appears in the doorway in longshot. As he moves forward, reaching the center of the screen, camera starts to TRACK LEFT with him, moving parallel to his walk , holding him in the same longshot distance.

This 'following movement'
in which the subject and
the camera are in a fixed
relation to each other is
a clearly 'motivated move'
and we have little sense of
the deliberate intervention
of the director.

The length of the track is
abouth three times the width
of the screen. It comes to
a stop as Grant reaches the
Reception Desk, static again
as we CUT TO:-

In contrast is the kind of camera move that is unmotivated,
where the director is deliberately telling us where to look. If the
camera either pans, tracks, cranes or tilts without motivation
from the subject (for example, when he or she start to walk out
of shot following the view of the camera, not leading it), this is
clearly intervention from the film-maker and is a much more
conscious move. The audience may sense it is therefore of some
significance and that they need to look carefully at where their
eye is being directed. As such, movements of this kind will usually be used when the film-maker wants to draw the audience's
attention to something that, hopefully, will contribute something to our understanding of the scene. Here, Hitchcock stages
the actor's move against the camera movement in order to create
dramatic suspense.

CLOSER ANGLE
Grant hands his slip of paper to the Receptionist. The girl reaches for the microphone to page the man that Grant has come to meet. Grant waits.

Camera now begins to TRACK in the opposite direction, to the Right, retracing the move in the preceding shot. As it does so, Grant is turning to the Left - away from the move of the camera. This gesture emphasise the deliberation of the camera move, making it a 'selfconscious' anticipatory intervention by the director.

Travelling back across the same distance, it reveals the figure of the killer - and, at that moment, turns from the sideways track to a very ominous move directly <u>at</u> the figure of the man who begins to pull on one black glove...

In 'North by Northwest' one sequence opens with a longshot of the Main Hall of Grand Central Station in New York. The people who stand about in groups are turned away from camera so that there is no focus of attention. It is a shot of the 'anonymous crowd' Then-

- a not particularly interesting looking MAN enters from behind camera Left, walking away towards background. Camera uses this move to 'motivate' a pan which follows him and scans the scene until it includes a row of telephone booths -

-inside which we now rediscover Cary Grant who has been absent from the story during the preceding sequence of exposition.

Cutting to inside the phone booth we pick up the dialogue of a phone call in which Grant is explaining his predicament to his mother.

BACKGROUND ACTION THAT 'MOTIVATES' CAMERA MOVEMENT

Between the deliberate and rather self-concious camera move and the more natural-seeming following move there is sometimes a compromise.

The director may stage a piece of background action which prompts the camera move which provides an excuse for an otherwise 'unmotivated' move.

The director who is experienced in handling the choreography of action that involved crowds and knows how to integrate their movement in background with the blocking of the action of the principals in foreground can achieve effects of which audiences are barely conscious but which help the flow of the scene.

As Grant hangs up we cut back outside again. Opening the door Grant comes abruptly face to face with a MAN who has been waiting to get in. (Grant is running away from the police and is nervous of being recognised)

Side-stepping, Grant walks back across the main hall. This time the camera follows him - a 'motivated' move -as he disapperas again into the crowd.

There is sometimes a compromise version of the motivated camera move, one that is to some extent deliberate but for which there is some incidental movement within the frame that helps the movement seem natural and unobtrusive. In a later sequence of *North by Northwest*, Hitchcock stages some background action among the crowd of extras, a piece of staging in the action of an unimportant figure that prompts an unselfconscious drift of the camera. It is a move that leads us to discover the major point of interest.

A further alternative is the zoom of the lens that produces an apparent move in or pull back, but from a stationary position. The disadvantage of the zoom effect is that it lacks the sense of movement within a solid, three-dimensional world (something that actually moving the camera closer to the subject would have). A zoom in enlarges the image. It brings the flat picture nearer to us, like optical enlargement of part of the screen image, merely giving the feeling of moving through three-dimensional space. But it provides no sense of a shift in space. The picture may look bigger, but we do not feel any closer. Consequently, many directors dislike the use of zoom lenses, and prefer to use tracking camera movements, though a director like Hitchcock enjoys the very self-conscious use of the zoom to highlight certain things at dramatically important moments.

CLOSE SHOT
Seeing his neice coming downstairs, Uncle Charles raises his glass to her.

MEDIUM LONGSHOT
From his point of view, As she descends, camera makes a fast ZOOM IN--

--to the hand that she is resting on the bannister. On it, she now has the incriminating ring--

--and the camera stops on it in BIG CLOSEUP which emphasizes its signifi- cance:

In 'North by Northwest', there is a very rapid, very brief camera ZOOM from a Close shot of Cary Grant to a Big Closeup. This is a fairly standard device for producing a 'shock impact' - in this case the effect of the big oil-tanker truck as it knocks him down.

ZOOM MOVEMENT FOR EMPHASIS

A tracking movement, or a lens zoom which moves us towards the subject, is a good deal more self-conscious than a pull back or zoom out. The pull back is adding new visual information: the track or zoom in is merely concentrating on information already there.

For some reason, the beginning filmmaker who uses a zoom effect for the first time is apt to become enamoured of it. It feels 'dramatic'. It has become a staple device in horror movies and something of a cliche.

Above is an example of its use in Hitchcock's 'Shadow of a Doubt'. It is perhaps excusable as a gimmick because it comes at a very climactic point in the story (the ring is the real evidence with which the girl can prove that 'Uncle Charles' is the murderer) - and it was used by Hitch before the zoom lens was a commonplace.

Hitch has admitted that in his earlier movies he took great delight in camera techniques that were complicated and ingenious; later his style became simpler and less self-conscious. It's a sound rule: as a beginner you are advised to experiment - if only to 'get it out of your system' and appreciate the values of simplicity.

RESUME CLOSESHOT
Uncle Charles reacts, the confidence in his manner vanishes. He makes his announcement.

Citizen Kane

1. This scene can be found in *The Citizen Kane Book* (Methuen, 1985) pp. 159–60.

As a way of bringing together our knowledge of screen sizes, framing, editing, and camera coverage, let's use as an example Orson Welles's *Citizen Kane*, regarded by many as the most important film ever made in Hollywood.

Arriving in Hollywood to direct his first film at the age of twenty-five, Welles was extraordinarily lucky to have Greg Toland as his cameraman. *Citizen Kane* is Welles's masterpiece, but much of its astonishing visual style must be due to Toland's contributions. Welles was interested in staging in depth and in the long take that was already being used by directors like Jean Renoir in France. This may have prompted Toland and Welles to explore elements of focus and depths of field.

Consider a scene that is not actually in *Citizen Kane* but theoretically might have been. The shooting script, if it had been prepared by another director, might have read something like this.'

FADE IN

1. DETAIL

Camera is close on a medicine bottle and an empty glass with a spoon, sitting on a bedside table. Overscene we hear the sound of laboured breathing.

FILM GRAMMAR

2. ANOTHER ANGLE

SUSAN ALEXANDER *lies in the ornate bed next to the table. She is alive but obviously in a stupor. Overscene we hear the noise of someone knocking on a door, the rattle of the door handle.*

3. CORRIDOR OUTSIDE

KANE's *hand is trying the handle of the bedroom door. It is locked from the inside.* KANE *knocks on the door with great urgency.*

4. LONGER ANGLE

Disturbed, KANE *stands at the door, resumes knocking with more urgency. The* BUTLER *is seen beyond him. Getting no response,* KANE *steps back and throws his considerable weight against the door.*

5. INT. BEDROOM

Breaking down the door, KANE *comes plunging into the room. The* BUTLER *is seen in the doorway behind him.*

6. REVERSE ANGLE

Shooting past KANE *to the figure in the bed. Beside the bed, on the small table, are the medicine bottle and spoon. In the bed beyond is the unconscious woman.*

7. CLOSE SHOT – KANE

KANE *reacts. Without turning he instructs the servant.*

> KANE
> Get Dr Corey.

He moves past camera toward the bed.

8. RESUME INT. BEDROOM

Camera moves with KANE *as he goes to the bed, kneels beside it. He picks up the medicine bottle from the table and examines it.*

SLOW DISSOLVE TO

9. INT. BEDROOM

In foreground, DR COREY *closes his black bag. The* NURSE, *in a white starched uniform, moves to join him. The camera eases back, panning to include more of the bedroom in background, and the figure of* KANE *who is seen sitting in a chair beside the bed where his wife is lying asleep.*

10. INT. BEDROOM

> DR COREY
> She'll be perfectly all right in a day or
> two, Mr Kane.

11. REVERSE ANGLE

*The NURSE and DR COREY in the background,
KANE and his wife in foreground.* KANE
studies the small bottle in his hand.

> KANE
> I can't imagine how Mrs Kane came
> to make such a foolish mistake. The
> sedative Dr Wagner gave her is in a
> somewhat larger bottle – I suppose the
> strain of preparing for the new opera
> has excited and confused her.

> DR COREY
> Yes, yes – I'm sure that's it.

> KANE
> There are no objections to my staying
> here with her, are there?

> DR COREY
> (*glancing at the Nurse in the background*)
> No – not at all. But I'd like the nurse
> to be here, too. Good night, Mr Kane.

*As the DOCTOR leaves, camera moves a little
closer on KANE, watching the woman in the
bed.*

12. CLOSE SHOT. SUSAN

KANE's *young wife lies in the bed, turned
away from him.*

FADE OUT

This scene might well have been covered in the set-ups seen above. According to conventional and routine formulas of film direction, each of these cuts is there for a purpose, to make a specific story point. In fact, Welles shot it very differently, in two quite rigid camera set-ups in place of the kind of cuts and movements outlined above. Welles and Toland used four primary elements of film grammar to create the scene.

1 The film frame and its potential for directing the attention of the audience through use of entrances and exits (the masking of the screen as a pictorial proscenium).
2 Masking within the frames, placing one object or character in front of another.
3 Patterning, in perspective depth, the design of the composition.
4 Chiaroscuro, the use of light and shadow, often in receding planes of depth (part of which is Toland's device of double exposure to achieve extreme depths of sharp focus).

In the actual sequence from the film, as detailed below, consider the use of the Doctor's bag to produce the effect of a fade in from black as it is picked out of the shot at the start of the scene. It reveals the Nurse who, being a relatively unimportant character, is back-lit so we do not see her face, and when she moves stands so her head disappears from frame. This focuses our attention, as she moves aside, on the one important character: Kane himself. The remarkable effect is that though there is only a single camera position, the speed at which the image tells the story is fast. The camera doesn't move, but the story sure does.

This is how the scene was actually shot by Welles and Toland.

1. INT. BEDROOM. NIGHT

A wide angle of the bedroom. Framed large in foreground is a medicine bottle and an empty glass with a spoon. Beyond, in middle distance, is the head of KANE's *wife,* SUSAN ALEXANDER. *Completely in shadow, her features are indistinguishable, but her breathing is heavy, drugged. Centre screen, in background and sharp focus, is the door of the bedroom. [Note: this deep focus was achieved by double exposure. The glass was shot first with the rest of the scene in darkness, then the film was wound back.]*

There is a knocking at the door. The door handle is rattled from the outside. A pause. Presently the door bursts open and KANE *plunges into the room, silhouetted in the doorway. The* BUTLER *is seen in the corridor behind him.* KANE *reacts to the figure in the bed.*

> KANE
> Get Dr Corey.

As the BUTLER *vanishes,* KANE *moves towards the camera, kneeling beside the bed and leaning over his wife. She moves her head weakly.* KANE *glances at the medicine in the foreground.*

DISSOLVE TO:

2. INT. BEDROOM. NIGHT

The dissolve is to almost the identical camera angle. The frame is filled with a doctor's black bag.

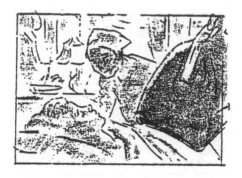

DR COREY
(*overscene*)
She'll be perfectly all right –

Entering frame, the hand of DR COREY *lifts the bag out of frame. This reveals* SUSAN ALEXANDER *lying in the bed in the same position. A* NURSE *in the white starched uniform is leaning over her.*

DR COREY
(*overscene*)
– in a day or two, Mr. Kane.

The NURSE *now stands up and again reveals* KANE *who is sitting in a chair beside the bed. As the* NURSE *moves out of frame,* KANE *examines the medicine bottle in his hand.*

KANE
I can't imagine how Mrs. Kane came to make such a foolish mistake.

DR COREY, *having collected his hat, comes back into the frame.*

KANE
(*continuing*)
The sedative Dr Wagner gave her is in a somewhat larger bottle – I suppose the strain of preparing for the new opera has excited and confused her.

DR COREY
Yes, yes – I'm sure that's it.

KANE
There are no objections to my staying here with her, are there?

The DOCTOR *glances at the* NURSE. *She has retired to a position near the door.*

DR COREY

No – not at all. But I'd like the nurse
to be here, too.

The DOCTOR *moves towards the door.*

DR COREY

Good night, Mr Kane.

The DOCTOR *leaves, closing the door behind
him. The* NURSE *in the background waits,
unmoving.* KANE *is left sitting in the chair
beside the bed, fingering the small bottle,
watching the figure in the bed. She stirs, a
very small movement that turns her head
towards the camera and away from* KANE.

Epilogue

No film schools existed when, as a youngster, I was obsessed with the dream of making movies, and there were few books about the craft. Accordingly, when after many years as a director I was invited to become a teacher, I realised I had come to theory (which far too many of the books 'about' cinema are concerned with) only after practice. For most directors, craft is based on a wealth of practical experience that has become second nature, a matter of instinct and intuition. In fact, a good director is likely to be as unaware of any logic to his working methods as a writer is of the grammatical sentence structure he uses while in the throes of creative work.

It is the same with grammar in any medium: one should have to think (or read) about it only if something isn't working properly, or if it is necessary to correct somebody else's error. The best defense I can offer for theory and the huge number of books about cinema is that they can be valuable when you run into problems, do not immediately see what is wrong, or need to revert from instinctual to more analytic thought processes. Remember: theory will not usually help you to do work that is good, though it may be of some help to identify your mistakes, and thus can sometimes be useful for corrective purposes.

These notes explore the processes through which certain common usages were developed by film-makers, and in turn became structures that were swiftly understood by audiences. The importance of studying conventional and established patterns of cinematic communication is not to lay down any immutable laws. It is rather to help you examine the always evolving processes: how they have worked and why they have had effect in the past. If you are able to understand such things, then you need no longer think in terms of 'rules.' Understanding the function of traditional usages will leave you free to invent and innovate as the need arises. I hope one of the underlying ideas throughout everything I have written for you, as students of cinema, is just how malleable I believe these ideas to be. I have, in the past, seen students go astray when they have buried themselves in the world of concrete rules and conventions.

A while ago, I had a response from an executive in a TV studio, a man in a position to offer career opportunities to graduating students. I had asked him what he was looking for in those people applying for a job, and he replied, 'The fact is we're not all that interested in what a youngster may have learned technically. It's a beginning, of course. His efforts in college can indicate his aptitude. But we reckon it will always be necessary to begin all over again, training our new employees in our own methods, our equipment and our technology. We're really much more interested in your students' imagination, their ideas, their impulses and compulsions, their creative abilities.'

To tell the truth, I was somewhat relieved by this potential employer's response to my question, because it means that as a faculty member of this institution, what I can most usefully spend my time doing is attempting to discover where students' real urges to make movies lie, and in turn how best to make the most of such impulses. After all, when young high school graduates come to me and claim to know exactly what kind of cinema it is they want to produce, I'm always a little uneasy. Perhaps all I can do in the negative sense is fail to encourage some of your less admirable compulsions. This is a negative way of putting it, but it seems a more constructive approach than merely imposing my own values upon you. The best thing I can do is to be a little less enthusiastic when you are too eager to do something which I don't think is very worthwhile.

Though I'm not really sure that one can ever teach anybody to have talent, it is possible to create an environment for study, and supply opportunities for the effort to learn. Occasionally a student has remarked that while the courses I preside over were (or were not) interesting, 'I didn't learn anything that I didn't already know – even if I didn't know that I knew it.' This may be as it should be. Weren't there some early Greek philosophers who believed that *all* knowledge and wisdom was already present inside man, that the meaning of the word 'education' ('e' for out, 'ducare' meaning to lead) was just a process of helping to bring it out into conscious awareness? It might be declared thus: as an instructor, the only things I can teach are what you already know, those ideas and opinions that if you were to stop and consider for more than ten seconds, you would probably intuitively understand at the most basic level. This is, I believe, what I have respectfully sought to do in these classes and notes. I hope you make the most of them.

Note on the editor

Paul Cronin was a researcher and translator on Ray Carney's *Cassavetes on Cassavetes* (Faber) and an editorial consultant on a forthcoming collection of interviews from Knopf, drawn from the archives of the American Film Institute, edited by George Stevens Jr. He is the editor of several books, including an acclaimed interview book with German director Werner Herzog, *Herzog on Herzog* (Faber) and two volumes – Roman Polanski and Errol Morris – in the Mississippi University Press 'Conversations with Filmmakers' series. He has written for various journals, including *Sight and Sound* and *Vertigo*. Co-founder of Sticking Place Films (www.thestickingplace.com), his films '*Look out Haskell, it's real!' The Making of Medium* Cool and *Film as a Subversive Art: Amos Vogel and Cinema 16* have been screened on television stations and at film festivals world-wide. Sticking Place Films recently completed *Mackendrick on Film*, which features footage of Alexander Mackendrick at work in the classrooms of CalArts, interviews with his students and colleagues, and extracts from archived interviews with Mackendrick about his career as a teacher of cinema. Currently he is writing a monograph about *Medium Cool* and working on a new film in West Virginia.